FAITH, THE FOUNT OF EXEGESIS

IGNACIO CARBAJOSA

Faith, the Fount of Exegesis

~

*The Interpretation of Scripture
in Light of the History of Research
on the Old Testament*

Translated by Paul Stevenson

IGNATIUS PRESS   SAN FRANCISCO

Original Spanish edition:

De la fe nace la exégesis:
La interpretación de la Escritura
a la luz de la historia de la investigación
sobre el Antiguo Testamento

© 2011 by Ignacio Carbajosa
© 2011 by Editorial Verbo Divino,
Estella (Navarra), Spain

Cover art:

Mosaic of three sacrifices pre-figuring the Eucharist:
Abel, Melchisedech, and Abraham and Isaac
Basilica San Apollinare in Classe, Ravenna, 6th century a.d.
© Alfredo Dagli Orti/Art Resource, New York

Cover designed by Roxanne Mei Lum

© 2013 by Editorial Verbo Divino
Published in 2013 by Ignatius Press, San Francisco
ISBN 978-1-58617-788-1
Library of Congress Control Number 2013930750
Printed in the United States of America ∞

Contents

Abbreviations

1. Journals and Series

ACJD	Abhandlungen zum christlich-jüdischen Dialog
AF	*Archivio di filosofia*
ATD	Das Alte Testament deutsch
BA	*Biblical Archaeologist*
BASOR	*Bulletin of the American Schools of Oriental Research*
BEstB	Biblioteca de Estudios Bíblicos
BEThL	Bibliotheca ephemeridum theologicarum Lovaniensium
Bib	*Biblica*
BS	The Biblical Seminar
BWANT	Beiträge zur Wissenschaft vom Alten und Neuen Testament
BZWAT	Beiträge zur Wissenschaft vom Alten Testament
BZAW	Beihefte zur Zeitschrift für die alttestamentliche Wissenschaft
CBQ	*Catholic Biblical Quarterly*
DJD	Discoveries in the Judaean Desert
EstBib	*Estudios Bíblicos*
EThL	*Ephemerides theologicae Lovaniensis*
Exp	*The Expositor*
FAT	Forschungen zum Alten Testament
GHZAT	Göttingen Handkommentar zum Alten Testament
HBT	*Horizons in Biblical Theology*
IEB	Introducción al Estudio de la Biblia

Interp   Interpretation

JBL   Journal of Biblical Literature

JBTh   Jahrbuch für Biblische Theologie

JNSL   Journal of Northwest Semitic Languages

JSNT.S   Journal for the Study of the New Testament Supplement Series

JSOT   Journal for the Study of the Old Testament

JSOT.S   Journal for the Study of the Old Testament Supplement Series

KuD   Kerygma und Dogma

MThZ   Münchener theologische Zeitschrift

OBO   Orbis Biblicus et Orientalis

OTL   Old Testament Library

OTS   Oudtestamentische studien

OTWSA   Oud Testamentiese Werkgemeenschap in Suid-Afrika

PD   Presencia y diálogo. Facultad de Teología "San Dámaso"

PhR   Philosophische Rundschau

PTMS   Princeton Theological Monograph Series

RB   Revue Biblique

RechBib   Recherches bibliques

RET   Revista Española de Teología

RevAg   Revista Agustiniana

RICP   Revue de l'Institut Catholique de Paris

SB   Studi Biblici

SBLSS   Society of Biblical Literature. Symposium Series

SBThS   Sources for Biblical and Theological Study

ScEc   Sciences Ecclésiastiques

SDSSRL   Studies in the Dead Sea Scrolls and Related Literature

SJOT   Scandinavian Journal of the Old Testament

SJT   Scottish Journal of Theology

STDJ   Studies on the Texts of the Desert of Judah

Sub   Subsidia. Facultad de Teología "San Dámaso"

SVal   Series Valentina

ThDiss   Theologische Dissertationes

ThT   *Theologisch Tijdschrift*

ThZ   *Theologische Zeitschrift*

TThZ   *Trierer Theologische Zeitschrift*

VT   *Vetus Testamentum*

VT.S   Vetus Testamentum Supplements

WMANT   Wissenschaftliche Monographien zum Alten und Neuen Testament

WUNT   Wissenschaftliche Untersuchungen zum Neuen Testament

ZAW   *Zeitschrift für die alttestamentliche Wissenschaft*

ZNW   *Zeitschrift für die neutestamentliche Wissenschaft*

2. Other Abbreviations

cf.   confer, compare

D   Deuteronomist (source)

DV   *Dei Verbum*

E   Elohist (source)

ed.   editor/editors

et al.   et alia

ff.   following

FR   *Fides et ratio*

ibid.   ibidem

J   Yahwist (source)

LXX   *Septuagint*

MT   Masoretic Text

NT   New Testament

OT   Old Testament

P   Priestly (source)

PBC   Pontifical Biblical Commission

R   Redactor

SC   *Sacrosanctum Concilium*

V.A.   Various authors

Introduction

In the Post-Synodal Apostolic Exhortation *Verbum Domini*, Pope Benedict XVI, returning to his speech in the Ordinary General Assembly of the Synod of the Bishops devoted to "The Word of God in the Life and Mission of the Church", underlines the need to bear in mind during exegesis "both methodological levels, the historical-critical and the theological", prescribed by *Dei Verbum* 12, so that one can "speak of a theological exegesis, an exegesis worthy of this book".[1] Behind this directive lies, in the words of Benedict XVI, "the serious risk nowadays of a dualistic approach to sacred Scripture",[2] whereby exegesis and theology are presented as irreconcilable fields.

This concern is not baseless. Indeed, the gap between "scientific" exegesis and theology, which the methodological directive of the Second Vatican Council wanted to close, has only grown in recent decades, and it is presented as one of the most worrisome challenges for the *intellectus fidei*. Since the promulgation of *Dei Verbum*, exegesis has yielded great fruits at the historical-critical level, but the same cannot be said about the theological level. Today we have much more data about each one of the books of the Bible and its setting, which can only serve as an aid to approaching Scripture. However, it cannot be said that the advances in historical-critical exegesis have really fed into theology or have caused the understanding of the Bible as the Word of God to grow among the Christian faithful. Rather, it can be said that perplexity has grown, among both the faithful and theologians, in the face of the results of this exegesis.[3] This situation, the Pope goes on to say in the *Verbum*

---

[1] *Verbum Domini* 34.

[2] Ibid., 35.

[3] A good summary of the problems raised by critical exegesis, including the preceding discussion, can be found in A. L. Nations, "Historical Criticism and the Current Methodological Crisis", *SJT* 36 (1986): 59–71. Cf. also F. Hahn, "Probleme historischer Kritik", *ZNW* 63 (1972): 1–17.

Domini exhortation, has a series of "troubling consequences, which are to be avoided". He himself lists them:

a) First and foremost, if the work of exegesis is restricted to the first level alone [the historical-critical], Scripture ends up being *a text belonging only to the past*: "One can draw moral consequences from it, one can learn history, but the Book as such speaks only of the past, and exegesis is no longer truly theological, but becomes pure historiography, history of literature". . . .

b) The lack of a hermeneutic of faith with regard to Scripture entails more than a simple absence; in its place there inevitably enters another hermeneutic, a positivistic and *secularized hermeneutic* ultimately based on the conviction that the Divine does not intervene in human history. According to this hermeneutic, whenever a divine element seems present, it has to be explained in some other way, reducing everything to the human element. This leads to interpretations that deny the historicity of the divine elements.

c) Such a position can only prove harmful to the life of the Church, casting doubt over fundamental mysteries of Christianity and their historicity. . . .

All this is also bound to have a negative impact on the spiritual life and on pastoral activity; "as a consequence of the absence of the second methodological level [the theological], a profound gulf is opened up between scientific exegesis and *lectio divina*. This can give rise to a lack of clarity in the preparation of homilies."[4]

One of the great challenges, therefore, that is faced by the *intellectus fidei* today is that of trying to restore the unity of the dual dimension of exegesis: being critical and theological at the same time. The modest contribution of this book is conceived as part of this great undertaking, which will yet require much reflection and, above all, much self-criticism within exegesis, and its results will still be a long time coming. I will try to offer some reflections that can contribute to clarifying this point, which is so decisive, by outlining the characteristic dimensions of the Catholic interpretation of Scripture. And I will do so without abandoning the practice of biblical exegesis itself. Specifically, I will concentrate on some aspects of the investigation of the

---

[4] *Verbum Domini* 35.

Old Testament (OT) and on the path that, over the course of time, this investigation has traveled.

After some 250 years of critical study of the OT,[5] we find ourselves with enough perspective to be able to look back and judge the path that has been traveled. It is now commonplace to say that our era is not an era of great certainties. Nevertheless, if it is propitious for anything, it is for the task of self-criticism. From the political and social point of view, the historical events through which we have lived in the last twenty years (such as the fall of ideologies) allow us to make a balanced historical judgment that until recently was almost impossible. From the point of view of biblical exegesis, the advances in general hermeneutics (well illustrated in the works of Gadamer and Ricoeur)[6] and the calling into question of some paradigms that seemed unquestionable have given new impetus for reflection on their methods and philosophical presuppositions.

Can the current scientific study of the OT continue feeding into theology? Can theologians build on the results of historical-critical exegesis? How should the OT be taught at a school of theology? And even more radically, does current exegesis truly get to the essence of Scripture, *the Word of God*? These questions arise today more naturally than they did only two decades ago, when they were, in a way, proscribed. The answers, however, are far from being unanimous.

At this point, it is necessary to clear the path of erroneous solutions that today, in certain circles, may appear attractive. In order to arrive at an exegesis that is critical and at the same time theological, it is crucial to avoid, both in the investigation and in the teaching of the OT, three temptations that would undermine at its base the very task that is being undertaken.

---

[5] As early as 1753, J. Astruc proposed three sources for the composition of Genesis and part of Exodus.

[6] Cf. especially H. G. Gadamer, *Truth and Method*, trans. J. Weinsheimer and D. G. Marshall, 2nd rev. ed. (New York, 2004); P. Ricoeur, *Le Conflit des interpretations: Essais d'herméneutique* (Paris, 1969); P. Ricoeur, *The Conflict of Interpretations: Essays in Hermeneutics* (Evanston, 1974); P. Ricoeur, "Contribut d'une réflexion sur le language à une théologie de la parole", in *Exégèse et herméneutique*, ed. V.A. (Paris, 1971), 301–18; P. Ricoeur, "L'Herméneutique du témoignage", in *Lectures 3: Aux Frontières de la philosophie*, ed. P. Ricoeur (Paris, 1994), 107–39; P. Ricoeur, "Herméneutique de l'idée de révélation", in *La Révélation*, ed. V.A. (Brussels, 1977), 15–54.

The first temptation is to eliminate the historical-critical method. Since the problem posed by modern exegesis has its origin in this method, it seems that the most suitable approach would be to set it aside. More than a few voices have spoken out in support of doing this. However, since historical fact is one of the dimensions that makes up our faith, and since Sacred Scripture is a privileged written testimony to this fact, we cannot approach Scripture adequately without the instruments that scrutinize history and study literature.

As long ago as 1943, the encyclical *Divino Afflante Spiritu* (written by Pius XII) not only encouraged studies of the biblical languages, archeology, the comparative study of ancient religions and literatures, textual criticism, and so on, but also considered providential the advances of exegesis in these fields during the twentieth century.[7] Twenty years later, the dogmatic constitution *Dei Verbum*, from the Second Vatican Council, underlined the double dimension of the Catholic interpretation of Scripture, which is based on its very nature: the Word of God in human words. Therefore, since God has spoken in Sacred Scripture "through men in human fashion, the interpreter of Sacred Scripture, in order to see clearly what God wanted to communicate to us, should carefully investigate what meaning the sacred writers really intended and what God wanted to manifest by means of their words."[8] This includes, as the Council explains, giving attention to literary forms and to the meaning that the sacred writer intended to express, especially through the study of the situation of his own time and culture as well as the characteristic styles of feeling, speaking, and narrating.[9]

Subsequently, the Pontifical Biblical Commission (PBC), which as of 1971 had ceased to be an organ of the Magisterium, in its document *The Interpretation of the Bible in the Church* (1993),[10] states that the historical-critical method is "indispensable" for the study of Sacred Scripture:

> The historical-critical method is the indispensable method for the scientific study of the meaning of ancient texts. Holy Scripture, inasmuch as it

---

[7] Cf. *Divino Afflante Spiritu* 11–15.

[8] *Dei Verbum* 12.

[9] Cf. ibid.

[10] Pontifical Biblical Commission, *The Interpretation of the Bible in the Church* (Vatican City, 1993).

is the "Word of God in human language", has been composed by human authors in all its various parts and in all the sources that lie behind them. Because of this, its proper understanding not only admits the use of this method but actually requires it.[11]

Although it does not constitute the Magisterium either, the book *Jesus of Nazareth*, by Joseph Ratzinger (Benedict XVI), expresses well the concern of the Pope, who, while conscious of the limits of the historical-critical method, tried to underline its validity, as it constitutes one of the fundamental dimensions of exegesis, although it does not exhaust the task of interpretation:

> The historical-critical method—specifically because of the intrinsic nature of theology and faith—is and remains an indispensable dimension of exegetical work. For it is of the very essence of biblical faith to be about real historical events. . . . The historical-critical method—let me repeat —is an indispensable tool, given the structure of Christian faith.[12]

Benedict XVI himself tried to make clear the value of the historical-critical method by highlighting its importance, this time in an authoritative manner, in his recent post-synodal exhortation *Verbum Domini*:

> Before all else, we need to acknowledge the benefits that historical-critical exegesis and other recently-developed methods of textual analysis have brought to the life of the Church. For the Catholic understanding of sacred Scripture, attention to such methods is indispensable, linked as it is to the realism of the Incarnation: "This necessity is a consequence of the Christian principle formulated in the Gospel of John 1:14: *Verbum caro factum est*. The historical fact is a constitutive dimension of the Christian faith. The history of salvation is not mythology, but a true history, and it should thus be studied with the methods of serious historical research."[13]

Since the historical-critical method continues to be indispensable, it will not suffice—and this is the second temptation—to "defend ourselves" from the most "harmful" results of it with a kind of self-affirmation of the faith and dogmas beyond history and reason. This

---

[11] Cf. ibid., I A.

[12] J. Ratzinger (Benedict XVI), *Jesus of Nazareth: From the Baptism in the Jordan to the Transfiguration*, trans. Adrian J. Walker (New York: Doubleday, 2007), xv–xvi.

[13] *Verbum Domini* 32.

position, which arose at the very dawn of critical exegesis, has contributed to the radical separation between exegesis and theology, which only coexist in an irreconcilable dualism. It is curious that this position is not exclusively that of the detractors of the historical-critical method but is shared by the very founders of the method. Let us consider a very illustrative example, although it relates to the study of the New Testament (NT).

To wit, in 1835 D. F. Strauss published his *Leben Jesu* (*The Life of Jesus*), which sets out to destroy the historical foundations of faith in Jesus as he appears in the Gospels. In the epilogue to this work, however, he undertakes the task of reconstructing this same faith on other foundations:

> The results of the inquiry which we have now brought to a close, have apparently annihilated the greatest and most valuable part of that which the Christian has been wont to believe concerning his Saviour Jesus, have uprooted all the animating motives which he has gathered from his faith, and withered all his consolations. The boundless store of truth and life which for eighteen centuries has been the aliment of humanity, seems irretrievably dissipated; the most sublime levelled with the dust, God divested of his grace, man of his dignity, and the tie between heaven and earth broken. Piety turns away with horror from so fearful an act of desecration, and strong in the impregnable self-evidence of its faith, pronounces that, let an audacious criticism attempt what it will, all which the Scriptures declare, and the Church believes of Christ, will still subsist as eternal truth, nor needs one iota of it to be renounced. Thus at the conclusion of the criticism of the history of Jesus, there presents itself this problem: to re-establish dogmatically [that is, on the theological level] that which has been destroyed critically [that is, on the historical level].[14]

As can be seen, the separation between reason and faith, and, consequently, between exegesis (critical and historical) and theology-spirituality-piety (uncritical, dogmatic, believing), is present at the very origin of the critical study of the Bible.

Nor will it suffice—and this is the third temptation—for us to adopt an "intermediate" position that affirms the need for the historical-

---

[14] D. F. Strauss, *The Life of Jesus Critically Examined*, trans. George Eliot, 4th ed., (London, 1902), §144.

critical study of Scripture but that chooses from it only the results that are compatible with the data of tradition. With regard to the OT, this "pliable" position has been found frequently in the second half of the twentieth century. Many theologians have constructed their theology on the basis of some information from historical-critical exegesis that it was possible to bring back and incorporate, in broad strokes, into a linear history of salvation, while discarding the more problematic information. For this position, the book *Old Testament Theology*, by G. von Rad,[15] was the mirror in which to look.

However, this position leaves open the breach between exegesis and theology, which only touch through an effort at conciliation that works in the always unstable zone where the fields intersect. As a consequence, the strength of the theological construction will be affected by the greater or lesser soundness of the exegetical information, which, as has been seen in recent decades, changes like fashions. The fact that in this position exegesis and theology affirm themselves while they use each other is a clear sign that the changes in paradigms in exegesis do not entail a crisis in theology: the same building remains standing while changing some foundations . . . that in fact are not the true foundations. Both disciplines maintain their principles unquestioned. With a division like this, Scripture can hardly be the *soul of theology*.[16]

In the first part of this work (chapters 1 and 2), I want to go down a different and little explored path that may truly contribute to the task of arriving at a non-dualistic exegesis. This will consist of carrying out a self-criticism of the historical-critical method beginning within this very method. In a lecture in New York in 1988, which quickly became a "classical" text, the then Cardinal J. Ratzinger, speaking of the crisis in modern exegesis, presented the need for self-criticism in this way:

> What we need is a criticism of the criticism. We cannot develop it from the outside, however, but only from the inside, from critical thought's

---

[15] G. von Rad, *Old Testament Theology*, one-volume ed. (Peabody, Mass., 2005).

[16] Cf. the expression from the encyclical *Providentissimus Deus*, picked up subsequently by the decree *Optatam Totius* 16: "The students are to be formed with particular care in the study of the Bible, which ought to be, as it were, the soul of all theology. After a suitable introduction they are to be initiated carefully into the method of exegesis; and they are to see the great themes of divine revelation and to receive from their daily reading of and meditating on the sacred books inspiration and nourishment."

own potential for self-criticism: a self-critique of historical exegesis that can be expanded into a critique of historical reason that both carries on and modifies Kant's critiques of reason.[17]

Of what does this "criticism of criticism" consist? Cardinal Ratzinger himself explains it, putting the emphasis on a *diachronic* reading of the results of exegesis:

> The historical method would have to begin its self-critique by reading its findings diachronically and so by taking distance from the impression of quasi-scientific certainty with which it has largely been accustomed to present its interpretations.[18]

> Exegesis can no longer be studied in a linear-synchronic fashion, after the manner of scientific discoveries, which do not depend upon their history, but only on how exactly they measure their data. Exegesis needs to recognize its own nature as a historical discipline. Its history belongs to its being. In critically classifying its respective positions within the whole of its own history, it will recognize the relativity of its judgments, on the one hand, while being better equipped to penetrate to the real, albeit always unfinished, understanding of the biblical Word, on the other.[19]

A diachronic reading of the results of historical-critical exegesis, in the present case in certain fields of the OT, can in fact be enormously instructive. It would be a matter of describing the evolution or development of biblical exegesis across time, situating it in its historical context, presenting the important figures who carry it out and the determining factors that lead them to their respective views. In this way it would become apparent that the supposed "objectivity" by which the exegete is moved is not always such. As a product of his time, the scholar approaches the Bible with a collection of prejudices or prior understandings, in most cases unconscious or at least unformulated, which condition the results of his research. In fact, a "history" of exegesis shows how great paradigms that at one point seemed irrefutable

---

[17] J. Ratzinger, "Biblical Interpretation in Conflict: On the Foundations and the Itinerary of Exegesis Today", in *Opening Up the Scriptures: Joseph Ratzinger and the Foundations of Biblical Interpretation*, ed. José Granados, Carlos Granados, and Luis Sánchez-Navarro (Grand Rapids, 2008), 8.

[18] Ibid.

[19] Ibid., 28.

wound up being abandoned after a time. This in and of itself says a great deal about the initial presuppositions. It also shows that the exegete is not free from the great ideologies or world views that dominate an era. In many cases they constitute his starting point or prior understanding when he approaches the Bible. Thus it is possible to understand why Ratzinger, in the lecture cited, asked for scientific exegesis to "recognize the philosophical element in a whole series of its basic axioms" and invited it to "test the findings that rest on these axioms".[20] John Paul II, years later (1998), gave an invitation to serious discernment before applying to the Sacred Scripture "the various hermeneutical approaches [which] have their own philosophical underpinnings".[21]

A paradigmatic case of diachronic reading of the results of historical-critical exegesis, with regard to the NT, is the work of Albert Schweitzer, published in 1905, in which he reviews more than a century of research on the life of Jesus, from Reimarus to Wrede.[22] In fact, it represented a turning point in the search for the historical Jesus and in the history of modern exegesis. In it, the ideal of objectivity free from interference on the part of the subject, which liberal theology had advocated, was shown to be unachievable. In spite of the use of methods that promised such objectivity, the divergence of the results revealed that it had been impossible to eliminate the subject who was using the method. The work of Schweitzer clearly showed the impossibility of an objective historical reconstruction of the life of Jesus.

In addition, it made it obvious that such research was very far from having been carried out because of true historical interest:

> The historical investigation of the life of Jesus did not take its rise from a purely historical interest; it turned to the Jesus of history as an ally in the struggle against the tyranny of dogma.[23]

As many models of Jesus appeared as there were biographers of him. They did nothing more than project their own categories onto the life of Jesus:

---

[20] Ibid.

[21] *Fides et ratio* 55.

[22] A. Schweitzer, *The Quest of the Historical Jesus*, rev. trans. (Minneapolis, 2001).

[23] Ibid., 5.

Thus each successive epoch of theology found its own thoughts in Jesus; that was, indeed, the only way in which it could make Him live.

But it was not only each epoch that found its reflection in Jesus; each individual created Jesus in accordance with his own character.[24]

Schweitzer made a great contribution to exegesis by underlining the ideological and philosophical presuppositions of each attempt to describe the life of Jesus. This is one way in which he became a precursor of the great hermeneutics of the twentieth century, which would definitively bring to the table, at least in theoretical discussion, the factor of prior understanding when approaching the text. So the radical statement of Ratzinger in the aforementioned lecture should not be surprising: "The debate about modern exegesis is not at its core a debate among historians, but among philosophers."[25]

Significantly, exegesis is a human "science", and therefore its results are absolutely conditioned by the position that investigators take with regard to the object. They cannot claim the objectivity characteristic of the natural sciences. If this is obvious in the case of historians, it is even more so in the case of exegetes. Indeed, the nature of their object (the event of the revelation of God in history as attested in Scripture) requires that they take a position that will condition their greater or lesser understanding of this event.

The work of Schweitzer can be a mirror in which to observe oneself when reviewing the history of the modern exegesis of the Old Testament. Ratzinger's suggestion that a criticism of criticism be performed from within critical thought itself, through a diachronic reading of the

---

[24] Ibid., 6.

[25] Ratzinger, "Biblical Interpretation in Conflict", 19. Along very similar lines, although with a very different analysis and proposal, J. Barr later expressed the view, "The methodological discussions in which biblical studies are now engaged seem to me to have rather little to do with the Bible itself. They are not based on the Bible, nor can they be settled by the Bible. . . . These discussions seem to me to be discussions of our own modern experience and it is our own modern experience in its many varied aspects that is the authority to which we are appealing" (J. Barr, "The Synchronic, the Diachronic and the Historical: A Triangular Relationship?" in *Synchronic or Diachronic? A Debate on Method in Old Testament Exegesis*, ed. J. C. de Moor, OTS 34 [Leiden, New York, and Cologne, 1995], 14). R. A. Harrisville and W. Sundberg start from this statement by Ratzinger and study the historical and philosophical context in which the main champions of historical criticism were born and moved (R. A. Harrisville and W. Sundberg, *The Bible in Modern Culture: Baruch Spinoza to Brevard Childs*, 2nd ed. [Grand Rapids, 2002]).

results of historical-critical exegesis, will be the method that I will follow. In the first chapters of this work (chapters 1 and 2), I want to direct that diachronic look toward the research in two central fields of the Old Testament: the formation of the Pentateuch and the introduction to the prophets. In spite of the fact that these are two fields with clearly differing outlines, the research that has been concerned with them has partaken of the same cultural context, so that many of the problems that will be seen during the review, and even the authors dealt with, will be common to both.

In the first chapter, I will carefully go over the history of research into the composition of the first five books of the Bible. The documentary hypothesis, the most refined form of which bears the imprint of J. Wellhausen, has provided the interpretive framework for the Pentateuch for almost a century. Only in the last three decades has it begun to be called into question. Today we have sufficient information, and sufficient historical perspective, to uncover the philosophical and cultural presuppositions that were behind that hypothesis. Part of this chapter will be devoted to this matter. Similarly, the passage of time, together with hermeneutical reflection, has made it possible to identify some methodological problems that served as the basis for the paradigm that was able to be so long dominant in biblical studies. In the final part, I will turn my attention to the alternative proposals for a synchronic reading of the Pentateuch.

In the second chapter, I will take a diachronic look at "critical" research into the prophets, the beginning of which is usually placed around 1875, starting with the works of Wellhausen and B. Duhm. In this case, too, statements about the role of the prophets in the history of Israel as well as the image of them that has been transmitted have been strongly conditioned by very specific philosophical and cultural presuppositions. In the final part of the chapter I will also present new interpretive proposals that represent a radical alternative to the preceding model.

But all this self-criticism of the historical-critical method, while enormously instructive, will require a *pars construens* to contribute effectively to the proposal for a new exegesis. This is precisely what I propose to do in the third chapter. In it, in the context of the information that has been brought to light in the first two, I will try to expound the characteristic dimensions of the Catholic interpretation of the OT.

The whole preceding exposition, which is of enormous hermeneutical significance, will provide the framework for discussing the most suitable way to approach Scripture and the factors that favor a correct interpretation of it. The overarching intention of this third chapter is to understand how it is possible to have an exegesis that is at once critical and theological and that therefore transcends the reason-faith dualism to which I referred above. The dogmatic constitution on Divine Revelation, *Dei Verbum*, which presents the fundamental principles of biblical interpretation, will serve as the framework for the discussion.

Finally, in the concluding section, I will first bring together the results of the study about the history of research on the formation of the Pentateuch and on the prophets, so that it will be possible to judge the fruitfulness of Ratzinger's *desideratum* that I have sought to fulfill: the need for a criticism of the historical-critical method from within the method itself. In addition, I will take a synthetic look at my attempt to bring the twofold task of exegesis back to unity.

Research on the Formation of the Pentateuch

That the Pentateuch is a "composite" work, that is, a work in which smaller units of different provenance, length, and era converge, is a fact that today is obvious in the eyes of literary criticism. It would suffice to read attentively the opening part of this work, Genesis 1–2, to realize this. Indeed, in Genesis 2:4 we find the end of one creation account and the beginning of another. In the first part of this verse (2:4a), one complete account ends that has seen the creation in six days, crowned by the appearance of man and by God resting. In the second part (2:4b), with no transition, a new account begins that starts with an earth on which there is still no vegetation or any man to work it:

> [2:4a] These are the generations of the heavens and the earth when they were created.
> [2:4b] In the day that the LORD God made the earth and the heavens, [2:5] when no plant of the field was yet in the earth and no herb of the field had yet sprung up—for the LORD God had not caused it to rain upon the earth, and there was no man to till the ground. . . .

In the first account (Gen 1:1–2:4a), the divine term *'Elohîm* is used, while in the second (Gen 2:4b–23) *YHWH 'Elohîm* is used. In one the verb *br'* ("create") is used, and in the other the verb *yṣr* ("form"). In addition, in the first, creation is carried out by means of the word, while in the second, it is achieved by work. These are all clear signs of literary composition.

What seems obvious today, though, has not always seemed so. On the contrary, the weight of the traditional attribution of the Pentateuch to Moses (an attribution external to the Pentateuch itself)[1] has for many centuries conditioned the reading of the first five books of the Bible,

---

[1] Cf. J. Blenkinsopp, *The Pentateuch: An Introduction to the First Five Books of the Bible* (New York, 1992), 1–2; J.-L. Ska, *Introduzione alla lettura del Pentateuco: Chiavi per l'interpretazione dei*

to the point of glossing over many pieces of information that should have called that attribution into question.

I will now review the stages through which the critical study of the formation of the Pentateuch has gone from its origin to the present day. This examination will not be guided as much by a zeal for exhaustiveness as by an interest in the factors that have been decisive in determining the path of exegesis and the methodological questions that are involved in the choices of this exegesis.

I. The Documentary Hypothesis

A. From the Beginnings to De Wette

Although some authors had earlier denied the Mosaic authorship of certain passages of the Pentateuch,[2] the true critical study of its sources would come in 1711 from the pen of Henning Bernhard Witter (1683–1715), who was the first to call attention to the differences in the divine appellations in Genesis 1–3, as has just been described. However, the one who claimed the honor of being the pioneer is Jean Astruc (1684–1766), who in 1753, on the basis of the same data, proposed three sources for the book of Genesis and for Exodus 1–2: one Elohist, one Yahwist, and a third composed of independent material. The basic contribution of Astruc was that of proposing a hypothesis about composition that covered the whole book of Genesis (and part of Exodus) on the basis of a fact that he considered the keystone: the revelation of the divine name YHWH in Exodus 3:14. The Elohist source would have to be the most ancient. The Yahwist source, from the time of Moses, must have projected back in time a divine name that only became known at the time of the departure from Egypt.

While Astruc was the first to propose a "theory of documents", he was also responsible for guiding the critical study of the Bible down a path loaded with hypotheses that were not always well founded. In-

---

primi libri della Bibbia (Rome, 1998), trans. Pascale Dominique as *Introduction to Reading the Pentateuch* (Winona Lake, 2006), 96–99.

[2] Abraham Ibn Ezra, in the twelfth century, and Baruch Spinoza, in his *Tractatus Theologico-politicus*, published in 1670. Cf. Blenkinsopp, *Pentateuch: An Introduction*, 2.

deed, while in the first chapters of Genesis there are enough elements to support its composite character, the step to a general theory that proposes, on the basis of the "key" of Exodus 3:14, complete documents that have been combined is a step that does not necessarily follow.

Astruc's theory would be expanded and presented in a systematic manner some years later by Johann Gottfried Eichhorn (1752–1827), whose *Einleitung in das Alte Testament* (Introduction to the Old Testament) would be widely distributed.[3] It was, at this first stage, the best representative of the documentary hypothesis, which supported the existence of several complete, parallel, and independent documents at the origin of the Pentateuch.

It is well worth noting that none of the authors cited so far openly called into question the Mosaic authorship of the Pentateuch. They were all able to make their theories compatible with the figure of Moses, who was believed to have played the part of a kind of compiler of materials.

A contemporary of Eichhorn was Alexander Geddes (1737–1802),[4] who supported the idea of the composition of the Pentateuch, not on the basis of complete documents, but on the basis of multiple small narrative units and other incomplete and independent texts. This theory would be known as the *fragmentary hypothesis*. In this view, the final compiler was no longer Moses, but an author or authors who were much later. As will soon be seen, historical circumstances would keep this theory from having as much prominence in history as its rival, the documentary hypothesis. Today, though, after two centuries, it is again gaining importance as a real alternative.

Wilhelm Martin Leberecht de Wette (1780–1849) was to be the author who would definitively break with the Mosaic authorship of the Pentateuch. His studies of the books of Chronicles, comparing them with the parallels in Samuel and Kings, led him to conclude that the chronicler wrote long after the events that he narrated (in the Persian or even the Hellenistic era) and that he projected the late institutions of the temple into the era of Moses. What seemed evident in the case of the chronicler became a plausible hypothesis in the case of the

---

[3] J. G. Eichhorn, *Einleitung in das Alte Testament* (Göttingen, 1780–1783).

[4] A. Geddes, *The Holy Bible as the Books Accounted Sacred by Jews and Christians* (London, 1792); A. Geddes, *Critical Remarks* (London, 1800).

Pentateuch: many laws and narratives of the first five books of the Bible could reflect the historical picture of later eras that were made to go back to the time of Moses (and thus derive support from it).

The great contribution of De Wette to the documentary hypothesis, however, was having found a point in history that served to date the different documents. In 1805 he published his doctoral thesis,[5] in which he identified the scroll discovered in the Jerusalem temple during the reform of Josiah (622 B.C.) with the book of Deuteronomy, or at least with an early edition of it. Not only did the hypothesis prove to be attractive, but once it was taken into consideration, it made it possible to discover a surprising coincidence between the spirit and the institutions of the reform (as shown in 2 Kings 22–23) and the content and demands of Deuteronomy. The date of Josiah's reform therefore became the key for dating the documents: those laws and accounts that presuppose the institutions and demands of Deuteronomy and 2 Kings 22–23 (the heart of which was the unification and centralization of the cult in Jerusalem) would have to be later than the reform, while those that show no knowledge of them would have to be prior.

Before moving on to the next stage, it is necessary to present a third theory, known as the *complementary* or *supplementary hypothesis*. Its paternity must be attributed to Heinrich Ewald (1803–1875),[6] who suggested considering the Elohist document to be the base document that supported the skeleton of the narrative of the Pentateuch, to which other "complements" had been added that did not form part of a complete document. In this way it would be possible to solve the problem of why the final redactor had not eliminated the inconsistencies that are found in the account: the "supplements" were later than his activity. This theory, displaced by the success of the documentary hypothesis, was to gain new prominence in the present day.

B. Wellhausen

In spite of the fact that authors such as Astruc, Eichhorn, and De Wette were present at the origin of the documentary hypothesis, it would be the name of the Protestant exegete Julius Wellhausen (1844–1918), the

---

[5] W. M. L. de Wette, *Dissertatio critica qua Deuteronomium diversium a prioribus Pentateuchi libris, alius cuiusdam recentioris autoris opus esse demonstratur* (Jena, 1805).

[6] H. Ewald, *Geschichte des Volkes Israels bis Christus* (Göttingen, 1843–1845).

son of a Lutheran pastor, that would become permanently associated with this theory. With him it would find its most classic, clear, and systematic formulation. For this, though, he needed the contribution of other exegetes, who honed the presentation of the documentary hypothesis and prepared the way for it.

First, Karl David Ilgen[7] (1763–1834) and, immediately afterward, Hermann Hupfeld[8] (1796–1866) distinguished two different sources within the Elohist account: E^1 (older) and E^2 (more recent). In this way the source that would later be called *Priestly*, to distinguish it from the *Elohist*, made its appearance. In 1866 Karl Heinrich Graf (1815–1869),[9] based on the studies of his teacher Edouard Reuss,[10] would assign a late date, subsequent to the exile, to one of the two sources, both of which were still called *Elohist*. Since the preexilic prophets show no familiarity with the Mosaic legal system and since, on the contrary, the ritual laws are clearly linked to the prophet Ezekiel, the first Elohist source, which contains these codes, must be moved back at least to the period of the exile. It is here that it is necessary to locate the origin of a revolution in Pentateuchal studies that would only catch on with the guidance of a historian's mind like that of Wellhausen. In the history of Judaism and of the interpretation of the Bible, the Torah had always been the center, the foundation on which the rest of the history of Israel developed. Thus it was natural that, in the early division into sources, the legislative core should be considered the most ancient. The intuition of Reuss, to which Graf gave voice, therefore looked like a genuine revolution.

It was to Abraham Kuenen (1828–1891)[11] that credit would go for coining the definitive name of *Priestercodex* (whence the initial P, which

---

[7] K. D. Ilgen, *Die Urkunden des Jerusalemer Tempelarchivs in ihrer Urgestalt, als Beitrag zur Berichtigung der Geschichte der Religion und Politik aus dem Hebräischen mit kritischen und erklärenden Anmerkungen, auch mancherley dazu gehörenden Abhandlungen* (Halle, 1798). The idea of written documents had already become so deeply rooted that Ilgen thought that both Elohist sources were part of the archives in the Jerusalem temple that were destroyed in 587 B.C.

[8] H. Hupfeld, *Die Quellen der Genesis und die Art ihrer Zusammensetzung von neuem untersucht* (Berlin, 1853).

[9] K. H. Graf, *Die Geschichtlichen Bücher des Alten Testaments: Zwei historischkritischen Untersuchungen* (Leipzig, 1866).

[10] Reuss had already expounded his theories about the formation of the Pentateuch in 1833, but he did not publish them until 1879: E. Reuss, *L'Historie sainte et la Loi* (Paris, 1879).

[11] A. Kuenen, "Critische bijdragen tot de geschiedenis van den Israëlitischen godsdienst. V. De priestelijke bestanddeelen van Pentateuch en Josua", *ThT* 4 (1870): 391–426, 487–526.

is used to distinguish the priestly document) to identify one of the two sources into which E had been divided, namely, the one that contained the legislative material. For his part, Eduard Karl August Riehm (1830–1888),[12] in 1854 isolated the fourth source in the classic theory, the Deuteronomist, responsible for the last book of the Pentateuch.

All the "ingredients" were now present for Wellhausen to make his particular collage. One of them, the most critical one, came to his awareness almost by chance. In the introduction to his *Prolegomena zur Geschichte Israels*[13] (1883), Wellhausen recounts that it was during a visit to Göttingen in 1867 that he learned, through Albrecht Ritschl, that Graf situated the Law chronologically after the prophets. He later learned that Graf owed this insight to his teacher, Reuss, and that other authors, such as Leopold George and Wilhelm Vatke,[14] had independently come to the same conclusion at the same time. The idea that the Law was a postexilic construct and that, therefore, it was not found at the origin of Israel immediately took hold in the mind of a Wellhausen already internally prepared to receive it.[15]

The possibility of understanding the origins of Israel without reference to the Law became the cornerstone of the historical reconstruction done by Wellhausen. In fact, this author must be considered more a historian (of the religion of Israel) than a theologian or scholar of biblical literature.[16] The classic sequence of the four sources of the doc-

---

[12] E. Riehm, *Die Gesetzgebung Moses in Lande Moab* (Gotha, 1854).

[13] J. Wellhausen, *Prolegomena zur Geschichte Israels*, 6th ed. (Berlin, 1905). Translated as *Prolegomena to the History of Israel* (Edinburgh, 1885).

[14] On the relationship between Wellhausen and Vatke, see L. Perlitt, *Vatke und Wellhausen*, BZAW 94 (Berlin, 1965).

[15] Cf. Wellhausen, *Prolegomena to the History of Israel*, 3–4.

[16] Wellhausen was well aware of the break with the classic (and thus ecclesiastical) interpretation that was entailed by delaying the Law. In fact, he resigned from a professorship in Greifswald when he found out that he had to teach candidates for church ministry. His letter of resignation, addressed to the Prussian ministry of worship, dated April 5, 1882, reads as follows: "I became a theologian because I am interested in the scientific study of the Bible, and I have only gradually become aware that a professor of theology also has the practical task of preparing students for service in the evangelical Church, and I am not prepared to undertake this task. Furthermore, in spite of all the discretion of which I am able, I cause my hearers to become unfit for their occupation. Since then, my responsibility as a professor of theology has weighed seriously on my conscience" (quoted in H.-J. Kraus, *Geschichte der historisch-kritischen Erforschung des Alten Testament*, 3rd ed. [Neukirchen-Vluyn, 1982], 256). Contrary to what was done by other major exegetes before him, Wellhausen did not seem willing or able to reconstruct "dogmatically" what had been destroyed "critically" (cf. Strauss, *Das Leben Jesu*, § 144).

umentary hypothesis in fact constituted an orderly linear view of the history of Israel. This view replaced the old one, the one presented by the texts themselves and calmly passed down by both Judaism and the Church for centuries: the Law, received at Sinai, precedes the entrance into the Promised Land.

On the basis of a careful study of the laws and narratives of the Hexateuch[17] (he considered that the conquest of the Promised Land was the true end of the primordial history and thus included the book of Joshua), Wellhausen offered the following sequence of written documents and combinations among them.

Chronologically, the first document was taken to be the Yahwist (J), who wrote in the early part of the monarchy in Judah (ninth century B.C.). Later was the Elohist document (E), which must have been situated in the context of the Northern Kingdom around the eighth century, by this time already under the influence of classical prophecy. Both documents include primarily narrative material, with the exception of some early legislative material (of an ethical nature, centered around the Decalogue and the Book of the Covenant) concentrated in Exodus 20–23 and Exodus 34. The reform of Josiah (end of the seventh century) was supposed to be the time frame for the redaction of the third document, Deuteronomy (D). With this document, the first systematic codification of written laws came onto the stage, and it would change the nature of ancient Israel. The last document was the Priestly one (P), from the postexilic era, although it included material from the time of the exile, as can be seen from its dependence on Ezekiel. The majority of the legislative material was concentrated in it. This last document, which contains the priestly material, is occasionally called *Quattuor* by Wellhausen, in reference to the historical framework of four covenants (with Adam, with Noah, with Abraham, and with Israel at Sinai). It should be emphasized that the documentary hypothesis does not speak generically of four sources but, rather, of four *written documents* or accounts that are considered to have internal *consistency*.

In Wellhausen's opinion, the first two documents were combined to form a consistent account by an editor whom he called the "Jehovist". Since Deuteronomy shows familiarity with that combination and not

---

[17] J. Wellhausen, *Die Composition des Hexateuchs und der historischen Bücher des Alten Testaments*, 4th ed. (1866; Berlin, 1963).

with the priestly account, it is logical to think that the D account would have been added to the JE document first, and only later would the collection be combined with P. The final edition of the Hexateuch as we know it would be linked with the reform of Ezra (fifth century B.C.).[18]

History and literary analysis depend heavily on one another and are often completely mixed together in Wellhausen's model. His historical reconstruction recognized three basic phases, which coincide with the three periods of literary activity: the beginnings of the monarchy (J–E), the reform of Josiah (D), the postexilic phase (P). The great institutions of Israel (places of worship, sacrifices, feasts, priesthood, offerings) can be studied during their historical development by following this tripartite division. Thus, for example, the places of worship in Israel went through three clearly differentiated phases:[19]

— In the first phase, which covers the time from the conquest to the seventh century B.C., YHWH was worshipped at different sanctuaries, both in those places of Canaanite origin and in those more recently founded. They are all the "dwelling" of YHWH, privileged places for relating to him. However, they are not exclusive; private worship of the same YHWH is also practiced at altars in the countryside, on hills, under trees.

Witnesses to this stage are the J and E documents, which show the patriarchs consecrating some sanctuaries (Shechem, Bethel, Beersheba) after receiving a divine manifestation.

— A second stage is said to have been inaugurated with the reform of Josiah, which entails the unification and centralization of the cult in Jerusalem and the elimination of the rest of the sanctuaries and places of worship.

The book that 2 Kings 22 presents as the origin of the reform of Josiah, discovered in the temple in 622 B.C., would be precisely the book of Deuteronomy (the D document), a witness to this phase.

— The third and final stage begins with the return from exile in Babylon and the reconstruction of the temple, which is when the centraliza-

---

[18] Cf. the promulgation of the "book of the law of Moses which the LORD had given to Israel" in Neh 8:1.

[19] Cf. Wellhausen, *Prolegomena to the History of Israel*, 17–51.

tion of the cult in Jerusalem really triumphs, almost like an institution that had never known any previous form.

The priestly document was believed to be a witness to this era, with its attempt to move the origin of the one temple in Jerusalem back in time to the construction of the tent of meeting on Mount Sinai.

What led to this view? Was a certain image of the historical development of the religion of Israel what guided the process of distinguishing documents? Or was it, rather, the results of literary criticism that revealed historical evolution in the institutions of Israel? There can be no doubt that both factors are often mixed together in Wellhausen's hypothesis, and this, as we will see later, is one of its weak points.

The "Wellhausian" model of the documentary hypothesis was rewarded with immediate success in the academic realm and gradually became established as the only model for explaining the formation of the Pentateuch. The clarity of its exposition and the historical reading that went with it constituted a new paradigm, a "scientific" one, that replaced the old and "naïve" paradigm received from tradition (whether Jewish or Christian). The strength and attractiveness of this new paradigm are shown by the fact that it was held for more than a century as the virtually exclusive model and that it also became established in the Catholic realm. But for that to happen, the involvement of some "unique" figures was necessary, people who made the model "kinder", although, paradoxically, they wound up undermining its foundations.

C. Gunkel, von Rad, and Noth

Hermann Gunkel (1862–1932),[20] the son of a Lutheran pastor, burst onto the scene of biblical studies with solid literary training and a broad knowledge of the discoveries that, in the second half of the nineteenth century, had brought to light a good part of the religious literature of the area around Israel. He himself can be considered a representative of the History of Religions school, an intellectual movement that placed great importance on the comparative study of religious texts. While

---

[20] For a study of the life and work of Gunkel, see W. Klatt, *Hermann Gunkel: Zu seiner Theologie der Religionsgeschichte und zur Entstehung der formgeschichtliche Methode* (Göttingen, 1969).

Wellhausen discounted (or rather ignored) all influence of the literature of the Middle East on the biblical corpus, Gunkel came to believe that there were strong connections between the religion of Israel and the religious life of Mesopotamia and Ancient Egypt.[21]

Gunkel never questioned the existence of written documents at the origin of the Pentateuch; in fact, he took them as his starting point. However, his real objective was to delve into their prehistory, into that non-literary phase of the period prior to the monarchy. Wellhausen insisted on one period, the monarchical one, as the origin of the literary activity and on one format, that of the written document, as the key to understanding the current Pentateuch. Gunkel, for his part, wanted to go back to the period of the judges and even earlier, to nomadic Israel, and study the oral traditions that only later would be written down.[22] Gunkel can be considered the father of *Formgeschichte*, or the *history of forms*, because he paid attention to the smaller units transmitted orally. However, he was to lay the foundations of what subsequently, with the work of von Rad and Noth, would be known as the method of the history of traditions, which investigates how the traditions about Israel's past came to be fixed and preserved before being put into writing.

What were the criteria and the instruments for identifying the orally transmitted units of which Gunkel spoke? Two terms are key for this task: *literary genres* (*Gattungen*) and the *social situation* (*Sitz im Leben*) in which they arise. Gunkel started with the narrative units of Genesis, the book to which he devoted the most attention. In his opinion, a careful look at their literary and esthetic characteristics would make it possible to identify key points that distinguished some units from others. These characteristics are the ones that make it possible to speak of literary genre. Gunkel lists three essential characteristics:

—A structure and a series of formulas.
—An atmosphere and a way of thinking.
—A social situation (*Sitz im Leben*).

---

[21] Wellhausen harshly criticized the use that Gunkel made of the literary sources outside the Bible, perhaps sensing the threat that it represented for his theory of the four documents. Cf. ibid., 70–74.

[22] The difference with Wellhausen is perfectly illustrated by the first thesis in the introduction to the third edition of his commentary on Genesis: "Genesis is a collection of sagas (*Sagen*)" (cf. H. Gunkel, *Genesis*, 3rd ed., GHZAT 1, 1 [Göttingen, 1910], vii).

The last of these characteristics, destined to become a commonplace in *Formgeschichte*, was key for Gunkel: "Whoever wants to understand an ancient literary genre must ask himself first where its roots are in the life of the people (*Sitz im Volksleben*)."[23] This social context, which is decisive for the different literary genres, can be quite varied. In the case of a great number of psalms (another of the books most studied by Gunkel), the context would be cultic. In the case of Genesis, especially in the patriarchal traditions, the genre is very much that of the family: the stories of the ancestors were transmitted from parents to children in the heart of the family. Gunkel called this genre the *saga*, using a term coined in the literary studies of the era to identify the great Nordic accounts that had been transmitted orally and that were only then beginning to be collected in writing.

The fact that Gunkel never openly challenged the dominant theory (on the contrary, he made use of the classic scheme of written sources in his commentary on Genesis) meant that his studies, which posed questions that were very hard for the documentary hypothesis to solve, had the effect of reinforcing this very theory by also covering the prehistory of the texts.

The figure who contributed the most, though, to the peaceful acceptance of Wellhausen's model was undoubtedly Gerhard von Rad (1901–1971), a Lutheran pastor, who managed to construct a beautiful theology[24] on the basis of the documentary hypothesis, which saved the basic historical core of the faith of Israel. As in the case of Gunkel, the studies of von Rad also contained at their base elements that undermined the heart of the classic theory, but exegesis would realize this only much later.

Without doubting the existence of large written documents at the origin of the Hexateuch, von Rad preferred to start from its final form and consider it a progressive expansion of an original historical credo that in its simplest and most primitive form contained the entrance of the ancestors into Egypt, the exodus, and the conquest of the land.[25] Its clearest formulation can be found in Deuteronomy 26:5–9:

---

[23] H. Gunkel, "Die israelitische Literatur", in *Die Kultur der Gegenwart: Die orientalischen Literaturen*, ed. P. Hinneberg (Berlin and Leipzig, 1906), 53.

[24] G. von Rad, *Theologie des Alten Testaments*, 4th ed. (Munich, 1962).

[25] For what follows, cf. G. von Rad, *Das Formgeschichtliche Problem des Hexateuch*, BWANT 78 (Stuttgart, 1938).

"A wandering Aramean was my father; and he went down into Egypt and sojourned there, few in number; and there he became a nation, great, mighty, and populous. And the Egyptians treated us harshly, and afflicted us, and laid upon us hard bondage. Then we cried to the LORD the God of our fathers, and the LORD heard our voice, and saw our affliction, our toil, and our oppression; and the LORD brought us out of Egypt with a mighty hand and an outstretched arm, with great terror, with signs and wonders; and he brought us into this place and gave us this land, a land flowing with milk and honey."

The *Sitz im Leben* of this small historical credo was thought to be liturgico-cultic: the feast of weeks, during the harvest, when peasants offered their firstfruits to Yahweh, precisely the context in which the passage of Deuteronomy is inserted. In von Rad's opinion, this credo goes back to the era of the judges and is linked to the sanctuary of Gilgal, the place where the entrance into the Promised Land is celebrated, which is the high point of this credo. In fact, Joshua 4:21–24, which is set in the framework of the first camp of the people in Gilgal, after crossing the Jordan, is another ancient, more synthetic formulation of the historical credo. Other formulations with the same content can be found in Deuteronomy 6:20–23 and Joshua 24:2–13.

In this formulation of the historical credo, no mention at all is made of the gift of the Law or of the primordial history either (Gen 1–11). In von Rad's opinion, the tradition of the delivery of the Law on Sinai probably belongs to a different stream, also of cultic origin: the feast of tabernacles (cf. Deut 31:9–13), linked to the sanctuary at Shechem. In Joshua 24:14–26, which is set in Shechem, Joshua seals a covenant between Yahweh and his people and imposes "statutes and ordinances", which he then writes in the book of the "Law of God". In the separation of the historical credo, on the one hand, and of the Law, on the other (both of which are present in chapter 24 of Joshua!), von Rad shows himself to be a disciple of Wellhausen, while in the search for a historical core (through the *Sitz im Leben*), he is indebted to Gunkel.[26]

---

[26] In this last case it is also necessary to recognize the influence of one of von Rad's teachers, Albrecht Alt (1883–1956), who likewise sought the original nucleus of Israel's faith in the period prior to the monarchy by identifying in the expression "the God of the fathers" the originality of a primitive personal cult linked to the nomadic (pre-Israelite) patriarchs and not to Canaanite sanctuaries. Cf. A. Alt, *Der Gott der Väter: Ein Beitrag zur Urgeschichte der israelitischen Religion*, BWANT 3 (Stuttgart, 1929).

The Yahwist redactor is taken to be the one responsible for joining the traditions of the historical credo with the legislative ones and, on the basis of these, creating a great narrative plot that goes from the primordial accounts (which he himself brought in as the great prologue to his history) up to the possession of the land (the book of Joshua). He also brings in the traditions of Abraham and Isaac, which he links to that of Jacob, which was already found in the historical credo. To join the patriarchal traditions to the exodus, he incorporates the story of Joseph. This grand narrative work is believed to have been carried out during the reign of Solomon, which satisfied all the requirements for the emergence of a "Solomonic enlightenment".

Although von Rad, like Gunkel, starts with oral traditions prior to written composition, he attributes a foundational role to the Yahwist writer, whom he considers a literary genius with great personal qualities. He considers the work of the Yahwist to be far above the Elohist and priestly accounts. His powerful theological plan stands out in it and serves as the connecting thread that runs through a very diverse collection of material. The monarchy that saw its greatest splendor with Solomon, the time when the Yahwist was writing, was the high point of the history of Israel. This monarchy even played an essential role in the universal plan of salvation, as can be seen from the presentation of the story of mankind: a story of division and sin, marked by the curse, is intersected by the story of Abraham, by whom "all the families of the earth shall bless themselves". The promise addressed to Abraham is fulfilled with the monarchy in the time of David.

A contemporary of von Rad was Martin Noth (1902–1968), a Lutheran theologian, who shared with him the conviction that the historical core of Israel should be sought in the cultic traditions of the pre-Israelite tribal confederations. While von Rad's reconstruction pursued a theological interest, Noth was moved by a historical interest: reconstructing the history of Israel.[27]

Several points, however, differentiated him from von Rad. First, from the literary point of view, Noth did not take as his basis the study of the Pentateuch or the Hexateuch; rather, he took the Tetrateuch, leaving out Deuteronomy, which he considered an introduction to the

---

[27] Cf. M. Noth, *Das System der zwölf Stämme Israels*, BWANT 52 (Stuttgart, 1930); M. Noth, *Überlieferungsgeschichte des Pentateuch* (Stuttgart, 1948); M. Noth, *Geschichte Israels* (Göttingen, 1950).

historical books (Joshua through 2 Kings). The D document did not
have any part in the Tetrateuch, nor did the JEP sources have any part
in the book of Joshua. The origins of Israel must be sought only in
the first four books of the Bible.

Second, Noth did not grant to the Yahwist the role that he had in von
Rad's reconstruction. On the contrary, for Noth the basic themes of
the Yahwist history as well as its content and even their sequence were
already fixed before the J document was written. Noth even seems to
suggest that the main traditions came through the hands of the final
redactor in written form. The same is supposed to be true of the E and
P sources. The redactors of all three documents added little to the previous material: J the primordial history and P the genealogies. In this
last document, he identifies two sources: one that is older, which contains the priestly account, and another (P^s) that is supposed to contain
the more recent supplements of a legislative character (such as most of
Leviticus).

As the name of his most important work, *Überlieferungsgeschichte des
Pentateuch* (*A History of Pentateuchal Traditions*),[28] indicates, Noth's interest is tracing the history of the traditions that have gone into the
Pentateuch (in reality, the Tetrateuch) and that are found at the origins
of Israel. He identifies five great traditions that had independent origins
and histories of transmission, linked to particular sanctuaries:

— Exit from Egypt.
— Stay in the desert.
— Entrance into the land.
— Promises to the patriarchs.
— Revelation on Sinai.

The real-life environment that made the transmission of these traditions possible is believed to have been the confederation of the twelve
tribes of Israel, which Noth compares with the Greek amphyctionies.
This is thought to be the earliest embryonic stage, in the era of the
judges, of the united monarchy.

Now that we have reviewed the theories of Gunkel, von Rad, and
Noth, we are in a position to understand why, even though they con-

---

[28] Noth, *Überlieferungsgeschichte des Pentateuch*.

tained elements that challenged the classic documentary hypothesis,[29] these theories only contributed to a wider acceptance of it.

— All three of these exegetes accepted the basic idea of the existence of four written documents and four original authors, however different the role was that each attributed to them.

— All three found the primitive core of the religion of Israel in the period that preceded the monarchy, thus neutralizing the impression that the postexilic origin of the Law left the traditions of Israel without historical foundation. Expressed in theological terms, it was possible to argue for the existence of a *revelation* at the origin of Israel, as opposed to the idea that this people represented nothing more than another expression of the *natural religions*.

— The dating of the first document, the Yahwist (J), was moved back a century, going from the ninth to the tenth century B.C. and thus strengthening the historical plausibility of the accounts. The proximity of the patriarchal traditions to the earliest writings restored a certain degree of confidence in the accounts concerning the origins of Israel.

— While von Rad insisted on theological continuity between primitive and more recent theologies in the Pentateuch (the latter do no more than complete or expand a core that is already present at the origins), Noth did the same with history and sociology, locating the roots of the basic institutions of Israel in the period of the judges.

— Von Rad's theology of the OT, which accepted and assumed the four documents of the Pentateuch, made it possible, by dating the Law late, to recover a theological reading enormously damaged by the fracturing of the collection into sources and by the rupture in the linear reading that the Bible offered. This theology had great influence in Catholic circles, where von Rad, who spoke of categories such as "history of salvation", "sin", "grace", and "promise", was the living example of the compatibility of the documentary hypothesis with the theological reading (which accepts an original revelation) of the Old Testament.

---

[29] Cf. the article by N. P. Lemche in which he states that Alt and Noth undermined the foundations of the method while they were working on it (N. P. Lemche, "Rachel and Lea. Or: On the Survival of Outdated Paradigmas in the Study of the Origin of Israel", *SJOT* 2 [1987]: 127–53).

The sense that the documentary hypothesis, especially on the basis of the labors of von Rad, had no reason to undermine the essential historicity of the origins of Israel was strengthened after the Second World War by the studies of notable authors such as William Foxwell Albright[30] (and his whole archeological school), Roland de Vaux, and John Bright. Taking advantage of the already huge amount of material available for comparison with the areas around Israel, they showed the parallels between the patriarchal stories and the laws and customs of the second millennium. Thus, for example, the Hittite vassalage treaties (dated around the fourteenth-thirteenth centuries B.C.), which showed surprising parallels with the covenant accounts in the Pentateuch, indicated the antiquity of this latter institution in Israel.[31] Likewise, some poems in the Pentateuch (Gen 49; Ex 15; Num 23–24; Deut 33) were considered, because of their form and language, to be of great antiquity, so that their content came to be seen as supporting the later narrative traditions. The great events that mark the early history of Israel were thought to have been transmitted orally in the form of songs that celebrated and memorialized epic exploits. These poems would have preserved the historical core that only later was to be developed by narrative.

The atmosphere just described, which extended up until the early seventies, is very well exemplified by two statements from authors of the stature of R. de Vaux and J. Bright. The former, referring to the traditions contained in the ancient poems of the Pentateuch, stated that "these traditions have a firm historical basis."[32] The American historian, for his part, stated, "Although we cannot undertake to reconstruct the lives of Abraham, Isaac, and Jacob, we may confidently believe that they were actual historical individuals"[33] and that "the patriarchal narratives are firmly anchored in history."[34] It is therefore not surprising that in the vast majority of schools of theology, well into the seventies, the documentary hypothesis was taught as a piece of information

---

[30] Cf. W. F. Albright, *From the Stone Age to Christianity*, 2nd ed. (New York, 1957); W. F. Albright, "Abram the Hebrew: A New Archeological Interpretation", *BASOR* 163 (1961): 36–54; W. F. Albright, *Yahweh and the Gods of Canaan: A Historical Analysis of Two Contrasting Faiths* (London, 1968); W. F. Albright, *Archeology and the Religion of Israel*, 5th ed. (New York, 1969).

[31] Cf. G. E. Mendenhall, *Law and Covenant in the Ancient Near East* (Pittsburgh, 1955).

[32] R. de Vaux, *Histoire ancienne d'Israel* (Paris, 1971), 194.

[33] J. Bright, *A History of Israel* (Philadelphia, 1981), 92.

[34] Ibid., 77.

acquired by biblical science, an indispensable foundation not only for all exegesis of the Pentateuch, but also for all theological study based on it. In fact, this hypothesis continued to be presented to students of theology practically up until the nineties, even though as early as the mid-seventies it began to be seriously called into question.

II. Presuppositions and Methodological Problems of the Documentary Hypothesis

A. Philosophical and Cultural Presuppositions of the Documentary Hypothesis

Before beginning to judge the value of the documentary hypothesis, we should stop for a moment to examine the philosophical and cultural context in which it arose, aware that theories tend to be products of their time and that the study of this time provides us with factors that are decisive for explaining them.

It is obvious that the documentary hypothesis, as Wellhausen formulated it, presupposed a certain kind of historical evolution of the religion of Israel. The four documents were just the crystallization in writing of four stages of that evolution. We have seen, as well, the decisive role that the late dating of the Law played in Wellhausen's evolutionary scheme. Now is the time to see how factors that went beyond the literary and historical realm came into play in this theory.

Indeed, in the nineteenth century, romanticism made great strides. This movement felt, in the study of cultures and history, a special attraction to what was "natural", "pure", "original", "spontaneous", as opposed to what was "formal", "complex", "regulated", "composite", which was understood to be secondary, considered to be a degenerate version of the former.[35] Darwinian evolutionism collaborated to reinforce this trend by transferring to the field of history and cultures the evolution that takes place in all living organisms: they are born, they develop, and they die.

---

[35] First among the romantic exegetes would be Johann Gottfried Herder (1744–1803), who had great influence on later generations, especially on authors such as Wellhausen, Duhm, and Gunkel. On Herder's relationship with the Bible, cf. the chapter devoted to this by H. W. Frei, *The Eclipse of Biblical Narrative: A Study in Eighteenth and Nineteenth Century Hermeneutics* (New Haven and London, 1974), 183–201.

In the biblical field, this "spirit of the times" was translated into a search for the most original manifestations of the religion of Israel, those moments in which religious expression was more genuine, more pure, less contaminated by the ritualism and legalism into which every institution inevitably degenerates with the passage of time.

It is not surprising that when Wellhausen learned that Graf placed the Law after the prophets he confessed that "almost without knowing the reasons for this hypothesis I was prepared to accept it."[36] Indeed, he was prepared to welcome the idea that what was original in the religion of Israel was, not the Law, but the spontaneity of the stories of Saul and David, of Ahab and Elijah, or the discourses of Amos and Isaiah. These accounts were fresh, clear, spontaneous, heroic, authentic, as opposed to the material that he considered late, such as Chronicles or the law codes, which were static, abstract, narrow, perverse, anxious.[37] It is noteworthy that both series of adjectives come from the analogy with living organisms, which in their evolution pass through a stage of vigor and splendor and move on to a progressive decay until reaching complete sclerosis.

Both the romantic movement and the idea of the evolution of living organisms promoted the idea of considering that which was simplest and most spontaneous to be original and the opposite to be later; and what was later was also judged to be degeneration, not advancement, progress, or a high point. In addition, these ideas turned out to be especially suggestive for a Protestant mentality that conceived of the Reformation as a movement of returning to the original purity of the Christian message, which had been betrayed by the ritual-legalistic apparatus of the medieval and Renaissance Church. In this sense, it should suffice to recall the Law-Gospel distinction emphasized by Luther. Wellhausen, a product of liberal Protestantism, would identify the Gospel with natural, rational, and humanistic religion.[38] It should not be surprising that the Yahwist, the most ancient source, is a faithful reflec-

---

[36] Wellhausen, *Prolegomena to the History of Israel*, 3.

[37] The first series of adjectives appears in the chapter that Wellhausen devotes to the books of Judges, Samuel, and Kings, while the second is predominant in the chapter devoted to Chronicles (cf. ibid., 171–294). Cf. R. A. Oden, "Intellectual History and the Study of the Bible", in *The Future of Biblical Studies: The Hebrew Scriptures*, ed. R. E. Friedman and H. G. M. Williamson (Atlanta, 1987), 1–18, esp. 5.

[38] Cf. Ska, *Introduzione alla lettura del Pentateuco*, 127.

tion of the spirit of the Reformation. He is opposed to the cult; he is not under the Law; and he shares the ethical concerns of the preexilic prophets.[39]

Another aspect in which the romantic spirit shows its influence on Wellhausen is in the idea of a writer with character (and not a mere redactor or compiler) at the origin of each of the four documents. One of the outstanding characteristics of romanticism is that of looking for literary geniuses at the origin and in the development of the great cultures.[40] After Moses' death, it was necessary to look for other strong personalities who would play the role of founders of the literature of Israel. It must be recognized that the mentality of this era had a decisive role when a step was taken that was not necessarily logical: from the composite character of the Pentateuch to the hypothesis of four complete documents with internal coherence (that is, the fruit of the literary activity of four different writers). If a century and a half ago the documentary hypothesis triumphed over the fragmentary hypothesis, it was in large part due to that cultural context. It is interesting to note that today the latter hypothesis is getting its full revenge on the former.

In addition, the parallelism between the four documents of the Pentateuch and the four Gospels seemed inevitable and favored the plausibility of a hypothesis that, it should be repeated, did not necessarily follow from the data.

Other authors think they also see a direct relationship between the admiration that Wellhausen felt for the Prussian monarchy, under which German unification came about, and the admiration he felt for King David and the first period of the united monarchy.[41] The golden age of the religion of Israel was believed to have come about precisely at this period, which is when the first document of the Pentateuch, the Yahwist, was written.

A more debatable question is that of the possible influence of Hegelian philosophy on Wellhausen's theories. All authors are in agreement about the decisive role of Hegelian dialectic in the *Biblischer Theologie*

---

[39] Cf. T. Römer, "The Elusive Yahwist: A Short History of Research", in *A Farewell to the Yahwist? The Composition of the Pentateuch in Recent European Interpretation*, ed. T. B. Dozeman and K. Schmid, SBLSS 34 (Atlanta, 2006), 9–27 esp. 14.

[40] Cf. A. Rofé, *La composizione del Pentateuco: Un'introduzione*, SB 35 (Bologna, 1999), 102, trans. Harvey N. Bock as *Introduction to the Composition of the Pentateuch* (Sheffield, 1999).

[41] Cf. Ska, *Introduzione alla lettura del Pentateuco*, 127.

of Vatke, one of the predecessors of Wellhausen.[42] Lothar Perlitt argues, though, that the work of Wellhausen, contrary to what many claim, was not established on Hegelian foundations and that this distinguishes it from Vatke's work.[43] H.-J. Kraus disagrees with Perlitt's opinion:

> It is clear that the Hegelian categories have in him [Wellhausen] the value of form and principle. This explains why (1) the history of the religion of Israel and of Judaism is conceived of as "evolution" and as "process", (2) this process unfolds in a succession of periods in three phases, (3) the whole evolution, carried out in three periods of time, is understood as "denaturalization".[44]

In reality, it must be admitted that Wellhausen does not behave like a perfect Hegelian in his exposition of the stages of the development of the religion of Israel. The final stage, which in the dialectic scheme would be represented by synthesis (as conquest and a step forward), in Wellhausen's scheme is nothing more than the period of decadence and degeneration of the initial idea. At this point, Wellhausen is more romantic than Hegelian. However, the German exegete's historical reconstruction seems to be determined by the kind of generalization characteristic of the Hegelian philosophy of history, in which ideas have an almost hypostatic character.[45] Wellhausen goes so far as to say, "The idea as idea is older than the idea as history."[46]

B. Methodological Problems with the Documentary Hypothesis

After reviewing the history of the research that led to establishing the documentary hypothesis, and after giving attention to the philosophical and cultural presuppositions that favored it, the time has come to judge its value, that is, to judge its ability to explain the text that has come down to us. In this judgment, a fundamental role will be played by the evaluation of the methodological options that led the different authors to propose, on the basis of the final text, four documents at its origin.

---

[42] Cf. Kraus, *Geschichte der historisch-kritischen Erforschung*, 189–99.

[43] Cf. Perlitt, *Vatke und Wellhausen*.

[44] Kraus, *Geschichte der historisch-kritischen Erforschung*, 264.

[45] Cf. Blenkinsopp, *Pentateuch: An Introduction*, 11.

[46] Wellhausen, *Prolegomena to the History of Israel*, 36.

When judging the documentary hypothesis, it is imperative to make an initial observation. When this hypothesis is called into question, it is not the composite character of the Pentateuch that is being called into question but, rather, a certain understanding of that character and its origin. Indeed, on the basis of data more or less accepted by literary criticism, the documentary hypothesis wants to follow a series of presuppositions and lines of reasoning back to four written, consistent, and continuous accounts, which would explain the final form of the Pentateuch. Our job, therefore, will be to judge the validity of the presuppositions and lines of reasoning that support that hypothesis as well as to assess its ability to explain the text that has come down to us.

We will begin with the use made by the documentary hypothesis of the literary data that point toward the composite character of the Pentateuch. It escapes no one's notice that the presence of different *divine names* was, from the beginning, one of the "star" criteria for differentiating sources in the Pentateuch, especially in the books of Genesis and Exodus. So much so that the first two continuous sources were called Yahwist and Elohist, following the divine names utilized in the respective accounts. The starting point was the first two chapters of Genesis, where two accounts of creation are found, with theological content and literary garb that are very different between them and where each account systematically uses its own divine name. It seemed logical to conclude that each account came from a different source; the character of each was expressed in its theology of the creation, and one of the signs of the identity of each was the divine name used. The revelation of the divine name (YHWH) in Exodus 3:14 (cf. Ex 6:3) provided the key piece of information for proposing two linear histories that ran through a large part of the Pentateuch: the Elohist, prior to the revelation at Horeb, and the Yahwist, a later source that told the same story, but now in the light of the divine manifestation to Moses.

However, the leap from the plurality of the divine names to the documentary hypothesis was not at all logical. Time showed that the necessary intermediate link entailed by the revelation of the divine name in Exodus 3:14 was an argument of little weight and, in fact, a rather naïve one. It was the product of a linear reading that still considered Moses the redactor of the Pentateuch who worked from two sources. Although the argument ceased to be used, the theory for which it had provided a basis remained. Somehow, this argument had managed to establish the use of the divine names as a factor for the distinction of sources. But if one factor, together with others, distinguishes two sources in Genesis 1–2, can it really be the discriminating factor for other texts? Furthermore, is it logical that on the basis of the two sources identified in Genesis 1–2 one should conclude that two consistent and continuous documents run through the first part of the Pentateuch?

From the study of the first two chapters of Genesis, it can be concluded that it is of composite character, but it does not at all follow, even on the basis of the datum of Exodus 3:14, that the two theologies in play are responsible for two written accounts that run through a large part of the Pentateuch. With regard to the divine names, the documentary hypothesis assumed that the authors of the first two written documents (or, in its classic formulation, three documents: J, E, and P) were necessarily consistent in their use (or omission) of the divine names, YHWH or 'Elohîm. According to this presupposition, the use of one name in a document prevented its author from using the other (an obvious conclusion, since the classic formulation of the theory could no longer argue that the first document did not know the divine name that was revealed). However, this is not the case in the first narrative attributed to the Yahwist: in Genesis 2–3 both names are combined: YHWH 'Elohîm.

Another problem for the documentary hypothesis is that the redactor who "stitched" the large accounts together could have added or combined the divine names in his redactional work. As will be seen later, the hypothesis in question rests on a baseless image of the redactors. U. Cassuto holds that YHWH and 'Elohîm are not synonymous (and thus alternative) names and that the use of one or the other depends on the end being pursued. Thus, 'Elohîm would be the divine name that expresses a universalist dimension of God, while YHWH would be the same God in his historical dimension, the God revealed to Israel.[47] Segal, for his part, speaks of stylistic variety (a concern attributed to a single author) to explain the presence of the divine names in some accounts.[48]

A similar problem is posed by the presence of *duplicates* (a single ac-

---

[47] Cf. U. Cassuto, *The Documentary Hypothesis and the Composition of the Pentateuch* (Jerusalem and New York, 2006) [Hebrew original, 1941; first English edition, 1961], 18–49.

[48] Cf. M. H. Segal, *The Pentateuch: Its Composition and Its Authorship and Other Biblical Studies* (Jerusalem, 1967), 8–14, 103–23.

count narrated twice) in the Pentateuch. From the beginning this was a criterion that seemed obvious for identifying more than one source in an account. Furthermore, it seemed to support the documentary hypothesis, since one author, if he really is such, does not bring duplicates into an account, which tends to be consistent. According to this hypothesis, the duplicates refer to two different accounts at the origin, which have been combined only over time. In these lines of reasoning there are a series of presuppositions about the character of the author and his activity (and about the redactor, as will be seen later) that do not necessarily follow.

Indeed, the author could have combined two stories received by tradition, avoiding the temptation to harmonize them in a single account. He could have done this as an author and not only as a redactor or compiler. That is, he may be the one responsible for the general outline of the account, and he may wish at the same time not to eliminate any material received or to harmonize it with other similar material. Another possibility for explaining the duplicates in an alternative manner is to consider them deliberate literary devices on the part of the author.

A "classic" case of duplicates is that of the three accounts in which a patriarch passes off his wife as his sister (Abraham: Gen 12:10–20; 20:1–18; Isaac: 26:6–11).[49] It is curious that the criterion of the divine names led to attributing to the Yahwist the accounts of Genesis 12 (Abraham) and 26 (Isaac), while Genesis 20 (Abraham), which uses the name 'Elohîm, was attributed to the Elohist. In this way the presence of a duplicate in the history of a single patriarch, Abraham, was avoided. It did not seem problematic, though, to attribute to a single author a duplicate that referred to two different stories. In fact, it was being admitted that a consistent account could contain duplicates. Wellhausen, perhaps conscious of the methodological problem that this case posed, had to resort to the (somewhat rival) hypothesis of complements and claim that Genesis 12:10–20 did not originally belong to J but that it was a supplement.[50]

This same series of duplicates, however, has been the object of other interpretations that do not need to resort to independent documents to

---

[49] Cf. R. N. Whybray, *The Making of the Pentateuch: A Methodological Study*, JSOT.S 53 (Sheffield, 1987), 76–77.

[50] Wellhausen, *Composition des Hexateuchs*, 23.

explain their origin. Thus, for example, some authors have recourse to the rabbinic model, in which it is shown how a single author perfects a previous account by telling it again.[51] In the case under consideration, two of the versions could be presented as an improvement on the third one. No material is eliminated, but rather more is added, and with the addition comes reinterpretation.[52]

Another possibility is to understand the duplicates as a deliberate literary device on the part of the author himself. All three accounts under consideration are situated at key moments in the story of the patriarchs. The divine promise, linked to descendants, finds a high point of tension in the three "repeated" stories (the wives of Abraham and Isaac run the risk of disappearing from the stage) that is always resolved in favor of the promise: God shows himself to be faithful and overcomes the adverse circumstance.[53] The duplicates can be considered to play the same role as the "repeated" circumstance of the barrenness of the wives of the patriarchs: objections to the divine promise that lend dramatic quality to the account and end up emphasizing the power of God, who is always faithful to his promises, able to bring life where it is not possible.

It is precisely the frequency of these stories that are repeated that should lead scholars to consider the possibility that what they are looking at is a basic device of the Hebrew narrative. In fact, one of the inconsistencies of the documentary hypothesis is that it pays attention to some duplicates, which are key for distinguishing documents, while it ignores many others (within a single account that is considered consistent).[54] In a way, Wellhausen and his school take as their basis a naïve image of the author, which corresponds more to that of a typical author of nineteenth-century Europe (consistent in his account, without repetitions) than to that of an author of antiquity, particularly of Semitic antiquity. Fortunately, recent decades have greatly enriched

---

[51] Cf. S. Sandmel, "The Haggada within Scripture", *JBL* 80 (1961): 105–22.

[52] "The haggadic tendency makes of Scripture a literature which grew by accretion. This seems to me exactly the way in which literary reflection of a live religious tradition would grow. From the oral to the written, and from the book to canonicity, and from canon to midrash, represents a continuous process" (ibid., 122).

[53] Cf. Whybray, *Making of the Pentateuch*, 77.

[54] Cf. examples of duplicates within a single "document" that go unnoticed by the documentary hypothesis in ibid., 78–79.

our understanding of narrative techniques in antiquity, not only classical (from which much direct information has come down to us), but also from the world of the Middle East. The methods of rhetorical and narratological analysis, applied to the texts of the Bible, have given us a more realistic image of the author and his techniques.

The work *The Art of Biblical Narrative*,[55] by R. Alter, has been a pioneer in this. The repetitions, which until then were considered a sign of the composite character of an account (and of the ineptitude of the redactor who did not eliminate them!), are considered in this work to be an expression of notable literary ability:[56]

> One of the most imposing barriers that stands between the modern reader and the imaginative subtlety of biblical narrative is the extraordinary prominence of verbatim repetition in the Bible. Accustomed as we are to modes of narration in which elements of repetition are made to seem far less obtrusive, this habit of constantly restating material is bound to give us trouble, especially in a narrative that otherwise adheres so evidently to the strictest economy of means. Repetition is, I would guess, the feature of biblical narrative that looks most "primitive" to the casual modern eye, reflecting, we may imagine, a mentality alien to our own and a radically different approach to ordering experience from the ones familiar to us.[57]

Alter further links the phenomenon of repetitions with that of parallelism, which is exceedingly well known in Hebrew poetic literature. In poetry, the form of repetition called parallelism goes hand in hand with the persuasive will of the whole collection: the argument grows, not in a linear form, but in a cyclical form. It is not a matter of mere repetition; in parallelism there is progress in the idea, which, after being expounded for the first time, is reinforced, intensified, contrasted, expanded, and so on.[58]

It seems more than plausible to think that the authors of biblical prose were familiar with this way of advancing in the presentation of an argument. In this sense, as R. N. Whybray states, once it has been shown that repetition in the form of parallelism forms part of the literary techniques of the Bible, it "lays the burden of proof on the

---

[55] R. Alter, *The Art of Biblical Narrative* (London, 1981).
[56] Cf. especially the fifth chapter, devoted to the "techniques of repetition" (ibid., 88–113).
[57] Ibid., 88.
[58] Cf. ibid., 97.

documentary critic". If he wants to consider the repetitions proof of multiple authorship, he "must demonstrate in each case that the text as it stands manifests a gross implausibility or absurdity, and that the two or more documentary strands into which he proposes to divide it manifest a literary quality superior to that of the original".[59] This is a methodologically decisive point to which I will return later. It is not enough to divide up a text in order to do away with its presumed inconsistencies; it is necessary that the text or texts that result from this division have a degree of plausibility and internal consistency superior to those of the text with which one started.

Another piece of literary information that has always been used by the documentary hypothesis to reinforce its theory is the presence of *contradictions* within a single account. For the present discussion, contradictions that may exist between two separate accounts will not be considered, since they could be resolved by reference to different traditions that a single author has joined. In the case of contradictions within a single account that attempts to present itself as unitary, the documentary hypothesis proposes seeing two different written versions that a redactor has clumsily "stitched together". It is worthwhile to note the different views of the roles of author and redactor found in these types of arguments that are so essential for the documentary hypothesis. The implicit presuppositions that this hypothesis uses when speaking about author (creator of a complete and consistent document) and redactor (compiler of two documents) will now be described.

One of the fundamental presuppositions underlying the division of the Pentateuch into documents, as done by Wellhausen, is that each of the authors tried to write a continuous and consistent account of the origins and early history of Israel in accordance with the religious, political, and cultural ideas of his era. It is plain that Wellhausen, concerned with describing the history of the evolution of the religion of Israel, conceived of the role of the different authors as that of historians. If each of them did not write a consistent history that reflected his era, it would in fact not be possible to reconstruct the true history of the institutions of Israel. But would this image of the author as historian not be something of an anachronism? We have no indication of any activity like this in Israel prior to the exile or of works of history such

---

[59] Whybray, *Making of the Pentateuch*, 82.

as those that supposedly would have come from the pen of the authors of the four documents. Wellhausen, who paid little attention to the material linked to the cultures around Israel, which were beginning to be discovered, took it for granted that the literary and historical criteria with which the scribes of ancient Israel worked were the same as those used in nineteenth-century Europe.

Among those criteria, a prominent one is that of rigorous consistency when giving a historical account (something that is to be required and expected in any work on history today). The authors of the four documents are required to show a level of consistency that is, in fact, a strange criterion for almost any literary creation, especially from antiquity. It is thus important to emphasize, in the words of Alter, that "we may still not fully understand what would have been perceived as a real contradiction by an intelligent Hebrew writer of the early Iron Age, so that apparently conflicting versions of the same event set side by side, far from troubling their original audience, may have sometimes been perfectly justified in a kind of logic we no longer apprehend."[60] As was said earlier, advances in comparative studies of literature and religion, on the basis of the abundant material discovered in the last century and a half in the Middle East, have made it possible for us to have a more realistic image of literary activity in antiquity and of the criteria that guided it, which helps us at least to avoid anachronisms such as the one just described.

It is remarkable that while consistency is required of the authors of the four documents, virtually the opposite is assumed about the redactors. Indeed, the documentary hypothesis rests upon the presupposition that the inconsistencies in the final text (an assembled work made by the redactors) make it possible to identify the different documents. Consistency in the work of the author and inconsistency in the labors of the redactor are simultaneously assumed. In fact, one of the decisive questions that literary criticism, long occupied with the search for sources, delayed in formulating was, "Why did the final redactor not eliminate the inconsistencies?"

On the other hand, the very idea of a redactor who combined complete and consistent documents (and not merely different traditions) is only a hypothesis that is not based on data or examples from ancient

---

[60] Alter, *Art of Biblical Narrative*, 20.

literature. Attempts have been made to present some examples of historical works created on the basis of the combination of several (complete) previous works.[61] But in none of the examples adduced are continuous and complete documents combined, which cover the period and the events that the resulting work includes. In fact, there is only one work that could be given as an example: the *Diatessaron*, the harmony of the four Gospels made by Tatian in the second century A.D.

In this case we are dealing with a complete work that is the product of the conflation of four complete works that cover the same events and the same period. Even so, a couple of observations about it are relevant. First, it is questionable that a work produced in the second century A.D., in the context of Christian Syria, under the influence of the Greek and Roman world, can serve as an image of the literary activity of the Semitic world of at least eight centuries earlier. Second, the end pursued by a *harmony* of the four Gospels is very far from the one imagined for the different editors of the Pentateuch. And the same could be said of the source material.[62] The editing work carried out by Tatian does not bring together works written in different eras or works that reflect different ideologies or religious institutions. Moreover, the *Diatessaron* is based on three very similar documents (the synoptic Gospels), which in turn are based on common subject matter. Without this fact, the idea of a harmonization would probably not have arisen.

Another of the basic characteristics of the redactor in the view of the documentary hypothesis is his "conservative" character. The redactor preserves, as far as possible, the material that comes to him, which is logical if it really is complete and consistent material. His redactional in-

---

[61] A. Bentzen alludes to Tatian's *Diatessaron* (with regard to the four Gospels), to the work of Chronicles (with regard to Kings), and to Ezra and Nehemiah (with regard to Jeremiah). De Vaux gives as examples the work of Ibn al-Athir as well as an anonymous Syriac work of the thirteenth century A.D., the same *Diatessaron* of Tatian, the book of Chronicles, the books of Ezra and Nehemiah, Deuteronomy (with regard to the scroll of the Law found in the temple), and the poem of Gilgamesh. Cf. A. Bentzen, *Introduction to the Old Testament* (Copenhagen, 1948), 2:61–62, and R. de Vaux, "A propos du second centenaire d'Astruc: Reflexions sur l'état actuel de la critique du Pentateuque", in *Congress Volume: Copenhagen 1953*, VT.S (Leiden, 1953), 182–98, esp. 185–86.

[62] Cf. Sandmel, "Haggada within Scripture", 107, which explicitly rejects the example of Tatian to illustrate the activity of the hypothetical redactor who joins the J and E documents (R^{JE}).

terventions are always minimal, aimed at "stitching" the different documents together and hiding (unsuccessfully!) the "scars" derived from his activity. In the documentary hypothesis, it is essential to argue for this conservative role, so that the different unitary accounts can be identified on the basis of the final form of the text. In fact, it allows the redactor to intervene here and there with a little more personality, coinciding precisely with those passages that are difficult to assign to a particular source. However, the personality will never go so far as to become intentionality or a plan that guides his redactional interventions. This is so much the case that in the exegesis of the Pentateuch one often speaks of the personality, the ideology, and the intention of J or E, for example, but one hardly ever hears about the intention of the redactor R[JE]. The following words of John van Seters summarize well the role that tends to be assigned to the redactor in the biblical field: "In the actual practice of literary criticism the redactor functions mainly as a *deus ex machina* to solve literary difficulties."[63]

This same question of contradictions has brought to light other weaknesses of the documentary hypothesis. It was said above that, in principle, the presence of contradictions in an account indicates that it has a composite character. The problem is that a strict application of this principle, together with the other principles of a lexicographical, stylistic, or thematic nature, has led many authors to propose new sources within the classical sources. While initially one spoke of two or three sources, which in the classic formulation of the documentary hypothesis became four, in time, and following the principles of the theory itself, the sources multiplied.[64] Moreover, this was normal, since consistency was required of the author of a continuous and complete document . . . and the four documents did not always have it. The problem is, in fact, hard to solve. If one argues that a single document could contain any kind of inconsistency or contradiction, like every ancient (and even modern) literary work has, in the end one is undermining the very principle that led to the division of the received text into sources. If a work can contain any kind of tension or inconsistency, why not propose a single author as the one responsible for the whole Pentateuch, on the basis of received traditions?

---

[63] J. van Seters, *Abraham in History and Tradition* (New Haven and London, 1975), 129.

[64] Cf. Blenkinsopp, *Pentateuch: An Introduction*, 14.

Another of the weaknesses of the documentary hypothesis was identified long ago by P. Volz,[65] who warned about the use of a *circular argument* (*circulus vitiosus*) when texts are assigned to a particular document
as a result of the theology they express, which would be a characteristic
of that very document. The problem is that the typical character of a
document—its theology—was determined on the basis of the texts that
had previously been assigned to it. A particular text is priestly because
it expresses the theology typical of the priestly document, a theology
that in turn is derived from those texts that have been assigned to the
priestly document.

Equally problematic is the methodological choice to which the supporters of the documentary hypothesis resort when a text does not
lend itself a priori to the usual analysis of documentary sources. First
Wellhausen and later Noth considered it methodologically adequate
to submit these texts to the same solution that had proven fruitful in other parts of the Pentateuch. This is what can be called the
"analogical" argument:[66] since in some parts of the Pentateuch the existence of documents (which are supposed to be continuous and complete) can be demonstrated, it seems logical, by analogy, to assume
that those same documents run continuously through the whole Pentateuch. Thus, commenting on the difficulties of some passages that
do not lend themselves to the classical analysis of documents, such
as Genesis 15, Exodus 19, and Numbers 22–24, Noth stated that "it
should suffice to offer the possibility of explaining them on the basis
of the results of the literary-critical analysis that has proved adequate
in other texts."[67] The same author, in his commentary on the book of
Numbers, begins by saying that he considers it justified "to approach
the fourth book of Moses with the results of the analysis of the Pentateuch obtained in other books and, therefore, to expect the presence
of continuous sources for the whole Pentateuch in this book too, even
if, as has already been said, the situation in the fourth book of Moses

---

[65] Cf. P. Volz and W. Rudolph, *Der Elohist als Erzähler: Ein Irrweg der Pentateuchkritik?* BZAW
63 (Giessen, 1933), 20. In this same work, Volz denies the E source its status as a continuous
and consistent document. Its material should not be separated from J, and, at most, it could
be considered a gloss or addition to this latter source.

[66] Cf. Whybray, *Making of the Pentateuch*, 117.

[67] Noth, *Überlieferungsgeschichte des Pentateuch*, 6.

does not at first lead, by itself, to these conclusions".[68] On other occasions, recourse is had to the redactor to resolve these same difficulties: contrary to the immediate literary evidence, the existence of the classical sources in a text is affirmed, and the introduction into each document of elements characteristic of other documents is attributed to the redactor.

The riskiness of these methodological choices is plain to see, especially because they replace the text as is, as an object of study and a starting point, with a model that is applied over the text. In this case, once again, a large part of the problem rests on the claim to identify, as sources of the Pentateuch, complete and consistent documents and not a multiplicity of traditions circumscribed to the passages under study. This claim turns exegesis into an exercise in the identification of previously known sources (with very specific characteristics) in a particular text. Everything revolves around this premise; those literary data that do not fit the model will be attributed to the clumsy editorial work of the redactor.

Precisely because this premise functions implicitly in the work of the supporters of the documentary hypothesis, it is not surprising that they were accused of dividing a text into various fragments, shattering a literary unit that was sometimes very elegant. Along these lines, Moses Hirsch Segal states that the search for the four documents in the texts under study "has broken up many a charming old tale into . . . fragments . . . and has thus destroyed the beauty and the symmetry of the tale and the coherence and logical sequence of its parts."[69] Noth himself, a supporter of the documentary hypothesis, recognizes the contribution of the literary analysis of Volz and Rudolph, which has "preserved the literary unity of many precious stories from the usual literary criticism".[70]

We can therefore conclude that what seemed to be solid foundations for the edifice of the documentary hypothesis in fact are not. On the contrary, based on data that point toward a broadly composite character (divine names, duplicates, contradictions, and so on), the theory that

---

[68] M. Noth, *Das vierte Buch Mose: Numeri übersetzt und erklärt* (Göttingen, 1966), 8.

[69] Segal, *Pentateuch*, 20.

[70] Noth, *Überlieferungsgeschichte des Pentateuch*, 24.

Wellhausen backed came to a conclusion that did not logically follow: the existence of four documents, with four different theologies, written in four different eras.

III. Calling the Documentary Hypothesis into Question

A. New Studies and the Multiplication of Sources

As was said earlier, the documentary hypothesis, in spite of the methodological problems that accompanied it (which have just been described), was maintained as the unquestionable paradigm until the early seventies. In reality, there was no lack of contrary opinions, although they were isolated and very much muffled by the consensus around the dominant theory.[71] The first cracks of any seriousness came, not from new comprehensive theories, but from particular studies of accounts in the Pentateuch, especially in the book of Genesis. These works began to have as their perspective, not the division of the account according to the paradigm of the four documents, but the careful study of the whole literary unit.

One of the most studied accounts in this period was that of the story of Joseph. In fact, starting in the late sixties it became a "testing ground" on which the different theories faced off. The studies on this long and complex account laid bare the inability of the documen-

---

[71] A clear example are the theories of three of the first Jewish scholars to contribute to the debate about the formation of the Pentateuch, U. Cassuto (1883–1951), M. H. Segal (1876–1968), and Y. Kaufmann (1889–1963), who were very critical of the documentary hypothesis. Cassuto believed that the sources of the Pentateuch were not complete and continuous documents, like books, but rather fragmentary traditions (cf. Cassuto, *Documentary Hypothesis*, 117–26). Segal, for his part, insisted that a continuous reading of the Pentateuch reveals *its theme*, the theme of the Pentateuch, showing that there is more internal unity and consistency in those writings than the documentary theory makes it possible to distinguish. For this, it is necessary to abandon the analytic method and accept the text that has been proposed for us as a unit. The true theme of the Pentateuch would be, according to Segal, "the selection of Israel from the Nations and its Consecration to the Service of God and His Laws in a Divinely-appointed Land" (Segal, *Pentateuch*, 23). Finally, Kaufmann, even while accepting the existence of documents, places P at a date prior to the exile, preceding the D document (cf. Y. Kaufmann, *The Religion of Israel, from Its Beginnings to the Babylonian Exile* [Chicago, 1960], 175–200 [original in Hebrew]).

tary hypothesis model to account for all the data.[72] In fact, the patient study of this great account, based on literary criticism, uncovered more sources than scholars were willing to accept up until then. The most serious problem was not so much that the number of sources was greater than four (because it was always possible to turn to the supplementary theory or even to redactional intervention), but that no trace was found of some sources that were *supposed* to be in the account.[73]

These first signs of alarm in the story of Joseph are the ones that led von Rad to consider, shortly before his death, the need for a new model, as he expressed it in the last edition (in an "Epilogue to the Story of Joseph") that he was able to prepare of his commentary on Genesis. In his words, there is already a noticeable "discomfort" that accompanies the supporters of the classic theory as they face the problems that it could not resolve:

> The interpretation of the Joseph story given here began from the presupposition, widely accepted today, that whole stretches of the Elohist have been incorporated into the main Yahwistic recension. It should not be forgotten, however, that voices are continually raised in support of the view that the source theory (apart from the undisputed contribution of the source P) is not applicable to this narrative complex. . . . Larger or smaller discrepancies are obvious. But they must be regarded as glosses, as subsequent interpolations or as constructions of whole narrative variants. By means of this explanation it is possible to argue for a single narrative complex. But the explanation fails in an analysis of all the Pentateuchal material, which both before and after leads to the assumption of the dualism of a Yahwistic and Elohistic recension. This is not, of course, an answer to the question whether the Joseph story also shares in the dualism. But the question cannot be answered on the basis of the Joseph story alone; it must come from a comprehensive new analysis of the Pentateuch narrative material, which we urgently need.[74]

---

[72] Cf., especially, R. N. Whybray, "The Joseph Story and the Pentateuchal Criticism", *VT* 18 (1968): 522–28; B. D. Redford, *A Study of the Biblical Story of Joseph*, VT.S 20 (Leiden, 1970).

[73] Another text that was problematic in the same sense is Genesis 14, where we find an Abraham very different from the one in the large documents. Cf. J. A. Emerton, "The Riddle of Genesis XIV", *VT* 21 (1971): 403–39.

[74] G. von Rad, *Das erste Buch Mose: Genesis: Übersetzt und erklärt*, 10th ed., ATD 2/4 (Göttingen, 1976), 362, trans. John H. Marks as *Genesis: A Commentary*, rev. ed., Old Testament Library (Philadelphia: Westminster Press, 1973), 439–40.

B. Van Seters and Rendtorff

Von Rad's request would soon find an answer in the work of two authors who, with very different points of view, would call into question the dominant model and would collaborate in the search for a new paradigm. One of them is a Canadian, John van Seters; the other, a German, Rolf Rendtorff, an evangelical theologian, successor to von Rad in the professorship of the University of Heidelberg.

I will begin with the studies of Van Seters, who, while sharing and developing some basic presuppositions of Wellhausen's system, winds up taking the documentary hypothesis to a kind of *reductio ad absurdum*.[75] While Rendtorff would challenge the presuppositions of the classic theory, Van Seters would collaborate in its destruction by taking them to their logical conclusion.

In 1975, Van Seters published his book *Abraham in History and Tradition*,[76] in which he openly questioned the consensus on the dating of sources (and thus on the stages of the history of the religion of Israel) that the twentieth century had established and attacked the essential historicity of the accounts of the patriarchs in Genesis, which, after the literary researches of von Rad and the archeological and historical ones of the Albright School, seemed to rest on firm foundations. As the very title of his book indicates, in the accounts about Abraham it is necessary to distinguish, according to Van Seters, history and tradition. It was not history that generated a tradition, but precisely the opposite: a late tradition generated accounts projected backward in history.

Indeed, in the opinion of Van Seters, the patriarchs' nomadic lifestyle fits better in the setting of Mesopotamia in the seventh-sixth centuries B.C. than in that of the second millennium, contrary to what the Albright School claimed.[77] Also in opposition to this latter school, Van Seters questioned the supposed parallelisms between the social customs and legislation of the second millennium in Mesopotamia and Egypt (with regard to marriage, adoption, contracts, and covenants), on the one hand, and the customs and legislation that appear in the patriarchal

---

[75] Cf. G. J. Wenham, "Pondering the Pentateuch: The Search for a New Paradigm", in *The Face of Old Testament Studies: A Survey of Contemporary Approaches*, ed. D. W. Baker and B. T. Arnold (Grand Rapids, 1999), 116–44, esp. 125.

[76] Van Seters, *Abraham in History and Tradition*.

[77] Cf. ibid., 13–38.

accounts of Genesis, on the other hand.[78] In his opinion, customs and legislation tend to be kept unchanged for a long time, so that comparisons with texts of the second millennium are not decisive. Many customs attested at the end of that millennium are kept intact several centuries later. Moreover, this time in a positive sense, some biblical customs find their real parallels in customs typical of the Middle East of the first millennium.

Van Seters' conclusions, reaffirmed and developed in later works,[79] can be divided into two fields: that of history and that of literary criticism. In the first, he denies any historical basis for the patriarchal accounts and, in general, for the narrative of the Pentateuch. For Van Seters, the period of the exile in Babylon represents the key that explains many texts of the Pentateuch. Thus, for example, behind Genesis 15 (the promise of descendants and a covenant with Abraham) would be the spirit of the deuteronomistic movement and the atmosphere of Deutero-Isaiah, which would be confirmed by the discovery of the coincidences between the boundaries of the land that Genesis 15:18–21 marks out and the borders of the exilic era.[80] Moses himself would be nothing more than a fiction projected backward from the sixth century B.C. Indeed, the resistance of Moses to being sent before the pharaoh would be inspired by the accounts of the vocation of the prophets Isaiah and Jeremiah, while the idea of an exodus from Egypt is indebted to the idea of exodus across the desert, from Babylon, in Second Isaiah.[81] Genesis 14 (battles between kings; Melchizedek and Abraham), however, would reflect an even later era. The presence of the kings from the east is a hidden reference to the Persians, while the scene with Melchizedek (who exercises the priesthood in Abraham's presence) would be an attempt to justify the syncretism of the end of the fourth century B.C.[82] This is the date, according to Van Seters, at which the book of Genesis would have achieved its final form.

This substantial modification of the historical framework of the Pentateuch necessarily had to see its reflection in the field of literary

---

[78] Cf. ibid., 65–103.

[79] J. van Seters, *Prologue to History: The Yahwist as Historian in Genesis* (Louisville, 1992); J. van Seters, *The Life of Moses: The Yahwist as Historian in Exodus-Numbers* (Kampen, 1994).

[80] Cf. Van Seters, *Abraham in History and Tradition*, 263–78.

[81] Cf. Van Seters, *Life of Moses*, 63.

[82] Cf. Van Seters, *Abraham in History and Tradition*, 304–8.

criticism. As in the case of Wellhausen, it is not entirely clear in this case, either, whether it is historical investigation that has influenced the analysis of the sources or whether this latter analysis has produced an image of history. Van Seters continues to hold to the idea of documents as the basis of the Pentateuch, but he considers the classic model to be outdated now, with regard to both the number of sources and dating. In his opinion, the material that was classically attributed to J and E should be considered a unit that came from the Yahwist, an author who should be situated, no longer in the tenth or ninth century B.C., but in the era of the exile in Babylon. In this way, Van Seters would establish the guidelines for a new generation that tend to make the E document disappear and move up the date of J. In the context of the changes in exegesis that came about in the seventies, Jean-Louis Ska commented that "the Yahwist left the comfortable court of David or Solomon to live in exile."[83] Contact with Greek mythology and with that of the Middle East, which is behind Genesis 1–11, would come precisely during this exile.

In Van Seters' opinion, the work of the Yahwist was an introduction to the deuteronomistic history (composed of the book of Deuteronomy and the historical books, from Joshua through 2 Kings). Thus a radical change came about in the understanding of the role of the book of Deuteronomy. While it was normally considered a late book that took for granted the history of the patriarchs and the episodes in Egypt and the desert, now it was understood as the basic source from which the great accounts of the Tetrateuch were born. Thus, for example, the Yahwist would have taken the allusions in Deuteronomy to the conquests in Transjordan (Deut 2–3) and to the episode of the golden calf (Deut 9:16–21) and would have turned them into complete accounts. The encounter of Joshua with the head of the army of Yahweh (Josh 5:13–15) would have become the model on which the account of the burning bush was constructed.[84] On this point, too, Van Seters was a pioneer: he inaugurated an era in which the hand of the Deuteronomist was seen everywhere.[85]

The P document did not have such a marked character as J. In fact,

---

[83] Ska, *Introduction to Reading the Pentateuch*, 128.

[84] Cf. Van Seters, *Life of Moses*, 36–41.

[85] Cf. L. S. Schearing and S. L. McKenzie, *Those Elusive Deuteronomists: The Phenomenon of Pan-Deuteronomism* (Sheffield, 1999).

Van Seters tended to consider it postexilic material (fifth to fourth centuries B.C.) that complemented the history of J.[86] With regard to the criteria to identify documents, Van Seters thought that only the duplicates were an incontestable sign of the plurality of sources. Repetitions within the same story and variations in vocabulary or divine names were not signs of this, as they could be merely stylistic.[87]

In a way, the position of Van Seters can be seen as a radicalization of the presuppositions of Wellhausen or, better still, as the most extreme consequence of these presuppositions. Indeed, the statement that the Law is later than the prophets had resulted, in the model of the documentary hypothesis, in isolating and moving up in time a large part of the legislation of the Pentateuch. With Van Seters, Wellhausen's principle led to moving up the whole Law or Pentateuch, both the legislation and the narrative, which was written after and modeled on the prophets.[88]

The criticism that Rendtorff directs at the classic model is very different. On the one hand, it is more radical, in that it involves an objection to the very idea of documents. On the other hand, though, it is not as devastating in the field of history as that of Van Seters. Rendtorff's positions are based on his work *Das überlieferungsgeschichtliche Problem des Pentateuch*,[89] published in 1977, two years after Van Seters' first work. Even so, Rendtorff gets the credit for being the first one to reject publicly the classic documentary model and strike out in another direction. Indeed, in 1974, during his talk at the congress of the International Organization for the Study of the Old Testament (IOSOT) that was meeting in Edinburgh, he called into question the dogma of the existence of complete documents that run through the whole Pentateuch and directly attacked the figure of the Yahwist, who in his view did not exist either as a person or as a theologian.[90] In his conclusions

---

[86] Cf. Van Seters, *Abraham in History and Tradition*, 309–13.

[87] Cf. the two chapters that Van Seters devotes to methodology, one to criticize the classic model and another to present his basic criteria (ibid., 125–66).

[88] Cf. Wenham, "Pondering the Pentateuch", 125.

[89] R. Rendtorff, *Das überlieferungsgeschichtliche Problem des Pentateuch*, BZAW 147 (Berlin and New York, 1977), trans. John J. Scullion as *The Problem of the Process of Transmission in the Pentateuch*, JSOT.S 89 (Sheffield, 1990).

[90] R. Rendtorff, "Der 'Jahwist' als Theologe? Zum Dilemma der Pentateuchkritik", in *Congress Volume: Edinburgh 1974*, ed. Anderson, VT.S 28 (Leiden, 1975), 158–66.

he wound up advocating the beginning of a new phase in the study of the Pentateuch.[91]

Rendtorff's criticism of the documentary hypothesis is based on the work of his predecessor and mentor in Heidelberg, von Rad. In a way, the disciple did no more than lay bare the tensions that existed between his mentor's model and Wellhausen's classic hypothesis. Surprisingly, as has already been emphasized, von Rad's studies, which introduced strong contradictions within the classic model, had contributed to supporting it. In Rendtorff's opinion, the basic tension is between the literary critical method based on written documents and the method of historical criticism of traditions as von Rad applied it:

> When one tries to follow the gradual formation of the Pentateuch starting from the 'smallest units' right up to its present final stage, one does not encounter the 'sources' in the sense of the documentary hypothesis; and when one tries to allege the currently reigning notion of 'sources' to answer the questions raised by the traditio-historical study, then there is no answer. The assumption of 'sources' within the meaning of the documentary hypothesis can no longer make any contribution today to the understanding of the formation of the Pentateuch.[92]

Von Rad had demonstrated that the Pentateuch was made up of a collection of traditions clearly separate from one another, each with its own prehistory.[93] Rendtorff, on the basis of these results, undertook to show that the degree of independence between the different complexes of traditions was much greater than what could be expected. Moreover, and this is what was key, the great thematic or theological lines that traditionally characterized a particular source or document were found in certain groups of traditions but not in others. Put another way, if we consider the great complexes of traditions, such as the patriarchal accounts, the stay in Egypt, the exodus, Sinai, or the passage through

---

[91] Ibid., 166.

[92] Rendtorff, *Problem of the Process of Transmission*, 179.

[93] Why then does von Rad speak of the Yahwist? In Rendtorff's opinion, von Rad was a product of his time, and thus he gave the name Yahwist to the great literary genius who in the period of the "Solomonic Enlightenment" was to gather, as redactor more than as author, the traditions of the historical credo and join them to the legislative ones, incorporating, in addition, other smaller stories. Confusion was now afoot, because the Yahwist of the documentary hypothesis is not a redactor but the author of one of the complete documents that run through the Pentateuch (cf. Rendtorff, "Der 'Jahwist' als Theologe?" 159–60).

the desert, we will not find a common thread in the areas of theme or theology. The most serious thing is that the texts assigned to the same document throughout these great traditions do not show that continuity.

Rendtorff's criticisms are based on a careful study of the great accounts of the Pentateuch, especially the patriarchal histories. One of his basic methodological emphases is that of starting from a literary study of the text as it has come down to us and drawing consequences based on it, not on the basis of the models with which we approach it. Indeed, up until this point classic literary criticism did not take the text as a starting point for its interpretation and for historical reconstruction but went directly to the text to analyze it in accordance with a particular hypothesis already previously accepted.[94] So Rendtorff's caution with regard to the methods of literary criticism of the last century and a half is understandable: "I am, however, highly distrustful of the traditional *Literarkritik* so far as it leads to a production of texts. The subject of any interpretation has to be first and foremost the given text of the Hebrew Bible."[95]

In the case of the history of Abraham, the documentary hypothesis required the study of fictitious literary units. Whoever studied the "Yahwist" history of Abraham *had* to skip chapters 14, 15, 17, and 20–22. It was assumed that they were added subsequently by a redactor and thus did not deserve consideration: they did not form part of the initial consistent, meaningful *unit*. Rendtorff, at this point, called for a "new beginning".[96] This new beginning consisted of trying to avoid preconceived decisions about whether a particular text belonged to a particular source, thus leaving the way open for the most objective analysis possible.

A detailed study of the patriarchal history uncovers a unity that is at once complex (composite) and complete (united). It is obvious that each of the stories of Abraham, Isaac, and Jacob has its own process of formation and its own character. In the task of integrating the different

---

[94] Cf. R. Rendtorff, "Between Historical Criticism and Holistic Interpretation: New Trends in Old Testament Exegesis", in *Congress Volume: Jerusalem 1986*, ed. J. A. Emerton, VT.S 40 (Leiden, 1988), 298–303, esp. 299.

[95] Ibid., 300.

[96] Rendtorff, *Problem of the Process of Transmission*, 183.

stories into a single account, the divine promises addressed to each of the patriarchs has played a decisive role.

Another case studied by Rendtorff was the story of Joseph, which, as has already been noted, had become the privileged "laboratory" to put theories to the test. According to the documentary hypothesis, in this long literary unit we should be able to identify the narrative framework provided by P, into which the rest of the sources or documents fit. If we eliminate that material, we would necessarily find ourselves with a continuous and consistent account. However, in the account of Joseph few characteristic signs are found that indicate a priestly origin.[97] Even so, since the priestly document was originally a consistent account without gaps, its presence *must* be identified in the story of Joseph, even if it is by dint of joining fragments dispersed here and there in the same story. In Rendtorff's opinion, "This once more is a clear case of a circular argument."[98] The possibility that perhaps that consistent account did not exist (or, minimizing the damage, that it did not include the complete story of Joseph!) was not contemplated, in spite of the fact that it would have been able to explain the situation more easily.

This does not mean that there is not a connecting thread *inside* the large narrative units of Genesis-Exodus (the primordial history, the patriarchal accounts, the narratives of Exodus 1–15, the Sinai pericope). In those units it is possible to identify a theology that joins shorter narratives together and gives unity to the collection. Thus it is possible to speak of a "theology of the primordial history", a "theology of the patriarchal histories", and so on. However, the attempt to present a "theology" of each of the sources or documents of the Pentateuch (as a connecting threat that runs through the different accounts) is incompatible, still according to Rendtorff, with the literary evidence available to us.

Rejection of the documentary hypothesis does not involve, as Rendtorff properly emphasized, the rejection of literary criticism. The German author, quite to the contrary, undertook to show how good literary criticism demonstrates that the fragmentation of the great literary units into four hypothetical documents does violence to the text itself.

---

[97] Cf. ibid., 138–39.
[98] Ibid., 138.

In Rendtorff's studies, literary criticism fulfills a basic role in helping us understand how each of the narrative units has been put together to form the large accounts.[99] At this point, too, a new beginning would be needed, since the notions of "redaction" and "redactor" are too closely linked to the action of joining sources, according to the image that the documentary theory has transmitted to us. It is curious that even Noth felt uncomfortable with that image and had to resort to the terms *Sammelnder* (editor or compiler) and *Bearbeiter* (reviser)[100] to identify those responsible for some "redactional" activity that did not fit with the classic model. Rendtorff issued a call for collaboration in the task of determining the proper criteria for discovering the process that led not only to linking the smaller units into large accounts, but that assembled the whole Pentateuch from the large units. At this point, Rendtorff himself made his contribution, especially in identifying themes that unite small stories among themselves, as is the case of the divine promises in the patriarchal accounts.

By studying this redactional process, Rendtorff only identified a group of texts with a common denominator that could be comparable to the "sources" of the classic theory. This is a rather homogenous group of "priestly" texts. By no means, however, is it possible to speak of a continuous priestly narrative, so that it is better not to use the expression "priestly document", because of its classic resonance.[101] Furthermore, Rendtorff placed great importance on deuteronomic-deuteronomistic circles in the final redaction of the Pentateuch and considered no other hand to be comparable to this one in the labor of giving final form to the collection of the work, and he went so far as to state that there is no pre-deuteronomistic redaction of the Pentateuch.[102]

With regard to the dating of the Pentateuch and its traditions or, what amounts to the same thing, with regard to the *history* behind the texts, Rendtorff also issued a call for a reconsideration of criteria. On this point he had in mind not only the classic dating of documents that had been dominant since the time of Wellhausen, but the "revolutionary" proposals of Van Seters:

---

[99] Cf. ibid., 191–92.

[100] Cf. the subtitle of his work: M. Noth, *Überlieferungsgeschichtliche Studien: Die sammelnden und bearbeiten Geschichtswerke im Alten Testament*, 2nd ed. (Tübingen, 1957).

[101] Cf. Rendtorff, *Problem of the Process of Transmission*, 191–92.

[102] Cf. ibid., 199–201.

First, it must be conceded that we really do not possess reliable criteria for dating the pentateuchal literature. Each dating of the pentateuchal 'sources' relies on purely hypothetical assumptions which in the long run have their continued existence because of the consensus of scholars. Hence, a study of the Pentateuch which is both critical and aware of method must be prepared to discuss thoroughly once more the accepted datings. Further, it must be granted that our traditio-historical reflections rely for a large part on hypotheses which on each occasion must undergo critical scrutiny. . . .

Under such criticism of opinions held to date, care must be taken that the pendulum does not swing too far to the other side. This holds especially when replacing current dating with new. There is a tendency among some scholars today to maintain an exilic or post-exilic date for the great mass of pentateuchal material. The methodological criteria for such dating, however, must still be carefully weighed. It is not enough to replace a common enough early dating by a late dating. . . . It is more a question, I think, of an approach which makes distinctions; it reckons with a rather long period of formation of the Pentateuch, and above all with the joining together of the individual larger units so as to form a *single* whole.[103]

In Rendtorff's view, the final state of the Pentateuch reveals a general intervention of a deuteronomistic character that must have been preceded by a long process of development with different strata. In this process, the small units grew until they constituted medium-sized units, then large ones, and they eventually reached the final stage that is shown to us in the text we now have. But to speak of "deuteronomistic" redaction or character does not imply a particular date. To assume dependence in relation to Deuteronomy says nothing about the amount of time. Many scholars, with well-founded arguments, locate the core of Deuteronomy in the eighth century B.C. Considering that we are talking about a school and not an author, and considering that there are early deuteronomistic texts that do not depend on Deuteronomy, we can place its redaction even before the eighth century. The very custom of dating the priestly sections to the era of the exile or after the exile rests more, in Rendtorff's opinion, on conjecture and on the consensus of scholars than on unequivocal criteria.[104]

Rendtorff also devotes some lines to the problem of the "silence" of

---

[103] Ibid., 201–3.
[104] Cf. ibid., 203.

a large part of preexilic literature (such as the prophets of the eighth-
seventh centuries B.C.) with regard to the themes and names of the
traditions of the Pentateuch. Obviously, this is a question linked to
the problem of dating. For Rendtorff, the data cannot be avoided; the
question is what conclusions can be drawn from it. The silence of the
preexilic literature certainly indicates that the great themes of the Pentateuch were not central in Israel in that era. But one cannot conclude
from that alone that they were unknown themes. In fact, some isolated
pieces of information warn us against the danger of the argument from
silence. Indeed, in Ezekiel 33:24, Abraham is spoken of as the one who
took possession of the land, a statement that is put in the mouths of the
people who had stayed in Jerusalem.[105] This shows that that tradition
was already popularly known in the land of Judah before the exile.[106]

Rendtorff concludes his first great contribution to studies of the
formation of the Pentateuch by reaffirming the invalidity of the old
paradigm and warning, in large part in opposition to Van Seters, against
a new model that is nothing more than a reformulation of the old one:

> It would be following a false trail methodologically, I think, if 'new' or
> 'late' sources were now to replace the 'old' pentateuchal sources, or if
> one wanted to try to repeat the global interpretation of the 'Yahwist'
> or other 'sources' with another dating and on the background of other
> time-conditioned circumstances. That would be to pour new wine into
> old skins. The problem of the process of tradition in the Pentateuch lies
> deeper. One must tackle it, as von Rad demanded in one of his last state-
> ments: 'we urgently need a comprehensive new analysis of the narrative
> material of the Pentateuch'.[107]

C. Recent Developments

Rendtorff can certainly be considered the author who has laid bare, in
the most orderly and intelligent manner, not only the limits and inconsistencies of the documentary hypothesis, but also its radical invalidity

---

[105] "Son of man, the inhabitants of these waste places in the land of Israel keep saying, 'Abraham was only one man, yet he got possession of the land; but we are many; the land is surely
given us to possess'" (Ezek 33:24).
[106] Cf. Rendtorff, *Problem of the Process of Transmission*, 204.
[107] Ibid., 205–6.

in explaining the formation of the Pentateuch. By highlighting its limits, he has pointed to an alternate path through which to lead future
studies: the analysis of the formation and growth of the large literary
units. On this point, though, Rendtorff has only played the role of
precursor. His disciple Erhard Blum has been the one who has gone
down this road applying the new analysis to the whole Pentateuch.

In his first work, devoted to the great patriarchal traditions,[108] Blum
describes the stages of growth through which these histories have
passed. In spite of the warnings of his teacher about the dating of
the different stages, Blum unites the analysis of the strata of tradition
with the history of Israel. He believes that the most original strata of
the patriarchal histories may go back to the reign of David, though certainly after the victory over Edom (Gen 25 and 27: tension between
Jacob and Esau; Gen 31: tension between Jacob and Laban). From that
time on, the histories grew, especially during the second half of the
eighth century B.C. and the second half of the seventh century. A second
great stage of growth of the material began with the exile. In this era,
a large part of the history of Abraham was completed, on the basis of
the connecting thread of the promises of descendants, the gift of the
land, and the blessing. The third great stage came with the return from
the exile, when the patriarchal histories were linked to the rest of the
Pentateuch due to the editorial labor of the Deuteronomist.

In his second work,[109] Blum expands his gaze to the whole Pentateuch. This is where he develops more clearly the "redaction stage"
that joins the different traditions to form a single work. Like Rendtorff,
he finds no sign of the Yahwist or the Elohist at this stage. The hands
of the Deuteronomist and the priestly writer are the only ones that can
be identified.

Another scholar who rejects the idea of the Yahwist as the author
of a complete document is Hans Heinrich Schmid,[110] who identifies
in the texts classically attributed to J features typical of the prophetic
literature and of Deuteronomy. For Schmid, it was the deuteronomistic
circle that first created a continuous narrative, joining the great tradi-

---

[108] E. Blum, *Die Komposition der Vätergeschichte*, WMANT 57 (Neukirchen-Vluyn, 1984).

[109] E. Blum, *Studien zur Komposition des Pentateuch*, BZAW 189 (Berlin and New York, 1990).

[110] H. H. Schmid, *Der sogennante Jahwist* (Zurich, 1976).

tions on the basis of the idea of the promise of the land, the nation, and the blessing.

The last twenty years have seen a succession of numerous works that attempt, in one way or another, to react to the crisis in the old paradigm provoked by Van Seters and Rendtorff. At present we do not have enough historical perspective to be able to put all these studies in order. Since my concern is methodological, it is not worth the effort to describe them exhaustively. I will limit myself to a few clear points.

One of the most heated battles has had the Yahwist as its protagonist. As we have already seen, for Van Seters the Yahwist played a decisive role in the redaction of the Pentateuch, but, as opposed to the ideas of Wellhausen and von Rad, he should be situated in the era of the exile and not that of the Davidic monarchy. While Van Seters sends the Yahwist into exile, Rendtorff, first, and later Blum and Schmid, proclaim his demise. Both consider it entirely unfounded to speak of the Yahwist as the author of a continuous history that runs through all or a large part of the Pentateuch. The Yahwist, as a person or as a theologian, is believed never to have existed. A review of titles in recent years gives a full idea of the present state of this battle.[111] What is ultimately at stake is a final farewell to the documentary hypothesis and, with it, the construction of a new paradigm.

Concerning the Elohist, however, the consensus is greater: no one takes him seriously now. In the view of some, he should be integrated with the Yahwist (at least partially); in the view of others, he never existed. The "families" that have come out of the crisis most strengthened are the priestly and the deuteronomistic. However, their role, in the view of many scholars, should be transferred from the table of the author to that of the redactor. The problem of the dating of both redactions is, as has been seen, another of the central issues of the last few decades. It is plain to see that the close relationship between

---

[111] J.-L. Ska, "The Yahwist, a Hero with a Thousand Faces: A Chapter in the History of Modern Exegesis", in *Abschied vom Jahwisten: Die Komposition des Hexateuch in der jüngsten Diskussion*, ed. J. C. Gertz, K. Schmid, and M. Witte, BZAW 315 (Berlin, 2002), 1–23; Dozeman and Schmid, *A Farewell to the Yahwist?*; Römer, "The Elusive Yahwist"; J. van Seters, "The Report of the Yahwist's Demise Has Been Greatly Exaggerated!", in *A Farewell to the Yahwist?*, 143–57.

literary criticism and history, which comes from Wellhausen, continues to have an enormous effect on the shape of the debate.

With regard to the priestly "source", it is worthwhile to highlight
the studies of I. Knohl,[112] who, following the methods used for critical
analysis of the Talmud, considers the school responsible for the laws
of holiness (Lev 17–26) to be the one that edited the material in P, and
not vice versa. In this way, what was considered simply material for the
priestly source (H, from "Holiness Code") would now be, in Knohl's
opinion, the key to the puzzle: the school that is behind H would not
only have edited the material of P, but would also be responsible for
"the great enterprise of editing the Torah, which included editing and
rewriting the legal scrolls of the PT [Priestly Torah] and blending them
with the non-Priestly sources."[113]

The role of the Deuteronomist in the final redaction of the Pentateuch has been strengthened on the basis of the studies of Rendtorff and Schmid. The great literary genius pursued by von Rad, and
whom Van Seters identifies in the late figure of the Yahwist, seems ultimately to have incarnated himself in the Deuteronomist, and to such
a point that there has begun to be talk of a phenomenon called Pan-
deuteronomism.[114] The problem is that this term has a very vague referent. In the old paradigm of Wellhausen, he was linked to the reform
of Josiah. J. G. McConville, however, has presented serious objections
to this linkage, which is so essential, between 622 B.C. and the book
of Deuteronomy, with the result that the book could be much earlier
than the reform.[115] Today the dating of the deuteronomistic school,
or of the redactor, "fluctuates" between the eighth century B.C. and
even earlier (a possibility that Rendtorff leaves open) and the postexilic
period.

That Wellhausen's paradigm is in crisis and that, in the form in which
it was transmitted until the seventies, it no longer works is something

---

[112] Cf. I. Knohl, *The Sanctuary of Silence: The Priestly Torah and the Holiness School* (Minneapolis, 1995).

[113] Ibid., 6.

[114] Cf. Schearing and McKenzie, *Those Elusive Deuteronomists: The Phenomenon of Pan-Deuteronomism.* On the deuteronomistic redaction and the priestly redactor, cf. the recent contributions in T. Römer and K. Schmid, eds., *Les Dernières Rédactions du Pentateuque, de L'Hexateuque
et de L'Ennéateuque*, BEThL 203 (Louvain, 2007).

[115] Cf. J. G. McConville, *Law and Theology in Deuteronomy*, JSOT.S 33 (Sheffield, 1984).

that most scholars recognize.[116] However, there is no sign that indicates that we are witnessing the birth of a new paradigm. In a way, our era, which is also in crisis, seems unfavorable for the emergence of new syntheses.[117]

IV. Proposals for a Synchronic Reading of the Pentateuch

As we have seen in the preceding overview, one of the sharpest criticisms directed against the documentary hypothesis by its detractors is that it works on highly hypothetical textual units and not on the received text as it appears before our eyes. Those who side with this criticism, however, share with the old paradigm a diachronic view of the Pentateuch.

The correction that, in a way, was already introduced by von Rad,[118]

---

[116] There are those who continue repeating, with few modifications, the old scheme of the documentary hypothesis. Cf. A. F. Campbell and M. A. O'Brien, *Sources of the Pentateuch: Texts, Introductions, Annotations* (Minneapolis, 1993); R. E. Friedman, *The Hidden Book in the Bible* (San Francisco, 1998); R. E. Friedman, *The Bible with Sources Revealed: A New View into the Five Books of Moses* (San Francisco, 2003). Campbell and O'Brien have radically changed their position in recent years, and they now support the idea of a Pentateuch without sources (documents), constructed on the basis of traditional histories that were available, not to the readers, but to the narrators of histories as material for their use. This would explain the numerous inconsistencies, duplications, and so on (cf. A. F. Campbell and M. A. O'Brien, *Rethinking the Pentateuch: Prolegomena to the Theology of Ancient Israel* [Louisville, 2005]).

[117] Cf. the analysis that Ska does of the cultural context in which studies of the Pentateuch have developed over the last forty years (Ska, *Introduzione alla lettura del Pentateuco*, 145–48). Cf. also his attempt to explain the origin of the multiplicity of (often contrasting) opinions that dominate exegesis today (J.-L., Ska, "Old and New Perspectives in Old Testament Research", in *The Exegesis of the Pentateuch: Exegetical Studies and Basic Questions*, ed. J.-L. Ska, FAT 66 [Tübingen, 2009], 246–66).

[118] It is worthwhile to quote at length the comment that B. S. Childs makes about the inheritance that some scholars received from von Rad and the atmosphere that was breathed in the seventies, which were decisive factors for the way to be opened, little by little, for a new direction in exegesis: "As a young student who had fallen under the spell of von Rad, I shared with many others the conviction that his brilliant method held the key to a proper understanding of the O.T. Von Rad saw his approach as one which would revitalize the entire theological enterprise. Significantly, even he, in his last years, began to have second thoughts. In time a new generation of highly competent form and redaction critics replaced the old masters within the German universities. Yet much of the excitement which his early post-war lectures evoked had died. The promise had not materialized. Biblical studies in the 70's has begun to look like

---

and which Rendtorff and others developed, led scholars to pay attention to the great traditions or great accounts just as they have come down to us, without chopping them up on the basis of a priori criteria. But these authors did not stop digging into those accounts to find smaller units and explain their growth process. Moreover, the concept of "received text" was restricted, in the best of cases, to large accounts (such as the history of Joseph or the history of Abraham) and not so much to the collection in a book (Genesis, for example) or group of books (Pentateuch), which were units that were a little "large" for this type of analysis. It is plain that it is precisely in the description of how the great traditions came to form a book, or the whole Pentateuch, that the new hypotheses show themselves to be most uncertain and, above all, most in disagreement among themselves. While the new studies have returned a little "common sense" to the study of the great accounts of Genesis, the same cannot be said of the proposals for an overall understanding of the final redaction of the Pentateuch. Van Seters' Yahwist in exile, the omnipresent deuteronomistic hand, or the post-priestly school of the laws of holiness are models loaded with poorly founded hypotheses.

In August 2006, in the framework of the Society of Biblical Literature International Meeting, Rendtorff returned to Edinburgh, thirty-two years after his famous talk, to give a speech titled *What Happened to the Yahwist? Reflections after Thirty Years*.[119] In it he stated, "It seemed to me to be one of the fundamental mistakes of the modern historical-critical analysis of the biblical texts, that it does not—or at least not sufficiently—ask the question regarding the meaning and significance of the given text."[120] In addition, he pointed out that this criticism was not directed only against the supporters of the classic documentary hypothesis.

When Rendtorff made this last statement, he obviously did not intend to include himself, but those who, like Van Seters, criticize the

those in the 20's. Slowly I began to realize that what made von Rad's work so illuminating was not his method as such, but the theological profundity of von Rad himself" (B. S. Childs, "A Response" *HBT* 2 [1980]: 208).

[119] R. Rendtorff, "What Happened to the Yahwist? Reflections after Thirty Years", in Ellens and Greene, *Probing the Frontiers of Biblical Studies*, ed. J. H. Ellens and J. T. Greene, PTMS 111 (Eugene, 2009), 39–49.

[120] Rendtorff, "What Happened to the Yahwist?" 42.

old paradigm at the same time as they support it.[121] However, that criticism is precisely the one that the supporters of a synchronic reading of the Pentateuch direct against those who use diachronic methods, including Rendtorff. Indeed, for these authors the "received text" is the whole Pentateuch, and it is linked to the rest of the books that make up a work that has come down to us already bound in a certain manner: the Bible.

Its background aside,[122] the new insistence on paying attention to the final form of the text has been part of the study of the first five books of the Bible for more than thirty years. However, dialogue between the diachronic and synchronic readings of the Pentateuch has been almost nonexistent.[123] One of the most important supporters of synchronic methods for the books under discussion here is David J. A. Clines. As early as three decades ago, he condemned the scant attention that was being paid to the final form of the Pentateuch and lamented the time lost in speculations about hypothetical documents dated to hypothetical periods and addressed to a hypothetical audience.[124]

Clines accused the dominant exegesis of not taking note of the theme or themes of the Pentateuch, which are precisely what give it unity and make it possible to speak of a work that was finished and delivered to a community with a precise intention. In Clines' view, the theme of the Pentateuch is the (at least partial) *fulfillment* of the promises or blessings directed at the patriarchs. The promises of land, descendants, and of a certain relationship between God and man unify the different sections and books and lend a final image of consistency that the diachronic methods do not manage to identify.[125]

Often the synchronic reading is conceived as an alternative to a sterile

---

[121] In the same book in which Rendtorff's talk in Edinburgh is collected, a response to it by Van Seters is included, which was made a few years later. Cf. J. van Seters, "The Yahwist and the Debate", in Ellens and Greene, *Probing the Frontiers of Biblical Studies*, 62–66.

[122] In fact, the whole approach to Scripture prior to the critical study of the Bible was based on the final text.

[123] Cf., however, the attempt to reconcile the diachronic and synchronic methods carried out by F. García López, "De la antigua a la nueva crítica literaria del Pentateuco", *EstBib* 52 (1994): 7–35.

[124] D. J. A. Clines, *The Theme of the Pentateuch*, JSOT.S (Sheffield, 1978), 14. Before Clines, although with almost no effect on the academic world, Segal tried to justify a synchronic reading of the Pentateuch in search of its theme (Segal, *Pentateuch*, 22–23).

[125] Cf. Clines, *Theme of the Pentateuch*, 29–43.

diachronic reading. One of the most successful attempts to offer a hypothesis for a global (synchronic) reading of the Pentateuch while entering into dialogue with the results of diachronic exegesis is that of R. W. L. Moberly in his work *The Old Testament of the Old Testament*.[126] Moberly begins by studying a pair of texts that are at the heart of the old documentary hypothesis: the revelation of the divine name in Exodus 3 and Exodus 6. As we already know, the two texts, considered duplicates, are supposed to justify the theory of sources. Exodus 3:14–15 is attributed to E, while Exodus 6:2–3 is supposed to be part of P. Both are taken to be in contrast with the J document, which uses the term YHWH in the patriarchal accounts and the primordial history, projecting backward a name that is supposed to have been revealed only to Moses.[127]

Moberly does not consider it justified to view Exodus 6 as a duplicate of Exodus 3. Furthermore, the narrative plot would require an episode like the former (in which it is clarified what God was called before: *'El Shaddai*) to continue the latter. In his opinion, the two texts insist on the difference between the religious experience of Moses and that of the patriarchs. The revelation to Moses marks a qualitative advance in this religious experience. There is, then, no need to resort to a different source (Yahwist) to explain why the name of Yahweh is used in the patriarchal accounts. This is not a case of a theological perspective characteristic of the Yahwist, but the explicit will, common to all the authors of the Pentateuch, to identify the God who spoke to the patriarchs with the God who revealed himself to Moses. The patriarchs were able to know God as 'El, 'Elohîm, or 'El Shaddai, but this is the same God who definitively reveals his name to Moses. The use of the name Yahweh in Genesis serves as a reminder that the God we see acting in those texts is the same one who will later take Israel out of Egypt. Moreover, it reminds us that the patriarchal history is told from the perspective of Mosaic Yahwism. In this way, all the possible sources of the Pentateuch converge on a single view: there is a difference between the patriarchs and Moses, against a background of continuity.

While respecting the continuity mentioned, some differences can be

---

[126] R. W. L. Moberly, *The Old Testament of the Old Testament* (Minneapolis, 1992).
[127] Cf. ibid., 5–78.

highlighted. The patriarchs worship a single God, but we do not find in them the exclusiveness that characterizes Mosaic monotheism. The patriarchs lived peacefully with the Canaanites without trying to exterminate or expel them as the Law of Moses demanded. The first fathers already had circumcision, but it is not clear whether they kept the Sabbath or certain dietary laws, which are elements that characterize the Mosaic discipline. In these contrasts it is possible to perceive the novelty that the divine revelation to Moses represents.[128]

Moberly shows himself to be truly original when he compares the relationship (of continuity and difference) between the patriarchs and the rest of the stories of the Pentateuch after Moses with the relationship that exists between the Old and New Testaments. The God who reveals himself in both Testaments is the same, but Christ introduces a new and radical perspective on his nature. In the same way, the Sinai revelation introduces a new perspective that explores the divine mystery that had entered into the lives of the patriarchs.[129]

With this model, Moberly calls into question the fundamentals of the old documentary paradigm.[130] The use of the divine appellations as a distinctive feature of sources is baseless. In his opinion, all the writers of the Pentateuch share a single view of the novelty that the divine revelation to Moses introduces into the history of Israel. However, they all alike feel free to use the new appellation, YHWH, in their patriarchal accounts. The differences between the J, E, and P sources are, in the classic paradigm, religious differences. In reality, those differences do no more than distinguish two periods in revelation: before and after Moses.

Moreover, Moberly's reading challenges the skepticism about the historicity of the patriarchal traditions that, starting with Van Seters' studies, became so widespread. The fact that the writers, all of whom are involved in the new order of Mosaic Yahwism, describe customs in the patriarchs that are opposed to or have been superseded or abolished by the new Law shows that they are not projecting a contemporary religious situation but describing the actual situation prior to the revelation at Sinai.[131]

---

[128] Cf. ibid., 79–104.
[129] Cf. ibid., 125–46.
[130] Cf. ibid., 177–202.
[131] Cf. ibid., 191–98.

V. Does a Theory about the Origins
of the Pentateuch Serve Any Useful Purpose?

To the lecture that Rendtorff gave in the summer of 2006 in Edinburgh, which was referred to above, Clines offered a rejoinder.[132] It is
worth looking closely at his reply, because he brings up fundamental
methodological questions that radically challenge the dominant line of
research and open new paths in the study of the Pentateuch.

Clines begins his contribution by remembering that for a long time
the most important question in research on the Pentateuch has been
the question about its origins, which started from the question: Is the
documentary theory, or another alternative theory, true? However, in
Clines' opinion, there is another series of questions that must be formulated, not so much about the question of the *truth* of a theory, but
about its *value*, such as: Is a theory of this type useful? Should we be
interested in it? What does it matter if we have a theory about the origins of the Pentateuch?

What is at stake, therefore, is not the truth of a particular theory
about the origins but the type of questions that exegetes direct at the
text, the basic interest that moves them. In Clines' opinion, a scholar
could consider other questions valuable, such as the theological value
of certain texts or their literary character, questions about which the
theories of origins have little to say. When answering questions about
the value of the final text, the only text that has existed for more than
two thousand years, one does not start with the sources that may have
come together in its production, however sure one may be of their
existence.

Why, then, have questions about the origins of the Pentateuch been
dominant? Why has the hypothesis about documents prevailed as the
dominant model for more than a century? At this point Clines' response leaves the bounds of the *politically correct* by putting on the table
a penetrating analysis of the role of *power* in the preservation of the
comprehensive paradigms.

---

[132] D. J. A. Clines, "Response to Rendtorff", in Ellens and Greene, *Probing the Frontiers of Biblical Studies*, 49–55.

No longer is it the truth or falsity of a particular theory that determines whether it will find favor in the guild. Bad arguments will not be driven out by good arguments. Reason will not be the arbiter.

Rational debate still happens in the academy, I allow, and issues are sometimes settled purely on their merits. But when it comes to grand theories like the documentary hypothesis there is too much investment in the power that worldviews and grand theories accumulate to themselves for that to happen. I do not mean that there is no longer any place for rational argument, but only that rationality is subordinate to the exercise of power. It is naïve to think otherwise, or to act as if our decisions on such matters were not bound up with where we stand in a world of power.[133]

When Clines speaks of *power*, he has in mind, he makes clear, two types of power. On the one hand, the power of the people and institutions who adopt a certain point of view and, on the other hand, the power of the theories and world views to convince a large number of followers.

In the first case, some important exegetes with great influence, attached to institutions of great prestige, have supported, and continue to support, the documentary hypothesis. As a consequence, it will be difficult for those who do not adopt the same position to get a position in those institutions; they will not be invited to contribute a presentation at seminars, and they will hardly be able to find recommendations to publish their research. It is not by chance that resistance to the documentary hypothesis has usually arisen outside the centers of power, often from young scholars who work in second- and third-ranked institutions. The case of Rendtorff is the exception that proves the rule.

In the second case, it cannot be denied that the documentary hypothesis triumphed because it offered some weighty arguments in its favor. However, it was not the existence of evidence in its favor that gave such a long life to Wellhausen's theory. It was, rather, its explanatory ability and its comprehensive claims. Indeed, the classic theory became a matrix in which all the questions about the history and literature of Israel found a place. In reality, it was a world view that deserved the name "paradigm". Whole generations of students have assimilated this

---

[133] Ibid., 52.

world view and have developed their research projects about ancient Israel within this framework. Not to have done so would have entailed remaining outside the academic community:

> The intrinsic power of the theory gave authority to the community that adopted the theory, but in so doing made every new member of the scholarly community a victim of its power.[134]

To understand the current situation of the dominant paradigm about the origins of the Pentateuch, Clines turns to the classic work of Thomas Kuhn, *The Structure of Scientific Revolutions*,[135] in which great changes in theoretical paradigms are analyzed. When a paradigm begins to show its weaknesses, it enters a period of crisis. This crisis does not bring about—and does not even come close to bringing about—the abandonment of the old paradigm. On the contrary, the adherents of a particular paradigm usually seek solutions to the problems discovered by slightly modifying the general hypothesis. In Kuhn's opinion, all the crises end in one of the following three ways:[136]

1. The classic paradigm shows itself capable of responding to the problem that brought about the crisis, and everything returns to normal.

2. The problem persists and is recognized as such, but it is perceived to be the result of the lack of tools necessary to resolve it. Scholars set it aside in the expectation that a new generation with new instruments can resolve it.

3. A new candidate arises to take the place of the paradigm, and a battle about recognizing it begins. This is known as a battle of paradigms.

In Clines' opinion, none of these three possibilities is a good description of the current situation of studies about the origins of the Pentateuch. We cannot speak of the appearance of a new theory capable of taking the place of the old paradigm. We are, rather, at the stage of exploring the problems that the classic paradigm presents, with the consequent loss of confidence in it, without that simultaneously leading to the establishment of a new world view. Precisely because a paradigm

---

[134] Ibid., 53.

[135] T. Kuhn, *The Structure of Scientific Revolutions* (Chicago, 1962).

[136] Cf. ibid., 84.

is considered invalid only when an alternative triumphs, the normal thing, according to Clines, is for the old documentary hypothesis to continue to reign in universities, albeit with multiple modifications.

Clines believes that the new questions surrounding the value, and not the truth, of the theories about the origins of the Pentateuch may favor a kind of "silent revolution", a revolution that does not resolve the problems of the old paradigm but moves them out of the way. As he wonders about the result of this possible silent revolution, Clines states:

> The physicist Max Planck said: "A new scientific truth does not triumph by convincing its opponents and making them see the light, but rather because its opponents eventually die, and a new generation grows up that is familiar with it." My forecast is that the new generation in Hebrew Bible studies will, in some parts of the world at least, grow up with other interests in the forefront of their attention, and lose interest in questions of origins. However, that will not be the end of the Documentary Hypothesis, only its marginalization. The question, How did the Pentateuch, in fact, come into being? will persist, as a minority interest, for a much smaller audience than this.[137]

VI. Conclusions

The history of the hypotheses about the formation of the Pentateuch is, without a doubt, one of the most instructive pages in modern exegesis. Indeed, it is precisely in this field that the historical-critical method has found its most important testing ground. The composite character of the first five books of the Bible, a plainly obvious fact from the literary point of view, has pushed scholars to try to reconstruct the stages of this composition by identifying its original elements, the processes of its formation, its intermediate stages, its redactional stages and, above all, historical contexts, and the theology that prevails in them. Literary analysis thus presented itself as the possibility for reconstructing the true history of Israel, beyond the "official" history that the Bible transmits to us. If by using literary criteria it became possible to identify and put in order the pieces that formed this mosaic called the Pentateuch,

---

[137] Clines, "Response to Rendtorff", 55.

we would be in a position to describe the true *history of the religion* of
Israel.

The interpretive model that prevailed above all others was the one
known by the name of the documentary hypothesis, the paternity of
which is attributed to Wellhausen, although in fact his was no more
than the final link in a chain of contributions that only in him came
together to form a final consistent portrait concerning the composition
of the Pentateuch. A fundamental presupposition of this hypothesis is
that four complete (written) documents were involved in the formation
of the first books of the Bible and that each of them is from a different
era and has its own particular theology. The Pentateuch is supposed
to be the product of the "fusion" of those four texts. A clear sign
of the success of this theory is that it was upheld as the authoritative
explanatory model for more than a century, so that until very recently
the J, E, P, and D documents formed part of the most basic baggage
of students of theology.

From the very beginning, though, this theory contained serious flaws
in its main principles. It had been constructed on very weak or extremely hypothetical premises, and it had arrived at principles based
on a series of steps that did not logically follow one another. Today
we have sufficient historical perspective to identify some philosophical
and cultural presuppositions that served as bridges to join the elements
of a causal chain that was not at all logical. It is curious that the second
generation of scholars, who took it upon themselves to shore up the
edifice and give it greater literary, theological, and historical consistency (Gunkel, von Rad, Noth), took as their starting point elements
that could potentially damage the system and that ordinarily would have
led to it being called into question. However, the persuasive strength of
Wellhausen's explanatory model (a unitary and comprehensive hypothesis for the whole history of Israel and for the formation of the Pentateuch), supported by a certain cultural context, made those elements
that in time would come to undermine the model at first serve only
to consolidate it.

In the mid-seventies, the model, because of its internal contradictions
and as a consequence of the criticisms of more and more exegetes, began to fracture. Since then, and up to the present, it has become ever
more obvious that the model stood on very weak bases and, above
all, that the idea of four complete documents, each with a consistent

theology, had no basis in reality. Rendtorff was the leading figure of this criticism, who called into question the existence of a Yahwist ideology that could have become established in a document that runs through the whole Pentateuch (or Tetrateuch). The Elohist suffered the same fate even earlier. At no time was the composite character of the Pentateuch called into question. What was being criticized was the hypothesis that proposed several connecting threads that consistently joined accounts and laws throughout the whole Pentateuch.

In the last thirty years, the evidence that the classic paradigm does not do justice to the data we find in the Pentateuch has only grown. But it is equally obvious that no other comparable paradigm has arisen, that is, one that is comprehensive and that is capable of bringing most exegetes into agreement. What has begun to make headway in exegetical discussion concerning the Pentateuch is the question of methods, which until very recently was practically forbidden in the name of the basic principle that an ancient composite text must be studied diachronically. Today, the voices that support a synchronic approach to the text are ever more numerous and important. This development has been facilitated by the circumstances that the world has experienced in the last twenty years due to the "fall of ideologies", which in the area that concerns us here have helped uncover the flawed presuppositions that upheld both the documentary hypothesis and some versions of the historical-critical method.

However, at least in the field of the Pentateuch, the methodological debate is often presented as a question of deciding between two more or less contrasting methods: the diachronic and the synchronic. The main champion of the synchronic approach to the Pentateuch, Clines, offers an interesting analysis of why questions about the origins of the Pentateuch according to a diachronic model have dominated the agenda of scholars for the last century. In addition, he uncovers not only the unfounded presuppositions of much diachronic analysis, but also the textual and literary data that this analysis does not take into consideration (the value, the function, and the intention of the final text as well as its theme). What is missing, though, is a look at the text that does not eliminate any element of its nature, a look that approaches it with the method that the text itself imposes. And we have before us a text of a composite nature that, at the same time, has been delivered in a very specific final form (which already contains a synthetic judgment about the material received) to a very specific community (which has been charged with transmitting it to us) that considers it normative.

I will wait for the third chapter, devoted to the characteristic dimensions of the Catholic interpretation of the OT, to go deeper into this methodological question raised by the very nature of the text. There, in the context of the discussions that have arisen in this chapter (about the Pentateuch) and in the next one (about the prophets), I will be able to discuss more fruitfully the most suitable way to approach Scripture and, specifically, the underlying question hidden behind the choice between diachronic and synchronic methods.

2

The Critical Study of the Prophets

After reviewing the history of research on the formation of the Pentateuch, it is now time to turn, in this second chapter, to another page in the paradigms of modern exegesis: critical research on the prophets. As in the preceding chapter, I will present the basic stages of this research and then study the philosophical and cultural presuppositions that shaped the image of the prophet transmitted by the dominant exegesis. After laying out the criticisms that exegesis itself has directed at this model, I will finish by presenting some alternative proposals that have emerged in recent decades.

I. The Traditional Image of the Prophets in the Church and in Judaism

While the critical study of the Gospels and the person of Jesus, as well as of the Pentateuch, date back to the eighteenth century, we must wait until well into the second half of the nineteenth century to find the first "critical" works on the prophets. Indeed, up until then all the interest of critical exegesis had been centered on the study of the life of Jesus, in the NT, and on the problem of the sources of the Pentateuch, in the OT. The prophets and their preaching were seen and subsumed within the two classic paradigms that transmitted the two great traditions that are based on the Bible: the Christian and the Jewish.

A. The Place of the Prophets in the Christian History of Salvation

In the Christian view of the history of salvation, the prophets—and in this there are no differences between Churches and ecclesiastical communities—are presented as those who announce a new economy, the one brought by Jesus of Nazareth, the promised Messiah. All the prophecies achieve their fulfillment in Jesus Christ, and therefore it is this last historical event that gives unity and meaning to the prophetic preaching.

The role of the prophets is reflected by the position they occupy in Christian Bibles. As early as *Codex Vaticanus*, the first complete codex (fourth century A.D.) that includes the OT and NT (both in Greek), the prophets occupy the last place in the arrangement of the books of the OT, after the Pentateuch and the wisdom books, and just before the Gospels, to which they are the gateway. Although there are codices from the fourth and fifth centuries that have another order,[1] this is the one that has "triumphed", especially because it was the arrangement of books in the Vulgate, which would later set the order in Catholic Bibles. This order simply reflects the understanding that the Gospels and the NT in general have of the prophets. For them, the saving event of Jesus Christ, his birth, his words and deeds, his Passion, death, and Resurrection, had been predicted in the Scriptures, especially in the prophets.

This image of the prophets penetrated deeply into catechesis and piety, and Christian iconography has been a sign of it throughout the ages, from the decoration of the first Roman basilicas in the fourth century (in which the great prophets predict the chief mysteries of the life of Jesus) to the frescos in the Library of the El Escorial monastery, in the sixteenth century (in which the biblical prophets compete with Greek philosophy as forerunners of wisdom incarnate).

In this linear understanding of the history of salvation, the prophets come after the Law. When we pay attention to the order of our Bibles and to the historical sequence they suggest, the prophets take on the task of reminding the people of the Law or Covenant that was sealed at Sinai, from which the people have done nothing but continually distance themselves. Only after the inability of the first Law to obtain the people's faithfulness became apparent would the prophets begin to announce a new covenant (Jer 31), a new creation (Is 43; 65), a new heart and new spirit (Ezek 36). The New Covenant sealed with the

---

[1] *Codex Sinaiticus* (fourth century) and *Codex Alexandrinus* (fifth century) place the prophetic books between the Pentateuch and the wisdom books.

blood of the lamb, Jesus Christ, would take the central place of the old Law. The Church, the bride of the lamb, the body of Christ, is the place where this New Covenant is fulfilled.

B. The Place of the Prophets in Jewish Tradition

The biblical reading of rabbinic Judaism that triumphed after the destruction of Jerusalem (first century A.D.) presents the prophets as transmitters of the Law, both written (Pentateuch) and oral (which over time would become crystallized in the Mishnah and the Talmud). The message of the prophets cannot contain anything new, since everything essential for the life of Israel was revealed with the Law on Sinai. At most, the prophets make explicit what was found implicit in the Law. In every case they refer to the Law as the basic norm.

An example of the role the prophets play in Judaism is found at the beginning of the tractate *Pirke Avot* (Sayings of the Fathers) in the Mishnah:

> Moses received the Torah from Sinai and transmitted it to Joshua; Joshua to the elders; the elders to the prophets; and the prophets handed it down to the men of the Great Assembly.[2] They said three things: Be deliberate in judgment, raise up many disciples, and make a fence around the Torah. (*Pirke Avot* 1)

As can be seen, the function of the prophets is to serve as a bridge between the primordial revelation on Sinai and the teaching of the rabbis (descendants of the Great Assembly). The prophets are therefore the custodians and transmitters of the Law. As part of the chain, they hold a historically circumscribed place. While in Christianity we speak of a linear history of salvation in which the prophets point toward a future fulfillment, in rabbinic Judaism we would have to use the image of the circle: everything revolves around the Torah. Present-day Judaism, as the prophets once did, continues to preserve and communicate the Law it has received.

---

[2] This is a reference to the tribunal of 120 members that began to function with Ezra after the return from the Babylonian captivity.

II. The Critical Study of the Prophets:
Toward a New Paradigm

The two traditional paradigms, held by Judaism and Christianity, have one point in common: the untroubled acceptance of the image transmitted by the Bible itself about the relation between the Law and the prophets. In both cases what the OT transmits is taken for granted: that the whole Law was given on Sinai, before the entrance into the Promised Land. The prophets represent a later stage, which already presupposes the Law.

The critical study of the prophets was inaugurated precisely by calling this common point into question.

A. Wellhausen: The Law Does Not Precede the Prophets

We previously saw, while studying the formation of the Pentateuch, the revolution in the exegesis of the OT brought about by the hypothesis, first suggested by Reuss, immediately supported by his disciple Graf, and finally divulged and systematized by Wellhausen, that the Law was not earlier than the prophets but later than them. Up to this point we have studied only the repercussions this hypothesis had on studies of the Pentateuch. Now it is time to study the consequences this theory brought to the understanding of the prophets.

We will first focus on the researches of Wellhausen, the author who most radically exposed the consequences of chronologically situating most of the Law after the prophets. It is worthwhile to quote at length a biographical note that Wellhausen himself provides for us, in which we can see the cultural milieu into which the new hypothesis came to be grafted:

> In my early student days I was attracted by the stories of Saul and David, Ahab and Elijah; the discourses of Amos and Isaiah laid strong hold on me, and I read myself well into the prophetic and historical books of the Old Testament. Thanks to such aids as were accessible to me, I even considered that I understood them tolerably, but at the same time was troubled with a bad conscience, as if I were beginning with the roof instead of the foundation; for I had no thorough acquaintance with the Law, of which I was accustomed to be told that it was the basis and postulate of the whole

[biblical] literature. At last I took courage and made my way through Exodus, Leviticus, Numbers, and even through Knobel's *Commentary* to these books. But it was in vain that I looked for the light which was to be shed from this source on the historical and prophetical books. On the contrary, my enjoyment of the latter was marred by the Law; it did not bring them any nearer me, but intruded itself uneasily, like a ghost that makes a noise indeed, but is not visible and really effects nothing. Even where there were points of contact between it and them [the Law and the prophetic and historical books], differences also made themselves felt, and I found it impossible to give a candid decision in favour of the priority of the law. Dimly I began to perceive that throughout there was between them all the difference that separates two wholly distinct worlds. Yet, so far from attaining clear conceptions, I only fell into deeper confusion, which was worse confounded by the explanations of Ewald in the second volume of his *History of Israel*. At last, in the course of a casual visit in Göttingen in the summer of 1867, I learned through Ritschl that Karl Heinrich Graf placed the Law later than the Prophets, and, almost without knowing his reasons for the hypothesis, I was prepared to accept it; I readily acknowledged to myself the possibility of understanding Hebrew antiquity without the book of the Torah.[3]

"Understanding Hebrew antiquity without the book of the Torah" is precisely what Wellhausen does in his *Prolegomena*. There he asserts, time and again, the creative role of the prophets, a role that does not depend on the Law:

> It is a vain imagination to suppose that the prophets expounded and applied the law. . . . The voice of the prophets, always sounding when there is need for it, occupies the place which, according to the prevailing view, should have been filled by the law: this living command of Jehovah is all he knows of, and not any testament given once for all.[4]

The hypothesis that the prophets precede the Law, which Wellhausen so effusively embraced, immediately threw a shadow of suspicion on those responsible for the final redaction of the Bible, those who transmitted to us the opposite image, that of the priority of the Law over the prophets. Wellhausen, as a good historian, took it upon himself to outline a new image of the historical evolution of Israel: the

---

[3] J. Wellhausen, *Prolegomena zur Geschichte Israels*, 6th ed. (Berlin, 1905), 3–4.

[4] Ibid., 399.

prophets, promoters of individual and ethical religion, were betrayed by the legalistic-ritual system of early Judaism, which was responsible for the final form of the Pentateuch. Wellhausen occupied himself with rewriting the history of Israel in the article "Israel" (1881) that Robertson Smith commissioned from him for the *Encyclopaedia Britannica*.[5] Postexilic Judaism, which puts the Law at center, was considered to be a "degenerative" time in the religion of Israel. Wellhausen describes the new religion this way:

> For what holiness required was not to do good, but to avoid sin. . . . The whole of life was directed in a definite sacred path; every moment there was a divine command to fulfil, and this kept a man from following too much the thoughts and desires of his own heart. . . . A man saw that he was doing what was prescribed, and he did not ask what was the use of it. . . . By the Torah religion came to be a thing to be learned. . . . The rule of religion was essentially the rule of the law. . . . It was the law that gave the Jewish religion its peculiar character. . . . It [Judaism] . . . has an entirely different physiognomy from that of Hebrew antiquity, so much so that it is hard even to catch a likeness.[6]

Thus, the Jewish paradigm of understanding the prophets as transmitters of the Law did not correspond to historical reality. It was a creation of Judaism that had put the Law in the center of its new religion.

But it should not be thought that the Christian paradigm emerges unscathed from this criticism. In fact, according to Wellhausen, Jesus, in his polemic with Judaism, recovers the true spirit of the prophets but is betrayed by the Church-institution:

> The Gospel develops hidden impulses of the Old Testament, but it is a protest against the ruling tendency of Judaism. Jesus understands monotheism in a different way from his contemporaries. . . . This monotheism is not to be satisfied with stipulated services, how many and great soever; it demands the whole man, it renders doubleness of heart and hypocrisy impossible. . . . The Church is not His work, but an inheritance from Judaism to Christianity.[7]

---

[5] This article was later added as an appendix to the English edition of the *Prolegomena* (J. Wellhausen, *Prolegomena to the History of Israel* [Edinburgh, 1885]).

[6] Ibid., 500, 502, 508–9.

[7] Ibid., 509, 510, 512.

If the prophets do not take the Law as their basis, what is the heart of their preaching? Far from being mere commentators or repeaters, they are the true creators of spiritual and ethical religion:

> Where do they [the prophets] ever lean on any other authority than the truth of what they say; where do they rest on any other foundation than their own certainty? It belongs to the notion of prophecy, of true revelation, that Jehovah, overlooking all the media of ordinances and institutions, communicates Himself to the *individual*, the called one, in whom that mysterious and irreducible rapport in which the deity stands with man clothes itself with energy. Apart from the prophet, *in abstracto*, there is no revelation; it lives in his divine-human ego. This gives rise to a synthesis of apparent contradictions: the subjective in the highest sense, which is exalted above all ordinances, is the truly objective, the divine.[8]

The freedom and the pure spirit of the prophets have been suffocated by the Law. The spirit-Law dialectic wages its first battle with the appearance of Jewish legalism on the scene:

> With the appearance of the law came to an end the old freedom, not only in the sphere of worship, now restricted to Jerusalem, but in the sphere of the religious spirit as well. There was now in existence an authority as objective as could be; and this was the death of prophecy. For it was a necessary condition of prophecy that the tares should be at liberty to grow up beside the wheat.[9]

> The introduction of the law, first Deuteronomy, and then the whole Pentateuch, was in fact the decisive step, by which the written took the place of the spoken word, and the people of the word became a "people of the book".[10]

> What distinguishes Judaism from ancient Israel is *the written Torah*. The water which in old times rose from a spring, the Epigoni stored up in cisterns.[11]

I have already emphasized several times that Wellhausen is, above all, a historian. He is interested in describing, above all, the stages through which the evolution of the religion of Israel goes. As has been

---

[8] Wellhausen, *Prolegomena zur Geschichte Israels*, 398.

[9] Ibid., 402–3.

[10] Ibid., 409.

[11] Ibid., 410.

seen, prophecy is the high point in this evolution, and it would be betrayed by Jewish legalism-ritualism. However, Wellhausen had no special interest in studying the prophetic books to rescue the true words that constitute the highest spirit of Israel. Other contemporary authors would take on this task, and they would fill out the content of what I have called the new paradigm of the studies of the prophets.

B. Duhm and Kuenen: The Spirit of Prophecy

Bernhard Duhm (1847–1928), an evangelical theologian, was a colleague of Wellhausen at Göttingen, and, like him, in his research he took as his starting point the revolution brought about by considering the Law later in time than the prophets. In 1875 he published a work whose title was in itself a whole program: *The Theology of the Prophets as the Foundation for the History of the Internal Evolution of the Israelite Religion.*[12] It is evident that Duhm's objective, like that of Wellhausen, must be understood as part of the attempt to rewrite the history of the religion of Israel. Duhm was to make his contribution to this effort through the study of the theology of the prophets.

The words with which Duhm opens his study are very illustrative of the spirit of the era:

> The investigations that I now present . . . are inductive and not of a didactic nature. They are not derived from any theological or philosophical premise about the religion of Israel and its evolution; they are, rather, intended to help find and build a foundation for a correct view of the latter.[13]

The image of the prophets transmitted by the two traditional paradigms, Judaism and Christianity, is considered "unscientific", the product of theological premises that have little to do with historical reality or even with the texts themselves. The late dating of the Law is the cornerstone on which is based the new scientific study that is now applied to the prophets. The work that lies ahead is that of bringing to light the true theology of the prophets by freeing it from the tangle woven by the legalistic-ritual Judaism that edited its books.

---

[12] B. Duhm, *Die Theologie der Propheten als Grundlage für die innere Entwicklungsgeschichte der israelitischen Religion* (Bonn, 1875).

[13] Ibid., 1.

Duhm presents the prophets as the men of spirit who tried to break the cultic bonds that kept the religion of Israel prisoner. The prophet Micah, who inaugurated classical prophecy in Judah (eighth century), can be considered a good example. His diatribe against the cult in Micah 6:1–8 is considered by Duhm to be the most important passage of prophecy, a text representative of the ethical idealism defended by the prophets:

> Arise, plead your case before the mountains,
>   and let the hills hear your voice.
> Hear, you mountains, the controversy of the LORD,
>   and you enduring foundations of the earth;
> for the LORD has a controversy with his people,
>   and he will contend with Israel. . . .
> "With what shall I come before the LORD,
>   and bow myself before God on high?
> Shall I come before him with burnt offerings,
>   with calves a year old?
> Will the LORD be pleased with thousands of rams,
>   with ten thousands of rivers of oil?
> Shall I give my first-born for my transgression,
>   the fruit of my body for the sin of my soul?"
> He has showed you, O man, what is good;
>   and what does the LORD require of you
> but to do justice, and to love kindness,
>   and to walk humbly with your God?

The religion of Israel, as it is shown in the prophets, has nothing to do with the fulfillment of a complex of laws that came before it; rather, it has to do with ethical and moral behavior in relation to God and man in the life of the community. With Micah, Hebrew prophecy begins to emphasize morality as an imperative addressed to every individual. So it is understandable why Jesus of Nazareth, with his insistence on a right personal relationship with God, is the heir of the spirit of the prophets. This "individual" view of religion is embodied in the lives of the prophets themselves. The ethical idealism that, according to Duhm, represents the essence of the true religion of Israel springs from the direct and profoundly personal experience the prophet has of God. In this sense, the scholar should pay special attention to the accounts of sending, the visions, and the other extraordinary experiences of those chosen men.

In his commentary on the prophet Isaiah (1892),[14] Duhm for the first time systematically applies the new reading key to a prophetic book. In this sense, it can be considered the first modern commentary on a prophet. One of the novelties of this commentary, in relation to his first work, is the special attention paid to the poetic way in which the prophet expresses himself. In fact, poetic language becomes for Duhm one of the basic criteria for distinguishing the original oracles of the prophet from later glosses or additions. The authentic words of the prophet can finally come to light, throwing off the tight attire with which they had been covered by late Judaism.

Abraham Kuenen, a Protestant theologian whom we already know for his studies on the formation of the Pentateuch, wrote in 1875, like Duhm, a monograph devoted to the prophets, although it would gain renown only two years later, when the English translation of the Dutch original was published.[15] Along the same lines as Duhm, his work aimed to uncover the true theology of the prophets. In one of the chapters of this work, titled "The Place of Israelite Prophecy in the Religious Development of Humanity", Kuenen explains at some length the original contribution of the spirit of the prophets to world religious history. I will now devote some attention to these pages.

Following the spirit of the time, Kuenen makes a point of emphasizing that the traditional view, in which the prophet started with the Law, has been superseded by a new "historical and critical investigation", as the subtitle of this work reads, which provides us with a new image of the role of the prophets. At this point Kuenen benefits from his own studies of the Pentateuch, in which he showed how a great deal of the redaction of the Law is exilic or postexilic. While speaking of the traditional view of the prophets (of both Judaism and Christianity), Kuenen states:

> We should, however, have to acquiesce in this view of the work of the prophets . . . if history recommended or even demanded it. But it is already well known to the reader that, on this point especially, history does not coincide with tradition. To express it briefly: for the traditional phrase "the Law and the Prophets" it substitutes "*the Prophets and the Law.*" For

---

[14] B. Duhm, *Das Buch Jesaia* (Göttingen, 1892).

[15] A. Kuenen, *The Prophets and Prophecy in Israel: An Historical and Critical Enquiry* (London 1877).

the final redaction of the present Pentateuch was preceded chronologically by the entire series of the canonical prophets.[16]

But criticism of the traditional view is not limited to the aspect of the subordination of the prophets to the Law (which would link them to the past). It also attacks the fundamentally Christian view that reduces the role of the prophets to visionaries capable of predicting and announcing what will happen in the future (and which would therefore link them to the future). The prophet has a role in the present for his world. If he is no longer linked to the past or lives for the sake of the future, what is the role of the prophet in the present?

Starting with this point, Kuenen takes on the task of identifying the original contribution of prophecy in Israel:

> For it is self-evident that the task of the prophets now becomes entirely different from what it was according to the traditional conception first described. We must now attribute to them a much greater degree of originality. It is true that, according even to the view defended by me, the place of honour belongs to Moses. He gave the impulse to the whole subsequent development, when he bound Israel to the adoration of Jahveh, and expressed once for all the moral character of the Jahveh-worship in "the ten words". But it makes certainly, in reference to the prophets, a very great difference whether we give them the historical Moses, or the writer of the Pentateuch, as their predecessor. If no such author preceded them, then, while their work still remains as it is, they had no model to follow; then, they themselves have produced what they seemed at first to have borrowed from another quarter. On a close examination their work is plainly seen to have been twofold. Jahveh, a holy god who prescribes moral requirements: this is the fundamental idea which was handed down to them from Sinai. They have now, *in the first place*, maintained and applied, expanded and purified, Jahveh's moral law. They have, *in the second place*, gradually formed a purer and more spiritual conception of Jahveh himself, and have finally reached the height of ethical monotheism.[17]

Ethical monotheism (an expression coined by Kuenen) is the great contribution of the prophets of Israel to the religious development of mankind. In the history of Israel there was supposed to be a progression from monolatry to monotheism and from this to ethical monotheism.

[16] Ibid., 561.
[17] Ibid., 562–63.

This last step was not taken until the arrival of classical prophecy in the eighth century. Two centuries earlier, at the moment of the greatest splendor of the monarchy of Israel, Solomon gave clear indications that strong monotheism did not yet exist when he tolerated the entrance of the cult of other gods into his own territory and his own house. And what can be said about the situation of the Northern Kingdom, dominated by the cult of Baal, during the ninth century? The tendency toward idolatry would certainly continue both in the Northern Kingdom and in the Southern one during the eighth century. But in fact, "the higher and purer conception of Jahveh's nature *is in existence* in the eighth century before our era and it is *prophets of Jahveh* who present it, and on the ground of it combat the sensuous and less developed popular belief."[18] The command to put preaching into writing, which was unknown until this time, says much about the novelty of what was emerging in the eighth century.

Prophecy itself had to make its own way, according to Kuenen. Indeed, long before reaching its peak in the eighth century, Israel knew two different prophetic traditions, as the two terms used to name prophets, even in a late period, reveal: *roeh* (seer) and *nabi* (prophet). At this point we find ourselves with a Kuenen trained by his literary studies about the sources of the Pentateuch, who is capable of identifying different traditions on the basis of the smallest signs. In his opinion, the term *roeh* identifies the old Israelite seer, opposed to the pagan diviners more by his faithfulness to Yahweh than by the nature of his actions, while the term *nabi* should be linked with the phenomena of ecstatic prophecy that originated in the Canaanite cult, which did not come from Yahwism but which the latter assimilated over the course of time. Yahwism itself was the "architect" in charge of transforming the "raw material" it received and converting it into the majestic edifice of classical prophecy:

> Everything depends ultimately, not on the raw material out of which prophecy was built up, but upon the architect who has made it what it has become—upon Jahvism, under whose inspiring and hallowing influence the transformation of "seer" and "nabi" to the prophet whom we know from his own writings has taken place.[19]

---

[18] Ibid., 571.

[19] Ibid., 558.

This prophet gradually left behind the extraordinary phenomena that characterized prophecy in another time, such as ecstasy and visions. These are phenomena that belong to a still early stage in the development of prophecy:

> We could formerly leave the question undetermined, whether the ecstasies and visions of the Israelitish prophets were of a different nature from that of similar phenomena which occurred elsewhere, and which are still seen. We now without hesitation affirm that the former did not differ from the latter; they too belong to the natural or materialistic basis of prophecy, and therefore also in course of its development they have gradually retired more into the background; the distinguishing characteristic of prophecy is *not* to be found in these phenomena, but in *the spirit* which partly excited, partly expelled them, or subjected them to itself.[20]

In the course of the development of prophecy, all the gestures intended to unveil the future would also be left behind. The disappearance of these "supernatural" elements should be considered, not a loss, but a step forward in the evolution toward a more pure and spiritual religion:

> Or would materials for admiration be wanting here? I can hardly conceive of any one answering this question in the affirmative. What the organic, in distinction from the supernaturalistic, view of prophecy places before our eyes, may in truth be called a spectacle altogether unique. The mechanical communications of God have disappeared, and with them also the progressive unveiling of the secrets of the future. But in place of these, what a memorable development! what a contest for the possession of truth! It is the earnestness with which the prophets enter upon their task, the sincerity with which they believe in Jahveh and in his moral requirements, which place them in a position not only to maintain what has been handed down to them, but also to purify and elevate it. Thus they rise to the knowledge of what in ancient times remained concealed even from the wise and prudent.[21]

Kuenen anticipates an objection that he himself must have come across in the context of his researches: If the supernatural decays, how does God manifest his presence? If God no longer acts powerfully and visibly, how does Israel differentiate itself from other peoples?

---

[20] Ibid., 573.
[21] Ibid., 574.

We do not allow ourselves to be deprived of the belief in God's presence in history. In the fortunes and development of nations, and not least clearly in those of Israel, we see Him, the holy and all-wise Instructor of his human children. But the old *contrasts* [between Israel and the rest of the nations] must be altogether set aside. So long as we derive a separate part of Israel's religious life directly from God and allow the supernatural or immediate revelation to intervene in even one single point, so long also our view of the whole continues to be incorrect, and we see ourselves here and there necessitated to do violence to the well authenticated contents of the historical documents. It is the supposition of a natural development alone which accounts for all the phenomena.[22]

From this peak of classical prophecy, which abandons inferior forms of communication, we can understand, according to Kuenen, the difference between the true prophets and the false prophets, a commonplace of prophetic literature. It is no longer possible to continue arguing that the difference lies in the fulfillment of prophecies. In fact, "the great majority of their predictions [those of the canonical prophets] have *not* been fulfilled."[23] In the immediate future the restoration of Israel that they expected did not come about. With regard to the more distant future, Christianity assumed, in some respects, more than they expected, but in others, just the opposite.[24] What is it, then, that distinguishes a true prophet from a false one? Kuenen responds with clarity: "*It is the moral earnestness combined with deep piety* which forms the characteristic mark of the canonical, as distinguished from the other prophets."[25]

We should let Kuenen himself explain in his own words what he understands by "ethical monotheism", the great contribution of the prophets of Israel to the religious development of mankind:

They [the prophets] have themselves ascended to the belief in one only, holy, and righteous God, who realises his will, or moral good, in the world, and they have, by preaching and writing, made that belief the inalienable property of our race.[26]

In order for that ethical monotheism to become "the inalienable property of our race", the mediation of Christianity was necessary,

[22] Ibid., 585.
[23] Ibid., 586.
[24] Cf. ibid.
[25] Ibid., 584.
[26] Ibid., 585.

for it was responsible for this spirit entering the popular mentality and being impressed upon our hearts. In fact, Jesus, the heir to this ethical monotheism, should be considered the greatest of the prophets. This inheritance is *religion*, not speculation, and can therefore be transmitted and can, as in fact did happen, be welcomed and become the property of the people. This spirit of the prophets, which has run through the history of Israel and the history of mankind, reaches us today, especially by way of all sincere religious *reform*:

> That there existed eighteen centuries ago a Jewish nation, from which a new religious life could spring, was the fruit of the work done by the prophets. Then, when their task had been completed, they had already long before disappeared from the stage of history. But did they not live again in Jesus of Nazareth? Does not he see his predecessors in the prophets of Israel? Does he not borrow from them some of his leading ideas? . . . Nay, is not every reformation in the domain of religion effected by following that path which they trod, and which, as the pioneers of all, they opened up?[27]

III. The Study of the Psychology of the Prophet

In the early decades of the twentieth century, there began to be perceived in exegesis a growing interest in the psychology of the prophet as a key element for understanding the prophetic phenomenon. This is not even close to being a paradigm change. The perception of the prophet as the creative element of the religion of Israel, not submitted to the Law, which defines the new paradigm, would still continue for decades. However, there is a noticeable shift in interest: up to this time, exegesis had concerned itself with the *message* of the prophet, who was seen as a theologian and moralist; now the *prophet himself*, and specifically his *psychology*, became an object of study. There was no doubt that this change of direction would correct or call into question some statements by earlier authors. But this new orientation was not presented as an alternative to the radical turn that the exegesis of the prophets had taken on the basis of Wellhausen. Duhm himself, who had applied Wellhausen's model to the prophets, is a witness to this shift in interest.

---

[27] Ibid., 592.

While at first he considered the extraordinary psychological phenomena of the prophets to be secondary, in his mature works, especially in his great commentaries, he began to recognize the importance of this dimension for an understanding of the phenomenon of prophecy.

Some factors can help us understand the origin of this shift in interest toward the psychology of the prophet. The second half of the nineteenth century and the early years of the twentieth saw a succession of archeological discoveries in the Middle East that brought to light abundant literary material from the world that surrounded Israel. The great figures of exegesis of the second half of the nineteenth century had not paid too much attention to all that material, which gradually began to be published and studied. Only with the change of century, and because of the drive of the School of the History of Religions, did the biblical world begin to pay attention to the religious literature of the environs of Israel. It was not by chance that Gunkel, a distinguished representative of that school, was one of the main people responsible for the new direction of studies about the prophets.

Among the new material available to scholars, some texts stand out that describe ecstatic experiences presented as ways of communication with the divinity. Following the trend of the era, which tended to reread all the biblical material on the basis of the literature that was coming to light, these texts about ecstatic experiences began to be read in parallel with the numerous biblical texts that describe prophets (false or true) entering into trances (cf. 1 Sam 10:5–6; 1 Kings 18:28–29). It seemed possible to understand the prophets on the basis of their inner experiences. Thus a new field of study was opened.

Another factor that can help us understand the new orientation of the studies is the birth of psychology as a science, which began to gain ground in European universities. In Germany, Wilhelm Wundt (1832–1920) would exercise a significant influence on the studies that I am going to present, especially through two of his works, *Grundzüge der physiologischen Psychologie* (1874) and the encyclopedic *Völkerpsychologie* (published in ten volumes between 1900 and 1920). Much greater would be the influence exercised by the studies of Sigmund Freud (1856–1939) in all the disciplines of academic life, including the theological and the exegetical. It was in 1900 that *The Interpretation of Dreams* was published, a work that would have a broad effect on the European cultural world. The unknown world of psychology and the subconscious emerged as a decisive factor in countless areas of human and social life.

A. Hölscher

Gustav Hölscher (1877–1955), a Lutheran exegete, published a study in 1914 that focused on the prophets in which he paid special attention to psychology.[28] In this work he compares prophecy in Israel with ecstatic mantic "prophecy". To do this, he reviews all the texts in biblical literature in which the prophet communicates his oracles in a state of trance that could be induced by music (cf. 1 Sam 10:5; 2 Kings 3:15) or by other rites of a mantic nature. This parallelism with the mantic world ran into a serious objection: Can the forms of the classical Greek world be utilized to illuminate a literature that belongs to the Semitic world? New archeological discoveries would remove this objection. In 1899, W. Golenischeff published the fragments of a hieratic papyrus that contained the text known as *Voyage of the Egyptian Wen-Amon to Phoenicia*, accompanied by a Russian translation. A year later a German translation became available. This text tells the ecstatic experience of a servant of the king of Biblos in the eleventh century B.C. who took a trip to present-day Lebanon to buy its famous cedar wood. We thus have a text that describes the Canaanite atmosphere with which Israel lived in the period immediately prior to the monarchy. The commercial negotiations this papyrus contains have their parallel in those that David and Solomon carry out with the king of Tyre, which are intended to supply wood for the work on the future Jerusalem temple.

On the basis of these texts, Hölscher deduces that ecstatic prophecy was not characteristic only of nomadic societies, such as Israel is supposed to have been before its settlement in Canaan. Farming cultures of Asia Minor, Syria, and Palestine also testify to this type of prophetic ecstasy, which Israel presumably adopted because of its contact with Canaanite practices. Taking into consideration some accounts from the cultures neighboring Israel and the data the Hebrew Bible provides when it describes this phenomenon in the premonarchical and monarchical stages, ecstatic prophecy was linked to cultic rites, especially

---

[28] G. Hölscher, *Die Profeten: Untersuchungen zur Religionsgeschichte Israels* (Leipzig, 1914). On the first page of his book, Hölscher acknowledges himself to be indebted to Wundt.

sacrifices (cf. the collective ecstasy of the prophets of Baal on Mount
Carmel: 1 Kings 18:28–29), and to holy places dedicated to the veg-
etable deities (the "reforming" prophets make continual reference to
the idolatrous cult on high places and under trees).

Moreover, this was a collective or community phenomenon, with
bands directed by a leader. The Hebrew Bible refers to this type of
phenomenon when it speaks of the "sons of the prophets" (cf. 2 Kings
2:3–15). It could happen, though, that at a particular moment an extraordinary figure could arise from these groups, someone like Samuel
or Elijah, who separated himself from the group to act independently.
This same movement would give rise to "higher" forms of prophecy,
such as those of classical prophecy.

Even so, Hölscher had to face a new objection: Did these "higher"
forms of prophecy have any relation to ecstatic prophecy? The Bible
itself seems to contrast classical prophecy with the early prophetic
form (diviners, soothsayers, enchanters) and the ecstatic forms of the
prophets of Baal. To respond to this difficulty, Hölscher decided to
undertake the study of one of the great classical prophets. It is hardly
surprising that the one chosen was Ezekiel, the prophet of the visions.
Indeed, in 1924 he published a commentary on the prophet Ezekiel
as an example of an ecstatic prophet.[29] One of the characteristics of
ecstasy is that of expressing oneself in poetic language, a sign of the
transformation of consciousness that is at work at that moment. As a
representative of this type of prophecy, Ezekiel would have expressed
his ideas in poetic forms (during trances). This would be the criterion
to distinguish between the authentic sayings of the prophet (sections
in poetry) and the editorial additions (the prose remainder).

B. Gunkel

Hermann Gunkel is already familiar to us from his studies on the formation of the Pentateuch. Extraordinarily well prepared because of
his knowledge of the languages and literatures of the Middle East, he
would be the best representative of the new orientation of the exegesis
of the prophetic books.

---

[29] G. Hölscher, *Hesekiel, der Dichter und das Buch: Eine literarkritische Untersuchung*, BZAW 39
(Giessen, 1924).

In 1914, coinciding with Hölscher's first work, he wrote an introduction to the work of Hans Schmidt, *Die grossen Propheten*, in which he devoted a section to "the secret experiences of the prophets".[30] The significance of this section is seen by that fact that it was published separately in 1924, in three articles in English translation.[31] I will now turn my attention to these.

Gunkel begins his exposition by making the orientation of his study very clear:

> The prophets *have* a secret, . . . certain inward experiences which cannot be understood by the uninitiated observer. . . . These strange men must ultimately remain unintelligible to us useless [*sic*] we understand these secret experiences.[32]

Gunkel himself undertook to explain why, until then, attention had not been paid to these inner experiences of the prophets. In his opinion, the "orthodox" view saw in them simply mechanical instruments of a supernatural revelation. For its part, the "rationalist" view, which succeeded the preceding one, was "too dry and blunt to see in the prophets more than pious teachers and respectable preachers".[33] On the positive side, Gunkel presented four intellectual trends that promoted the new orientation of the studies. The first was the historical approach, which had been growing in importance during the nineteenth century and which had fortunately been completed by the Neo-romantic movement (of which Gunkel was a good representative), with great sensitivity for perceiving the details of the lives of men and peoples. The second trend was the comparative study of religions, which had been extending its influence by doing away with the "naïve" view that the prophets of the OT were a unique phenomenon. The third trend was the study of the literary history of the OT, which, by analyzing the

---

[30] Here I will quote the second edition of the work of H. Schmidt, since Gunkel made some corrections to his contribution: H. Gunkel, "Die geheimen Erfahrungen der Propheten", in *Die grossen Propheten*, ed. H. Schmidt, 2nd ed. (Göttingen, 1923), xvii–xxxiv.

[31] H. Gunkel, "The Secret Experiences of the Prophets", *Exp* 9 (1924): I: 356–66, 427–35; II: 23–32. A clear expression of the tendency of this era to explain everything on the basis of "inner experiences" is the article that follows the first part of Gunkel's exposition in the journal *The Expositor* (in the year 1924): "The Temptations of Jesus Christ—Were They Trance or Historical Experiences?"

[32] Gunkel, "Secret Experiences of the Prophets I", 356.

[33] Ibid.

forms of prophetic discourse, arrived by an indirect route at the inner life of the prophet of which they are the expression. The final trend that collaborated in the new orientation was, according to Gunkel, the emergence of psychology as a scientific discipline.

Once he had presented the background, Gunkel established some basic presuppositions:

> The fundamental experience of all types of prophecy is "ecstasy." That is a state of consciousness entirely outside the experience of the ordinary man of to-day, and not easily intelligible to him.[34]

Gunkel began by describing the outward actions and the symptoms of this ecstatic phenomenon as they appear in the Bible. There we find prophets in a "trance", who live grouped in communities (the *benê hannebî'îm*), whose status probably passes from some to others. Music and, in time, poetry play a very important role in prophetic expression. The preparation to receive revelation is also decisive: a kind of concentration that "scans" the horizon and for which the prophet seeks out remote places, like a mountain or a spot beside falling water, exerting a hypnotic power. This is how they receive revelation, although it can arrive without any prior preparation. When the ecstasy arrives, there are strong convulsions and even self-mutilations, such as those seen in the prophets of Baal whom Elijah challenges on Mount Carmel. At that moment the prophets express themselves, not quietly, but in shouts. The excitation is such that they can do no more than shout. But when the ecstasy is communicative, there is a transformation: "The prophet's words, as soon as they pass from stuttering to actual language, automatically take metrical form."[35]

This is one of the key characteristics of classical prophecy, which Hölscher also made it his job to highlight: the poetic form as an expression of a consciousness possessed by the deity.

In view of the more than likely perplexity that his description of the prophecy of Israel (and in it he also includes the highest forms of prophecy) could cause to the ears of his contemporaries, Gunkel reminds us of the distance in time and space from a culture that is not our own:

[34] Ibid., 358.
[35] Ibid., 365.

Some of these phenomena might seem to us cases of nervous or mental derangement, but we should remember that our Psychiatry has till now been exclusively occupied with the psychic life of civilised people of the present day, and that different criteria must be used for these passionate children of the hot East.[36]

After describing the outward manifestations of ecstatic prophecy, Gunkel directs his gaze to the inner life of the prophet. His first observation touches on "the religious passion of great intensity" that animates and sustains that life. It is the passion that, at the lowest stages of prophecy, was spurred by music and dancing, by shouting and singing. But it is also the passion that fills the great prophets who despise those external aids. At the height of that passion, the ecstasy arrives. Having arrived at this point, Gunkel is careful to underline that the ecstatic phenomenon should not be considered a strange and irrational mystery:

> The science of Psychology does not see in religious ecstasy any inexplicable mystery. It is aware there have been many religious ecstatics in the world besides the prophets, and that every human emotion is capable of being raised to the pitch of ecstasy.[37]

So what is there that is "divine" in these ecstatic phenomena? Can we speak of originality in the prophets of Israel, who claim to receive the Word of God in these circumstances? If we are faithful to the data of the Bible, the prophet claims to enter into contact with the deity, to feel his hand, to receive visions. And, of course, the ecstatic prophet claims to hear the words of Yahweh himself. "He feels himself to be Jahveh's messenger with the duty of announcing to whom it may concern the divine will which he has thus learned."[38] At this point the scholar forged in the comparative study of religions emerges:

> In all these manifestations of ecstasy both prophets and people believed they recognised the act of God. The investigator is in no way surprised at this, for he knows that wherever such phenomena are found all over the world, there also is the conviction that they are due to the deity. How should men in these ancient days think differently? . . . This inference

---

[36] Ibid., 366.
[37] Gunkel, "The Secret Experiences of the Prophets II", 428.
[38] Ibid., 429.

is so easy and natural, that it was universal throughout antiquity, and it reappears from time to time amongst ourselves. The ancient Israelite believed so too. He referred the ecstasy of the prophets to Jahveh's spirit. By "spirit" was meant in Hebrew antiquity that divine power which found expression in these and similar phenomena. . . . According to the belief current in Israel, God's spirit was the cause of all that found expression in any superhuman mysterious power in man. . . .

It must of course be said emphatically, that modern science meets this interpretation of the prophetic state with an unqualified denial. Whilst the modern investigator must inevitably try to understand such phenomena psychologically, the ancient mind sees in them simply a divine marvel.[39]

Gunkel also asks himself about the self-consciousness of the prophet. The question of human and divine cooperation (to put it in classical terms) in prophetic inspiration is a *topos* in exegesis. In Gunkel's view there is no doubt: the personality of the prophet disappears completely:

And what of the *self-consciousness* of the prophets, who like the people were certain that Jahveh Himself was working in them? What a consciousness such a man must have had! Under the thrill of this conviction, the personality of the ecstatic could entirely disappear and the deity take complete possession of him, so that he could now act and speak as God! The "I" that speaks through him is God Himself![40]

In the last part of his exposition, Gunkel tries to trace a *history* of Israelite prophecy by describing its most significant stages. In the story of Saul and Samuel we find the most ancient stage of prophecy. In it we find groups of prophets, established around the country, who experience ecstatic phenomena. They cause astonishment in people, but they are not particularly esteemed. At this stage they resemble the ecstatics of other nations. Gunkel does not believe that this ecstatic prophecy originates in Canaan, since it maintains a number of characteristics of its own.

From these circles, and through a long course of development, will come the prophets we know by name. They have many points in common with the *nebî'îm* of the early stage, although at the same time great differences separate them:

---

[39] Ibid., 429–31.
[40] Ibid., 431.

The similarity is in the form of the psychical processes. From the outside, the conditions seem the same, although their violence is diminished. The difference lies in the intellectual content. It is the highest thoughts that fill the ecstasy of the later prophets. And it is this supremely valuable content, though it took this form, that should warn the present day student not to estimate too lightly these strange phenomena. It was not ordinary men, but strong enthusiastic personalities who underwent these experiences.[41]

In the transition from the earliest stage to the more evolved one, a very important role was played by the emergence of the oracle. The first prophets simply entered into ecstasy. That in itself was an action of God. But it implied a step forward when the ecstatic state began to be accompanied by the profession of an oracle. This circumstance made the popularity of the prophets grow, and they started to be respected and sought out to deal with the vicissitudes of public and private life. They must also have been powerful because of their healing abilities, although their methods were far from those applied by pagan sorcerers. In Gunkel's opinion, the root of their healing power must be sought in the absolute trust that the sick placed in them.

Among these prophets there yet arose some even greater men who helped to take one more step forward in the history of Israelite prophecy. These are the prophets who no longer waited to be consulted in order to give an oracle. They prophesied the great events that affected the life of the nation: the defeats or victories in battles, the fate of a besieged city, the fall of a dynasty. It can confidently be said that their speech is more "rational" than the mad shouting of the prophets of the early era. But even in these men the "amateur" element is quite perceptible, although their violence has gone down. In this stage of prophecy, two types can be distinguished: the prophet of good fortunes and the prophet of misfortunes. The least important are the former: in them the interests of Yahweh are mixed with the interests of the kings. Much superior to them are the prophets of misfortunes, who are capable of confronting the kings or the whole nation, driven by the zeal of Yahweh.

The last stage of prophecy is reached with classical prophecy starting in the eighth century. When the Assyrian threat begins to draw near, these prophets are capable of announcing destruction and accusing the

---

[41] Ibid., Gunkel, "Secret Experiences of the Prophets III", 24.

people of the unfaithfulness and sin that are their cause. Their ideals
are noble and elevated, and with them they judge a people approaching
disaster. Monotheism and moral religion are their great contributions:

> It was they who welded together, as with bands of iron, religion and
> morality. Above all it is to them that we owe monotheism: to the feet
> of the God of their nation they brought all peoples and powers of the
> world and all the gods. From the eighth century onward these prophetic
> voices never ceased: they accompanied the history of Israel and Judah and
> outlasted both.[42]

These prophets received a superhuman knowledge of the future and
were therefore capable of predicting great events. Gunkel, though,
thought that their greatest virtue was not found in the ability to make
predictions, as important as that was:

> Were that all, the value of their words for us to-day, who have but little
> interest in by far the majority of their predictions, would be very small.
> Even their strange experiences, their phantastic visions and their strange
> symbols are but externals. There is more in them than that. They pro-
> claimed to their day the thoughts of God. They even gave Jahveh's *reasons*;
> they know why their words are true. . . . The new element in these men
> was that in their work prophecy assumed a spiritual and moral content.[43]

Did the ecstatic element still remain at this high point of prophecy?
Gunkel states that this element never disappeared, although in this last
period it would find itself clearly restrained by the higher inner experiences of the prophet:

> It is in this change of content that we find the reason why the vehement
> element in the outward form of their experiences subsides (although it
> never quite disappears), and is replaced by inward experiences which we
> can understand.[44]

The history of prophecy in Israel could be described synthetically, in
Gunkel's words, as "a steady transition from prophet to preacher and
religious thinker".[45]

---

[42] Ibid., 29.
[43] Ibid., 30.
[44] Ibid., 31.
[45] Ibid.

This journey through the study of the psychology of the prophets can be closed with the description that Theodore H. Robinson, another well-known representative of this trend, gives of a normal day in the life of the prophet:

> He [the prophet] might be mingling with the crowd, sometimes on ordinary days, sometimes on special occasions. Suddenly something would happen to him. His eye would become fixed, strange convulsions would seize upon his limbs, the form of his speech would change. Men would recognise that the Spirit had fallen upon him. The fit would pass, and he would tell to those who stood around the things which he had seen and heard.[46]

IV. Philosophical and Cultural Presuppositions of the Critical Study of the Prophets

In the study devoted to the formation of the Pentateuch we have already stopped to analyze the philosophical and cultural presuppositions hidden behind the image of the historical evolution of the religion of Israel that was derived from the documentary hypothesis as Wellhausen formulated it. In the present study, I began by presenting the role that Wellhausen assigned to the prophet in that evolution. It is therefore understandable that, in a first approximation, the same philosophical and cultural presuppositions that we studied then should likewise determine the image of the prophet as this first author now presents it to us.

However, in the investigation of the nature and role of the prophet in the history of Israel, we will see that new philosophical and cultural presuppositions come into play that up until now had not been contemplated. In fact, the exegesis that was concerned with the sources of the Pentateuch was still firmly anchored, because of its very object, in literary discussion. In the exegesis of the figure of the prophet, however, the literary question plays a more secondary role. The original nature of the religion, and thus of Christianity itself, is at stake. It is not surprising that there are many factors, some of them new, that condition this great battle.

---

[46] T. H. Robinson, *Prophecy and the Prophets in Ancient Israel* (London, 1923), 50. Cf. T. H. Robinson, "The Ecstatic Element in O. T. Prophecy", *Exp* 21 (1921): 217–38.

I will start, though, by reviewing the philosophical and cultural presuppositions shared with the previous investigation and by taking the opportunity to illustrate, qualify, or expand them on the basis of the new context and the texts and authors now being studied.

We have already had occasion to see the influence that the romantic movement and the idea of evolution in living organisms had on Wellhausen's historical model. We have also seen how these influences converged with the ideology of the liberal Protestantism of which this author was a part. In the image of the prophet that Wellhausen presents to us, the convergence of these three lines of influence only increases.

Indeed, in the history of Israelite religion that the German author portrays, we clearly see the romantic spirit that privileges the "pure" above the "complex", according to a clearly Darwinian evolutionary scheme. It is worth noting that the ninth edition of the *Encyclopaedia Britannica*, of which William Robertson Smith was coeditor in the years 1881–1888 and in which Wellhausen wrote his article "Israel", would go down in history for its strong defense of biological evolution (or what amounts to the same thing, the theories of Darwin) and of the critical study of the Bible, two fields in which, at that time, fierce battles were being waged.

In this evolutionary scheme, the prophet occupies the place of what is "original", as the founder of the spiritual, individual, and ethical religion. This religion degenerated over time, betrayed by the ritualism-legalism of Judaism. The prophetic spirit that was reborn in Jesus of Nazareth was again betrayed, degenerating into an ecclesiastical institution centered on the cult, law, and dogma. This prophetic spirit was precisely what the Lutheran Reformation inherited, and it claimed to be returning to the pure religion of Jesus and the prophets, which had been suffocated by the stagnation of the Catholic Church.

In that new spirit which the Reformation embodied, liberal Protestantism represented a drive that radicalized this return to the origins. To do this, it could count on the invaluable help of critical exegesis, which, just as in the field of the Gospels it looked for the historical figure of Jesus by freeing it from the "believing" redactions, in the field of the prophetic books looked for the authentic message of the prophets by rescuing it from the "secondary" redactional additions that smothered it under the weight of the cult and the Law. This task was precisely the one carried out by Duhm and Kuenen, who looked for the true spirit of prophecy in their exegetical studies. And this spirit turned out to be a deeply Protestant spirit.

Indeed, the Law (slavery)-spirit (freedom) opposition found in the background of the drastic separation between Law and prophets starting with Wellhausen is very sharply felt in Protestantism. The Law came to put out the spirit, turning it into rules to which we become slaves. Statements like those of Wellhausen "this living command of Jehovah is all he knows of, and not any testament given once for all"[47] or "With the appearance of the law came to an end the old freedom", reflect well that Protestant mentality.

The polemic with the cult, which the prophets, according to these authors, seem to champion, is another of the great historical claims of the Protestant Reformation. Just as the prophets attacked the empty cult that had paralyzed Israelite religion, Luther began a reform intended to rescue the true religion of Jesus from the ritual-ministerial-legal-dogmatic chains with which the Catholic Church had imprisoned it. This polemic with the cult was an expression of that other, more radical dialectic, strongly felt by Lutheranism, which exists between works and faith.

But it is in the description of the content of the true, pure, and spiritual religion brought by the prophets where the exegetes of interest here (Wellhausen, Duhm, and Kuenen) show themselves to be most "Protestant". "Ethical monotheism", the great contribution of the prophets to the religious development of mankind, could be considered a manual for the "good Protestant". The heart of this "manual" is a relationship with the only God based on ethics and moral consistency. Just as in the era of the prophets, so also now the fulfillment of some commandments or the mechanical performance of a series of empty rituals is not what links us to God. Now it is a matter of true religion, one with a sincere attitude toward God that expresses itself in right behavior, without duplicity, in all areas of life.

It is important to emphasize that, according to these authors, in the pure religion inaugurated by the prophets, to which every true religious reform returns, the relationship with God is always *individual* and *direct*, not mediated by any institution or ritual. When Wellhausen underlined

---

[47] Unless otherwise stated, in this section the quotes from the authors studied and their corresponding references are taken from the two previous sections.

this dimension by saying, "It belongs to the notion of prophecy, of true revelation, that Jehovah, overlooking all the media of ordinances and institutions, communicates Himself to the *individual*", he also showed himself to be a child of liberal Protestantism, which feels every form of institutional, sacramental, ministerial, or magisterial mediation to be an enemy of pure faith. For this reason, he identified the death of prophecy with the appearance of an objective authority: the Law.

The step from collective piety to individual piety is conceived as progress in the history of Israelite religion and a victory of the prophets. In the stages that Gunkel traces of the history of prophecy, the earliest stage corresponds to that of the prophets, who formed groups or communities (the *benê hannebî'îm*). The highest stage is that of the classical prophet, who has an individual and direct relationship with God.

It is precisely that personal, direct, and intimate relationship with God, which the Protestant mentality strongly underlines, that is found in the background of Hölscher's and Gunkel's studies on the psychology of the prophet. It is obvious that these studies could not be understood without the academic context of the era, in which psychology was gaining ground as a science and in which works like that of Freud were revolutionizing so many disciplines. But it is also true that the application of psychology to the study of the prophets and its use as a key explanatory factor for their lives and their messages find fertile ground in Protestantism: the relationship with God is an inner experience that could properly be called *mystical*. In this sense, Gunkel finds himself at home when he begins his article on *the secret experiences of the prophets* with the statement that "the prophets *have* a secret, . . . certain inward experiences which cannot be understood by the uninitiated observer."

Indeed, the Protestant mentality intensely feels the enormous distance between God and his creature. How is it possible to fill up this distance completely? Only God can do it through his spirit, which illuminates the heart and "by inspiration" makes the truth of his presence felt. It is thus an inner, mystical experience. More correctly speaking, only in Christ could a real contemporaneousness between God and man have come about. Today we can achieve the certainty of this presence through the illumination of the heart by the Spirit, who makes us taste or feel the presence of Christ.

These authors thus try to understand "the inner experiences" of the prophets starting from the image they have of the man-God relationship, based on the experience of inner illumination. This image of a "subjective" experience feels that "the enemy to beat" is the "objective" relationship the Catholic Church proclaims through her prolongation over time, in the body of Christ, of the Incarnation of God and his presence among men. The ecclesiastical institution, dogma, and the sacraments are the diametric opposites of subjective or mystical experience.

I will now go on to deal with other philosophical and cultural presuppositions that were less identifiable in the investigation of the sources of the Pentateuch (because of the very object of that investigation) and that play a very important role in the study of the prophets. This does not mean that the great authors who held the documentary theory were not under the influence of these "new" presuppositions. In fact they were, for the two courses of investigation we are looking at ran parallel to one another. But in the case of the investigation of the sources of the Pentateuch, for the reasons I have already mentioned, the presuppositions now being studied were reflected less in the results of exegesis.

In the positions of the authors who dealt with the prophets, and this is especially evident in Kuenen and Gunkel, a decisive influence was exercised by the rationalism that sprang from the Enlightenment, which limits the domain of reason to that which is empirically verifiable and which thus excludes from its field all supernatural elements. From this position there additionally springs, quite consistently, a new conception of religion: natural religion compatible with reason.

In the texts by Kuenen and Gunkel that have been studied here, it is especially striking that they attempt to reduce the extraordinary phenomena we find described in the prophetic books to mere natural development or to "scientifically" explainable psychological processes. Kuenen sees in the disappearance of the supernatural phenomena (attributed to a "naïve" view of reality) a sign of the progress of the religion of Israel. The exegete, by following the scientific and rational method, cannot, says Kuenen, continue to "derive a separate part of Israel's religious life directly from God", nor can he allow "the supernatural or immediate revelation to intervene in even one single point". This, he goes on to say, would go against history and would twist the documents. Instead of this, "It is the supposition of a natural development alone which accounts for all the phenomena."

For his part, Gunkel contrasts the ancient mentality, which attributes the ecstatic phenomena that are found among the prophets to divine intervention, with modern science (of which his exegesis is an expression), which attributes them to psychological processes: "Whilst the modern investigator must inevitably try to understand such phenomena psychologically, the ancient mind sees in them simply a divine marvel."

In both cases, there is the underlying, typically rationalist, prejudice that excludes the supernatural from the domain of reason. This is a dominant position in most of the critical exegesis of the nineteenth and early twentieth centuries, which is very well illustrated, for the study of the Gospels, by the work of A. Schweitzer.[48] This mentality, an offspring of the Enlightenment, can be traced back, in its approach to Scripture, to the work of the Jewish author Baruch Spinoza (1632–1677).[49] Born during the Thirty Years' War, a clear expression of the "conflict" of religions, Spinoza was convinced that the hatred and animosity of the Christians who were confronting each other could end if it was possible to arrive at a careful separation of the spheres of theology and philosophy. Then reason could guide the minds of men to truth and wisdom, while theology would continue to give rise to piety and obedience:

> To extricate ourselves from such confusion and to free our minds from theological prejudices and the blind acceptance of human fictions as God's teaching, we need to analyse and discuss the true method of interpreting Scripture. For if we do not know this, we can know nothing for certain regarding what the Bible or the Holy Spirit wishes to teach. To formulate the matter succinctly, I hold that the method of interpreting Scripture, does not differ from the [correct] method of interpreting nature, but rather is wholly consonant with it. The [correct] method of interpreting nature consists above all in constructing a natural history, from which we derive the definitions of natural things, as from certain data. Likewise, to interpret Scripture, we need to assemble a genuine history of it and to deduce the thinking of the Bible's authors by valid inferences from this history, as from certain data and principles. Provided we admit no other

---

[48] Schweitzer, *The Quest of the Historical Jesus*.

[49] With regard to Spinoza, his life, the context in which he acted, and his relationship to the historical criticism of the Bible (with abundant bibliography), see T. L. Frampton, *Spinoza and the Rise of Historical Criticism of the Bible* (New York, 2006).

criteria or data for interpreting Scripture and discussing its contents than what is drawn from Scripture itself and its history, we will always proceed without any danger of going astray, and we shall have the same assuredness in discussing things that surpass our understanding as in discussing things that we learn by the natural light of reason.[50]

Following the method that he has imposed on himself, Spinoza denies the possibility of miracles, although to do this he uses a deistic argument (which, when all is said and done, is a form of rationalism):

But since nothing is necessarily true except by divine decree alone, it most clearly follows that the universal laws of nature are simply God's decrees and follow from the necessity and perfection of the divine nature. If anything therefore were to happen in nature that contradicted its universal laws, it would also necessarily contradict the decree and understanding and nature of God. Or if anyone were to assert that God does anything contrary to the laws of nature, he would at the same time be compelled to assert that God acts contrary to his own nature, than which nothing is more absurd.[51]

How then should the accounts of miracles, which appear so abundantly in Scripture, be interpreted? It should not be thought that things happened as they are recounted in the miracles, since they are told to move the common people to devotion:

Without doubt, therefore, everything narrated in Scripture actually happened naturally, and yet it is all ascribed to God, since it is not the intention of the Bible, as we have shown, to explain things in terms of natural causes but only to speak of things that commonly occupy people's imaginations, and to do so in a manner and style calculated to inspire wonder about things and thus impress devotion upon the minds of the common people.[52]

The influence of these principles of interpretation of Scripture lets itself be felt in Kuenen's generation, as is clearly seen in his contemporaries David Friedrich Strauss (1808–1874) and Ernest Renan (1823–1892). In the following way, Strauss denies to the Absolute the possibility of interrupting the natural causal chain:

---

[50] B. Spinoza, *Theological-Political Treatise* (Cambridge, 2007), 98.

[51] Ibid., 83.

[52] Ibid., 90.

That an account is not historical—that the matter related could not have taken place in the manner described is evident,

First. When the narration is irreconcilable with the known and universal laws which govern the course of events. Now according to these laws, agreeing with all just philosophical conceptions and all credible experience, the absolute cause never disturbs the chain of secondary causes by single arbitrary acts of interposition, but rather manifests itself in the production of the aggregate of finite casualties, and of their reciprocal action.[53]

Renan, for his part, from the outset discounts miracles as irrational and therefore unhistorical:

We take for granted . . . that the miracles related by the Gospels have had no reality, that the Gospels are not books written under the inspiration of Divinity. Those two negations are not with us the result of exegesis; they are anterior to exegesis. They are the outcome of an experience which has not been denied. Miracles are things which never happen; only credulous people believe they have seen them; you cannot cite a single one which has taken place in presence of witnesses capable of testing it; no special intervention of the Divinity, whether in the composition of a book, or in any event whatever, has been proved. For this reason alone, when a person admits the supernatural, such a one is without the province of science; he accepts an explanation which is non-scientific, an explanation which is set aside by the astronomer, the physician, the chemist, the geologist, the physiologist, one which ought also to be passed over by the historian. We reject the supernatural for the same reason that we reject the existence of centaurs and hippogriffes; and this reason is, that nobody has ever seen them. It is not because it has been previously demonstrated to me that the evangelists do not merit absolute credence that I reject the miracles which they recount. It is because they do recount miracles that I say, "The Gospels are legends; they may contain history, but, certainly, all that they set forth is not historical."[54]

This is the context in which Kuenen and Gunkel write, determined by the a priori exclusion of every supernatural element from the terrain of history. Both, though, continue to be *religious* men. The religion in

---

[53] D. F. Strauss, *The Life of Jesus Critically Examined*, trans. George Eliot, 4th ed. (London, 1902), § 16.

[54] E. Renan, *The History of the Origins of Christianity. Book I: Life of Jesus* (London, 1890), xi–xii.

which they believe, and which will inevitably be projected in their studies, is natural religion that excludes every extraordinary phenomenon, the kind that moves "within the boundaries of mere reason".[55] This type of religiosity was to become very widespread in the nineteenth century, especially in academic and intellectual circles.

Of that religion it can be said that it is "Christian", and therefore the OT interests it, because it sees in Jesus of Nazareth the highest expression of human religiosity, one in which a man calls God "Father", one that has as its content the sublime ethic of the Sermon on the Mount. However, this religion, characteristic of liberal Protestantism, is now scandalized by Christian dogma as it has been transmitted by the Church (Catholic or Protestant), which is branded as irrational. That a man could have a divine nature, that a piece of bread could be the Body of Christ, that a woman could be Virgin and Mother at the same time, or that a minister of the Church (the bishop of Rome) could be infallible are irrational holdovers from another age that should be abandoned for the sake of a more pure, ethical, and rational religion.

In reality, the basic scandal, the root objection that enlightened reason sees in Christianity, is its claim that an event that is historical, and thus framed in space and time, can be *the decisive, saving factor* for the whole human race. Immanuel Kant (1724–1804) is the author who has best formulated this objection, promoting the development of a religion within the limits of reason, a Christianity without dogma:

> The only faith that can found a universal church is *pure religious faith*, for it is a plain rational faith which can be convincingly communicated to everyone, whereas a historical faith, merely based on facts, can extend its influence no further than the tidings relevant to a judgment on its credibility can reach. Yet, due to a peculiar weakness of human nature, pure faith can never be relied on as much as it deserves, that is, [enough] to found a Church on it alone.
>
> Conscious of their impotence in the cognition of supersensible things, and though they allow every honor to be paid to faith in these things (as the faith which must carry conviction for them universally), human beings are yet not easily persuaded that steadfast zeal in the conduct of a morally good life is all that God requires of them to be his well-pleasing subjects in his Kingdom. They cannot indeed conceive of their obligation

---

[55] Cf. I. Kant, *Religion within the Boundaries of Mere Reason and Other Writings* (Cambridge, 1998).

except as directed to some *service* or other which they must perform for God—wherein what matters is not the intrinsic worth of their actions as much as, rather, that they are performed for God to please him through passive obedience, however morally indifferent the actions might be in themselves.[56]

That "peculiar weakness of human nature" of which Kant speaks, which is at the origin of resistance to pure religion, seems to be the one that Wellhausen, Kuenen, and Gunkel spy in the people of Israel (and, later on, in Judaism and in the Church), which takes refuge in rites and resists welcoming the ethical and individual religion that the prophets inaugurate. The pure religious faith that Kant demands is the one that the prophets began when they introduced "ethical monotheism" in Israel. In Kuenen's words, "They have themselves ascended to the belief in one only, holy, and righteous God, who realises his will, or moral good, in the world, and they have, by preaching and writing, made that belief the inalienable property of our race." Thanks to them, Gunkel would say, "religion and morality" have been welded together with "bands of iron".

What value does Scripture have for Kant, since it is no more than a document of a historical or ecclesiastical faith? Just like statutory ecclesiastical faith, which it must uphold, Scripture is the "vehicle and the means for the public union of human beings in promoting it [pure religious faith]".[57] That is why, having as a clear reference the Scripture of the West, namely, the Christian Bible, Kant adds a *desideratum*:

> How fortunate, when one such book, fallen into human hands, contains complete, besides its statutes legislating faith, also the purest moral doctrine of religion, and this doctrine can be brought into the strictest harmony with those statutes (which [in turn] contribute to its introduction).[58]

This is precisely the task that authors like Wellhausen, Kuenen, Duhm, and Gunkel have carried out in the field of the OT: bringing

---

[56] Ibid., 112–13. The same contrast between natural religion and positive religions is contemporaneously developed by G. E. Lessing in writings such as "On the Origin of Revealed Religion" (1763 or 1764) and "The Education of the Human Race" (1780). Cf. G. E. Lessing, *Philosophical and Theological Writings*, trans. and ed. H. B. Nisbet (Cambridge, 2005), 35–36, 217–40.

[57] Kant, *Religion within the Boundaries*, 116.

[58] Ibid.

to light "the purest moral doctrine of religion" that, by kindhearted Providence, was found hidden in Scripture, obscured by the predominance that the statutory apparatus had in it.

Kant himself reserves a special role for scholars in interpreting Scripture, and in addition he asks for them "public freedom of thought":[59]

> Religion of reason and scriptural scholarship are, therefore, the properly appointed interpreters and trustees of a sacred document. It is self-evident that they must not on any account be hindered by the secular arm in the public use of their insights and discoveries in this field, or be bound to certain dogmas.[60]

In Kant's logic, and from the historical point of view, the Protestant Reformation was the providential instrument that had made it possible to recover "the purest moral doctrine of religion" that was found in Scripture by promoting, in addition, biblical scholarship.[61] Adolf von Harnack (1851–1930), a contemporary of Gunkel, who in his work *What Is Christianity?*[62] published in 1900 gave one of the most refined descriptions of spiritual and ethical religion, in fact sees in the Reformation a sublime incarnation of this religion:

> But no one can survey the history of Europe from the second century to the present time without being forced to the conclusion that in the whole course of this history the greatest movement and the one most

---

[59] Ibid., 122.

[60] Ibid., 120.

[61] Lessing, though, saw in Joachim de Fiore (1135–1202) and his movement the first historical turn that, in his case, already sensed the "third age of mankind", in which reason would reach the truths of natural religion all by itself, without the need for a pedagogue: "No—it will certainly come, the time of fulfilment, when man, the more convinced his understanding feels of an ever better future, will nevertheless have no need to borrow the motives for his actions from this future; when he will do good because it is good, not because it brings arbitrary rewards which previously served only to fix and fortify his capricious gaze so that he might recognise the inner and better rewards of such action. It will certainly come, the time of *a new, eternal gospel*, which is promised to us even in the primers of the New Covenant. Perhaps even certain enthusiasts of the thirteenth and fourteenth centuries caught a glimpse of this new eternal gospel, and erred only in proclaiming that its coming was so close at hand. Perhaps their *three ages of the world* were not just an empty fancy; and they certainly had no ill intentions when they taught that the New Covenant must become just as *antiquated* as the Old has become" (G. E. Lessing, "The Education of the Human Race", in *Philosophical and Theological Writings*, 237–38, §§ 85–88).

[62] A. von Harnack, *What Is Christianity?* (New York, 1903).

pregnant with good was the Reformation in the sixteenth century; even
the great change which took place at the transition to the nineteenth is inferior to it in importance. What do all our discoveries and inventions and
our advances in outward civilisation signify in comparison with the fact
that to-day there are thirty millions of Germans, and many more millions
of Christians outside Germany, who possess a religion without priests,
without sacrifices, without 'fragments' of grace, without ceremonies—a
spiritual religion![63]

Liberal Protestantism and critical exegesis, of which the authors being studied are representatives, present themselves as privileged (and
providential) instruments in historical development that help to recover
the true spirit of the Reformation (which the "peculiar weakness of
human nature" always tends to betray), the spirit of pure religion, of
Jesus, the heir to the prophets.

V. Calling the Postulates of the New Paradigm into Question

As happened in the case of the investigation of the formation of the
Pentateuch, a considerable amount of time had to pass before the fundamental postulates of the new paradigm for the interpretation of the
prophets were questioned. Even so, in the latter case it was not necessary to wait until the seventies. Shortly after the Second World War
elements of change could be noticed. One of the authors who contributed most to the criticism of these postulates was Ivan Engnell
(1907–1964), an exegete of the Uppsala School. In 1962 he published
an article in Swedish that, in turn, was based on two previous articles,
from 1947 and 1949. Only in 1969 did the English translation of it see
the light, in a collected work that made his most important researches
known to the academic world.[64] Already in this article we find most
of the axioms of the then-dominant paradigm questioned in a reasoned
manner.

---

[63] Ibid., 268.
[64] I. Engnell, "Prophets and Prophetism in the Old Testament", in *A Rigid Scrutiny: Critical Essays on the Old Testament by Ivan Engnell translated from the Swedish*, ed. J. T. Willis and H.
Ringgren (Nashville, 1969), 123–79.

A. The Relation of the Prophets to the Law

One of the pillars of the new paradigm in the study of the prophets is the claim that the prophets precede the Law and that they therefore are not the transmitters of a tradition but the true creators of a new religion. Engnell considers this claim unjustified:

> Here, it is important to emphasize once again that the prophets should not be regarded as founders of a new era in Israelite religion, much less as founders of a new religion, a characterization which has been propagated for a long time. Actually, to a great extent, the great prophets were bound to earlier forms and inherited traditions. They adopted and developed ideas and complexes which had already originated in the Israelite religion, especially in the forms which were associated with the cult. There is no need to question the fact that an actual development took place, but we should avoid a one-sided anachronistic view of this development.[65]

Indeed, it would be unfair to deny the decisive role Wellhausen's work played in understanding the development of the Law in Israel, especially in separating the different *redactions* of it. He made it possible to understand that there existed late redactions of the Law that should be placed after the prophets in time. But what was really "one-sided" and "anachronistic" was placing *all* the Law after prophecy. In fact, the very investigation of the composition of the Pentateuch eventually took on the task of showing that before the appearance of classical prophecy (in the eighth century B.C.), legislative traditions already existed in Israel (especially the Decalogue and the book of the covenant).[66] Moreover, detailed studies on each prophet made it clear that they had a tradition to which to refer, although on many occasions they did not make it explicit.

In a study published in 1975, devoted precisely to the relationship between prophecy and tradition, R. E. Clements managed to describe

---

[65] Ibid., 172.

[66] H. Gressmann and P. Volz were pioneers who placed the Decalogue before the prophets. Cf. H. Gressmann, *Mose und seine Zeit* (Göttingen, 1913); P. Volz, *Mose und sein Werk*, 2nd ed. (Tübingen, 1932) (the first edition came out in 1907). The studies of Mendenhall were also very significant, as they underlined the literary similarities between the Hittite vassalage treaties from the end of the second millennium B.C. and biblical legislative texts such as the Decalogue and the framework of the laws of the Covenant (cf. G. E. Mendenhall, "Ancient Oriental and Biblical Law", *BA* 17 [1954]: 26–46; G. E. Mendenhall, *Law and Covenant in the Ancient Near East* [Pittsburgh, 1955]).

the path that relationship had traveled in the previous hundred years and underlined the correctness of the new direction of the studies, based on a reassessment of the traditions prior to the prophets:

> The understanding of prophetic originality among earlier scholars had led to a considerable underestimating of the importance of the place of tradition in the prophets' preaching, and the redressing of the balance in this rightly represents a 'growing point' of Old Testament study. . . . What is particularly new [today] is a deepening awareness that such a sharp conflict with tradition, and such a negative attitude toward it, does not characterize the prophet throughout, however valid it is at certain points. Furthermore, there can be no doubt that, in the past, scholarship has sometimes found conflicts where none existed, or has wrongly credited the prophets with originating ideas and attitudes which they in fact inherited.[67]

B. The Prophets and the Cult

Another of the pillars that upheld the image of the prophet that Wellhausen inaugurated was that of radical opposition to the cult. On this point Engnell's criticism proves lucid when it attributes to a Protestant mentality the negative image of the cult that is deduced from that opposition:

> This understanding [of the prophets as those who create a new, "spiritual" form of religion that is "without cult"] . . . is undoubtedly prompted by a Protestant tenet that cultic piety is of inferior power, a view inherited from the Age of the Enlightenment and Rationalism. Advocates of this position operate on a purely anachronistic assumption that the prophets propagated a "spiritual" religion which was independent of the cult. But, in reality, this is completely foreign to ancient Israel, including her prophets.
>
> No fundamental declarations of anti-cultic principles are to be found in the prophets, no matter how diligently scholars persist in their attempt to find them. In an unprejudiced, true exegesis, which takes the context of the sayings into consideration, it is evident that, in reality, these so-called anti-cultic sayings refer to special cases: they are directed either against certain definite forms of the cult (foreign types, or types which claim to be Yahwistic but are not acknowledged as such by the prophet

---

[67] R. E. Clements, *Prophecy and Tradition* (Oxford, 1975), 1–2.

in question—which first of all is true of all North Israelite cults without exception), or against a cult whose advocates are incriminated in one way or another, especially in their inferior ethical and social practices. The polemical sayings which have been interpreted as essentially anti-cultic (for example, Amos 5:21ff.; Hos. 6:6; Isa. 1:11ff.; Jer. 7:21ff.) fall into one of these categories.[68]

What then was the relationship that the prophets established with the cult? The first thing that must be avoided, according to Engnell, is the temptation to consider that all the prophets had the same attitude toward the cult. Their positions were in large measure marked by the fundamentally religious and political historical circumstances in which their ministries were carried out. The context of the Northern Kingdom in the eighth century, in which Amos preached, dominated by the spread of idolatry, social injustice, and the empty cult, has little to do with that of Ezekiel, in the exile, or with that of Haggai, demanding the reconstruction of the temple upon return from the exile.

Another false image to avoid, Engnell goes on to say, is the one associated with the idea of justice. In the prophets this term has a totally different meaning from the one the modern mentality attributes to it. It does not have that marked ethical and social nuance. Justice has a cosmic dimension that finds expression in the cult. When the prophets demand justice, it is not outside the sphere of the cult. That justice has a cultic dimension: the prophets demand a just cult, a true Yahwist cult, free of the impurities of idolatry and pagan rites, one that is accompanied by innocence from the ethical and social point of view. This cult, far from being dispensable, is essential to preserve equilibrium in the cosmos in the continual battle against chaos.[69]

Nonetheless, even before Engnell's observations, the anticultic presupposition that Wellhausen's paradigm implicitly carried with it had been the target of criticism from the second generation of scholars, to which Gunkel belonged. In his studies on the psalms, by pursuing the real-life context of each composition, Gunkel identified the presence of oracles that, because of their form and content, can be called prophetic.

---

[68] Engnell, "Prophets and Prophetism", 137, 139. A similar criticism of the Protestant mentality hidden behind the wariness of exegesis in relation to the cult is found in S. Mowinckel, *Offersang og sangoffer: Salmediktingen i Bibelen* (Oslo, 1951), 24.

[69] Cf. ibid., 138.

His disciple Sigmund Mowinckel (1884–1966) was the one who, on the basis of these studies, drew the most important conclusions for the cult-prophecy relationship.[70] In Mowinckel's view, most of the psalms are linked to a liturgical or cultic (ritual) context, especially to certain festivals, some of which he himself made a point of "supposing" (since no word of any of them has come down to us). The oracles of a prophetic nature that can be identified in some psalms (60; 65; 82; 110) would indicate the existence of a type of prophet linked to the cult. It was Mowinckel himself who coined the term "cultic prophet" or "cultic prophecy", and in fact he considers Habakkuk, Nahum, and Joel to be included in this category.

Moreover, it must not be forgotten that although the prophets were in some cases extremely hard on the cultic rules of their contemporaries, other data reveal a close relationship with the cultic environment. Thus, Isaiah's calling takes place in the context of the temple, the place of the cult (Is 6:1). The prophets Jeremiah and Ezekiel introduce themselves as priests, descendants of a priestly caste (and therefore linked to the temple), which gives authority to their preaching. Moreover, some prophets (such as Haggai, Zechariah, and Malachi) were interested in the welfare of the temple and its cult.

Now that the image of the cult-prophecy relationship transmitted to us has been balanced out, it is only fair to recognize, according to Engnell, that prophetic preaching contributed to the weakening of the official cult and to shaping the conditions that it would have in the future.[71]

C. The Prophets and Ethical Monotheism

Kuenen's expression "ethical monotheism" had the virtue of condensing into two words what the early critical scholars considered to be the great contribution of the prophets to the history of mankind. Only with the arrival of classical prophecy, in the eighth century, was the ideal of a strong monotheism proclaimed, which left behind the "primitive"

---

[70] Cf. S. Mowinckel, *Prophecy and Tradition: The Prophetic Books in the Light of the Study of the Growth and History of the Tradition* (Oslo, 1946); S. Mowinckel, *Religion und Kultus* (Göttingen, 1953); S. Mowinckel, *The Psalms in Israel's Worship* (Nashville, 1962).

[71] Cf. Engnell, "Prophets and Prophetism", 142.

images of God, both polytheism and idolatry, as well as the "more evolved" monolatry. In addition, the belief in a single God was linked to a certain image of him that the prophets began to describe: a God who wanted an individual relationship with every person, based on moral consistency and ethics.

Again, this evolutionary scheme of the religion of Israel corresponds more to the presuppositions of the authors who proposed it than to the texts and data that history provides. In order to unmask this reconstruction of the history of the religion of the OT "based on a preconceived idea of historical development throughout",[72] Engnell thinks that, in the first place, it is necessary to review the terminology used. Indeed, for Engnell the term "monotheism" is ambiguous: sometimes it identifies an "affective monotheism" and sometimes a "rational and theoretical philosophical monotheism":

> Affective monotheism means that the god who stands in the center, the one to whom the worshipper is praying and offering sacrifice and to whom he is turning, is also *de facto* considered to be the only god. This type of monotheism is characteristic not only of the Mosaic religion, but also of the patriarchal religion; in other words, it is not limited to any particular time period nor is it the result of historical evolution.[73]

If we accept this de facto monotheism, of which we have innumerable testimonies in the OT, we can better understand that the previously mentioned evolutionary scheme grossly oversimplifies the matter. The position of the prophets should not be considered an absolute novelty, but rather a development of that exclusivistic attitude which is one of the most powerful elements in the traditional image of God in Israel. In this development, the exclusive role of Yahweh was more and more heavily emphasized, with the result that he gradually became, not just the only powerful God, but the only God.[74]

This "empirical" monotheism, says Engnell, "is not exactly the same thing as a thought-out, well-reasoned, rationalistic, philosophical monotheism", which is what critical scholars project onto prophetic preaching. This second type of monotheism would not ever have entered the world view of the prophets.

---

[72] Ibid., 143.

[73] Ibid., 143.

[74] Cf. ibid., 144.

Engnell also casts a critical eye on that other characteristic which scholars attribute to the monotheism supposedly inaugurated by the prophets—its ethical and individual dimension:

> As heirs to the period of enlightenment and liberalism and, to some extent, also the heirs of a persistent doctrine of verbal inspiration, contemporary scholars still exaggerate the idea that the great prophets were solitary figures—inspired, great individuals who stood outside the community and, for this very reason, represented the high point of Old Testament religion. . . . In connection with an evolutionistic view of Israelite religion, even in our day, scholars often interpret these prophets as the conscious champions of individualistic religion in contrast to the collective piety connected with the cult.[75]

If we had to base ourselves on studies of the history and the sociology of religions to evaluate this idea that the individualism of the prophets is a victory in religious evolution, we would have to describe it, along with Engnell, as "a veritable caricature".[76] Comparative studies of religions show that individualism is not a stage in evolution that leaves an earlier stage of collectivism behind. In addition, if we simply start with the texts of the OT, we will see that the community dimension is one of the most peculiar and distinctive traits of the religion of Israel and one that remains such throughout its history. Moreover, individual religious experience is found at all times, not just during the late period of the prophets. Perhaps one of Israel's strokes of genius is the experience that individual piety reaches its height within an keen awareness of belonging to a people and a history.

Engnell calls attention to some data that, far from highlighting the individual figure of the prophet, place him in his community context:[77]

a. The prophets belong to an organic social structure, the "prophetic group", a community that cannot be considered a form of primitive organization that was later superseded. Engnell believes that the classic prophets such as Amos, Hosea, and Isaiah moved within that structure.

b. The fact that the great prophets left books is due, in large part, to the existence of a circle of "disciples" of the prophet who received his words, preserved them, and put them into writing.

---

[75] Ibid., 152.
[76] Ibid.
[77] Cf. ibid., 153–54.

c. In their preaching, the prophets do not address individuals, nor do they create circles of chosen ones to whom they privately and individually pass on a hidden doctrine. The prophets address groups of people: the inhabitants of a city, rulers, those who practice injustice, or the entire people.

d. The content of the prophets' preaching shows their conscience quite clearly: all they say revolves around Israel, the chosen people with whom Yahweh has established a covenant; around their sin of infidelity to the covenant, about the remnant that will remain, and so on.

It is certainly a caricature to conceive of the prophets as the founders of a religion based on an ethical and individual relationship with God, as opposed to a community religion. All their preaching falls within the great dialogue between Yahweh and his people, and they move as required by this dialogue (with words of warning, punishment, conversion, comfort, hope, news, and so on). Only the projection onto the text of a certain religious model foreign to it, as we have had occasion to see, can lead one to hide what otherwise seems evident.

D. Ecstatic Prophecy

The question of the psychology of the prophet and the study of his ecstatic experiences, which would become the distinctive element of prophecy, were the focus of attention of a large part of OT exegesis in the first half of the twentieth century. We have already seen how this trend was set within the broader and more comprehensive academic trend that tended to study all human sciences on the basis of psychological processes.

In this case it was not necessary to wait long for the first "dissonant" voices to be raised, which tended at least to qualify the evident excesses of the "psychologizing" trend in the study of the prophets. In 1934, Mowinckel, two years after the death of Gunkel, his teacher, published an article in which he greatly diminished the importance of ecstasy in the classical prophets.[78] In fact, the characteristic that distinguished the "reforming" prophecy from the earlier prophecy was the

---

[78] S. Mowinckel, " 'The Spirit' and the 'Word' in the Pre-exilic Reforming Prophets", *JBL* 53 (1934): 199–227.

progressive attenuation of the ecstatic element. In the two centuries
that preceded the exile, the great prophets based their preaching, not
on the claim that they were *possessed* by the *spirit*, but on the claim that
they had *received* the *Word* of Yahweh. In fact, it was precisely possession by the spirit (*rûaḥ*) and the ecstatic manifestations that took place
that characterized "false" prophecy in the canonical writings of Israel.
While Gunkel came to the point of claiming that the personality of
the (ecstatic) prophet could completely disappear, Mowinckel argued
for the spiritual clarity and judgment that the great preexilic prophets
maintained in their ministries:

> On the whole little remains of the ecstatic element, apart from that which
> is the sound psychological substratum and core of religious ecstasy: the all-
> predominating, all-exclusive consciousness of having been called by Yah-
> weh to deliver a religious and moral message. All external stimuli, such as
> dancing and music, have been abandoned. True, the state in which they
> deliver that message is "elevated", but it is also characterized by spiritual
> clarity and reasoned judgment.[79]

Shortly afterward, Norman W. Porteous already managed to make a
general criticism of the "psychologizing" trend when he stated, "We
must further insist that it is a mistake to assume *a priori* that the experience of the great prophets is directly accessible to modern psychological methods."[80] Another criticism, this time technical, was to come
from the pen of H. Wheeler Robinson in 1946. In a study devoted to
the "psychology of inspiration", he made an interesting observation
about the term "ecstasy" and its inappropriate use in the context of
the prophets of Israel:

> 'Possession', or some equivalent term denoting invasion, is preferable to
> the commonly used 'ecstasy', because the latter springs from a Greek
> conception of personality, which does not at all harmonize with Hebrew
> psychology. 'Ecstasy' (*ekstasis*) implies that the *psyche* can leave its usual
> earthly dwelling, the human body, and travel into other regions, as in the
> Shamanistic belief of Mongolia. But the Hebrew *nephesh* is *not* conceived
> as such an entity, potentially independent of the body; it is no more than

[79] Ibid., 207–8.
[80] N. W. Porteous, "Record and Revelation", in *Record and Revelation: Essays on the Old Testament by Members of the Society for the Old Testament Study*, ed. H. W. Robinson (Oxford, 1938),
227.

the animating principle of the body, and it is the body which constitutes
the real personality for the Hebrew. For this reason belief in any real life
after death could not be held until belief in the resurrection of the body
had been reached. The Old Testament offers no example of a disembod-
ied 'soul' or 'spirit', however frequent that idea in the later apocalyptic,
possibly through Greek influence. Thus the very word, 'ecstatic', as applied to the psycho-physical phenomena of Hebrew prophecy, helps to
perpetuate a misconception.[81]

But Robinson himself goes on to call attention to another emphasis
—in his judgment mistaken—of the study of the psychology of the
prophet: the overvaluing of the emotional element:

> The emotional element in both human and divine personality as presented
> in the Old Testament is not the most fundamental for the religion of Is-
> rael. This is beyond question the volitional; the prophet is above all else
> a man of God under orders to utter and perform the *will* of God. It is the
> prophet's will, rather than his emotions, which reproduces the divine.[82]

Engnell, for his part, makes it his job to break, or at least weaken, the
connection (supported especially by Duhm and Hölscher) that closely
linked ecstasy and poetry. The studies of the Uppsala School had underlined the importance of the phase of oral transmission of prophecy
in the formation of the prophetic books. Engnell, a disciple of this
school, points out the consequences for the matter of interest here: the
idea that literary analysis could distinguish the authentic words of the
prophet, the ones expressed in poetic language during the trance or
ecstasy, from the later additions in prose turns out to be at the very least
naïve. The text that has come down to us is, in its entirety, composed
of the memories that some disciples preserved of the preaching of the
prophet.[83]

VI. New Interpretive Trends

Just as happened in the study of the composition of the Pentateuch, the
seventies also brought about a change of course in the literature on the

---

[81] H. W. Robinson, *Inspiration and Revelation in the Old Testament* (Oxford, 1946), 180–81.
[82] Ibid., 185.
[83] Cf. Engnell, "Prophets and Prophetism", 169.

prophetic books. Robert P. Gordon, in an article published in 1995 and titled "A Story of Two Paradigm Shifts",[84] reviews the history of the critical investigation of the prophets and divides it into two clear stages: from 1875 to 1975, in which the paradigm that arose from putting the prophets before the Law was dominant, and the present stage, starting in 1975, in which the old paradigm is abandoned in favor of new perspectives. In fact, he does not at all justify the choice of a specific date, 1975, to signal the end of the classic paradigm. Rather, it seems that it is based on the approximately one hundred years that the previous model was in force (from 1875). What is clear is that starting with the second half of the seventies, a good part of exegetical literature began to steer itself into new courses.

In spite of this, we cannot speak of a new paradigm in the studies of prophetic literature. Our era, as we have already seen in the case of the study of the Pentateuch, is not an era of great certainties or great syntheses. A multiplicity of methods and approaches have taken their places in exegesis, but it is impossible to distinguish (or intuitively sense) a dominant trend that is prevailing (or could prevail) over the rest.[85] Here I will present two radically opposed trends that, in the study of the prophets, have produced abundant literature in the last three decades: the canonical approach and the approach from the social sciences. In both cases, the problems the old paradigm generated, or those it did not resolve, turn out to be decisive in the justification of the new trend.

A. The Canonical Reading of the Prophets

The canonical approach to Scripture, understood as a modern exegetical trend, finds its foundational document, in regard to the prophets, in an article by Brevard S. Childs published in 1978, titled "The Canonical Shape of the Prophetic Literature".[86] It is necessary to establish a certain relationship between this new approach and the trend of syn-

---

[84] R. P. Gordon, "A Story of Two Paradigm Shifts", in *"The Place Is Too Small for Us": The Israelite Prophets in Recent Scholarship*, ed. R. P. Gordon, SBThS 5 (Winona Lake, 1995), 3–26.

[85] Witness to this is borne by the multiplicity of methods and approaches in the document *The Interpretation of the Bible in the Church* by the PBC.

[86] B. S. Childs, "The Canonical Shape of the Prophetic Literature", *Interp* 32 (1978): 46–55. In fact, as early as 1970 Childs had presented his canonical approach to Scripture, but only now, in a more systematic manner, did he apply it to a biblical corpus such as the prophets (cf.

chronic reading of the Pentateuch that we saw in the previous chapter. It was also in 1978 that Clines published his work *The Theme of the Pentateuch*, in which he insisted on a unitary reading of the first five books of the Bible. Both movements start from a criticism of the dominant exegetical literature rooted in the historical-critical method, which is of a diachronic nature. Both argue for an exegesis based on the text as it has come down to us.[87] However, the approach backed by Childs contains a hermeneutical foundation that Clines' synchronic reading lacks, as the latter's *pars destruens* (highlighting the limits of the diachronic reading) is more developed than the *pars construens*.

The canonical approach or method[88] refers, obviously, to the whole of Scripture (including the unitary Old-New Testament reading). Even so, in the article cited, Childs chooses the prophetic literature[89] to exemplify for the first time this type of reading and to establish the fundamentals that will serve for his approach to all Scripture. I will now take some time to study this article, which, although it has been developed and illustrated later on in the rest of his work,[90] already contains the essential elements of the method presented in a clear and synthetic fashion.

Childs begins by reviewing the results of the historical-critical method applied to biblical literature. In his opinion, and in spite of some

---

B. S. Childs, *Biblical Theology in Crisis* [Philadelphia, 1970]; it can even be said that Childs had already made a note of some elements of the method in 1964: B. S. Childs, "Interpretation in Faith: The Theological Responsibility of an Old Testament Commentary", *Interp* 18 [1964]: 432–49). The studies of J. A. Sanders on the formation of the canon and on its different forms, prior to 1978, operate from a perspective very different from that of Childs.

[87] In fact, J. Barr states that one of the two pillars on which the canonical method rests is a particular literary trend that privileges the study of the texts from the synchronic point of view. See J. Barr, *Holy Scripture: Canon, Authority, Criticism* (Oxford, 1983), 78.

[88] In the document *The Interpretation of the Bible in the Church* by the PBC, the trend that Childs leads was classified as an "approach" as opposed to other trends, for which the term "method" was reserved. In the last few years, though, most authors have referred to this trend using the name "canonical method".

[89] Significantly, Childs has devoted a large part of his attention to the prophetic literature, especially to the book of Isaiah. See B. S. Childs, *Isaiah*, OTL (Louisville, 2001), and *The Struggle to Understand Isaiah as Christian Scripture* (Grand Rapids, 2004).

[90] Cf., especially, B. S. Childs, *Introduction to the Old Testament as Scripture* (Philadelphia, 1979); B. S. Childs, *Old Testament Theology in a Canonical Context* (London, 1985); B. S. Childs, *Biblical Theology of the Old and New Testaments: Theological Reflection on the Christian Bible* (London, 1992); B. S. Childs, "Retrospective Reading of the Old Testament Prophets", *ZAW* 108 (1996): 362–77.

impressive gains, this methodology has not contributed to—quite the contrary, in fact—a better understanding of the prophetic books as Scripture of the Church, which is rather worrying, given the normative role they have in the formation of the Christian life. There are three criticisms that Childs directs at the dominant exegesis of the historical-critical variety. In the first place, the distinction between "genuine" oracles of the prophet and "non-genuine" oracles, characteristic of the literary-critical method, has interjected a pejorative category that impedes a unified view of the prophetic books. Secondly, form-critical analysis has "atomized" the text, dividing it into ever smaller units on the basis of fragile and often highly speculative hypotheses. Thirdly, redactional criticism and sociological methods have tended to politicize the biblical material and render it into a type of political propaganda.[91]

In the article under consideration here, and faced with the problems that historical-critical exegesis creates, Childs proposes a different approach to the biblical material that starts with one factual datum: the Hebrew Bible, in its final form, has been shaped by a major literary and theological force. Its task consisted of collecting, selecting, and ordering the biblical traditions in such a way as to allow the material to function as authoritative Scripture for the Jewish community, that is, as a normative expression of God's will to later generations of Israel who had not shared in those original historical events. In the case of the prophets, oracles that were directed to one generation were fashioned by a canonical process that turned them into Sacred Scripture for another generation.

Interest is therefore concentrated on the final form of the text, which is the canonical or normative one. On this point, the synchronic reading of Clines and the canonical approach of Childs agree. However, unlike Clines, Childs posits a theological basis for this decision, because of the text as it has come down to us. This decision starts with the peculiar relationship that exists between the text and the people of God, a relationship that is an essential element of the canon. The canon describes the history of the encounter between God and Israel, defines the scope of a unique relationship, and establishes an end to the whole process, "canonizing" a thoroughly delimited segment of history as normative (always in the form in which it is transmitted)

---

[91] Cf. Childs, "Canonical Shape", 47.

for all generations. The final form of the biblical literature is the only one that bears authoritative witness to the full history of revelation. This is so much so that there has been no interest in transmitting the "original" strata of the prophetic oracles, and we have scarcely any word about the process of canonization of the sacred books.[92]

Does this preference for the final form imply scorn for the original historical contexts in which a prophetic oracle arises? No, Childs would say; it implies, rather, taking seriously the critical function the canon exercises on the early stages of the process of formation of the prophetic literature. On some occasions, the original material is transmitted together with its historical context; on other occasions, the canonical process selects, reorganizes, or expands the traditions received. The final form of the text is the only one that provides us with the critical theological judgment that has presided over the process of the formation of a corpus that is canonical or normative for us. Therefore, this final form plays a hermeneutical role of the highest order when interpreting a text: in fact, it underlines certain elements and diminishes the importance of others. In the exegetical literature of the historical-critical variety, there has often been a desire to replace this criterion, which is ultimately canonical, with another criterion that reorganizes the material in a different way. This new criterion can be judged to be more or less adequate according to different parameters, but what cannot be doubted is that it is not normative for any community of faith.

The canonical process appears, not simply as an external valorization of successive stages of literary development, but as an integral part of the literary process. Thus, beginning in the preexilic era and increasing in significance during and after it, a canonical process was unleashed by Israel's religious use of its own traditions. This resulted in a process of collecting, selecting, and ordering of the texts that have gone into the Hebrew Bible as it has come down to us. Furthermore, the alternative criteria that we might want (or like) to apply have never been applied in the history of the text and have never given rise to a literary process.[93]

In a second part of the article, Childs concentrates on the prophetic

---

[92] Cf. ibid., 47–48.
[93] Cf. ibid., 48.

books to show examples of how the canonical process, in very diverse manners, has shaped the traditions to turn them into Sacred Scripture.[94] Below are listed the eight methods that Childs derives from the examples:

a. An original prophetic message was expanded by being placed in a larger theological context. This is the function performed by chapter 9 of Amos, which places all the harsh preaching of the prophet in a broader theological context that includes hope and final redemption.

b. The shaping process changed the level on which the original prophecy functioned, so that it came to function, in another context, in a metaphorical manner. The classic example is the vicissitudes of the marriage and the preaching of Hosea in the eighth century B.C. and the metaphorical function they fulfill in the book.

c. A collection of prophetic material has been detached from its original historical moorings and subordinated to a new theological context. This is the case of the so-called "Deutero-Isaiah" (Is 40–55), which has left behind its historical context of the exile only to be placed in the context of the first Isaiah, in the eighth century B.C.

d. A body of prophetic tradition was edited in the light of a larger body of canonical literature. This is the relationship that holds between the original message of the prophet Jeremiah and the Deuteronomic school that edited the book.

e. The original historical sequence of a prophet's message is subordinated (and changed) to a new criterion for the organization of the material of a radically theocentric book. The difficulty in situating the sequence of Ezekiel's oracles spatially, and sometimes chronologically, can be attributed to the radical theocentric perspective that has shaped the book and diminished the importance of the historical context.

f. The original prophetic message was placed within a rule-of-faith that provided the material with an interpretative guideline. The final verses of the book of Malachi (which are an appendix) play this role of an interpretive guideline.

---

[94] Cf. ibid., 49–53.

THE CRITICAL STUDY OF THE PROPHETS

g. Prophetic oracles that originated in different historical settings have been rearranged to form an orderly collection of models that play a typological role in relation to the coming rule of God. This is the case with the alternative blocks of oracles of judgment and salvation in the first four chapters of Isaiah. The alternation seems to be due not so much to a historical sequence as to a theological intention.

h. Prophetic symbolism undergoes an eschatological reinterpretation by shifting the initial referent of the original oracle. This is what happens with the initial oracle of the book of Joel (Joel 1–2), which, in its new context, announces the Day of Yahweh.

   In the third and final part of the article, Childs expounds the theological implications of the canonical process that has given the texts their final shape.[95] In this case, too, I will list his conclusions:

a. The task of Old Testament exegesis is the interpretation of the canonical text as it has been shaped in the history of Israel's experience with God. The content of the prophets' message is first and foremost a theocentric word. Concern with Israel's own identity is always secondary and derivative from a prior understanding of God.

b. Since the Reformation period there has been a tendency among Protestants, especially from the Reformed wing, to deprecate tradition as a threat to the integrity of the divine word; however, Scripture and tradition belong together. The active participation of the tradents in transmitting and shaping the biblical witness in no way calls into question its divine source. Rather, Israel registered the word of the prophets along with its own reception and saw in both the Spirit of God at work. The canon seeks to preserve the authority of the whole biblical witness and to resist all attempts to assign varying degrees of theological value to the different layers of Scripture on the basis of historical judgments.

c. To assume that the prophets can be understood only if each oracle is related to a specific historical event or located in its original cultural milieu is to introduce major hermeneutical confusion into the

---

[95] Ibid., 53–55.

discipline and to render an understanding of the canonical Scriptures virtually impossible.

d. Biblical texts are made relevant to today's community of faith and to the world, not by first decanonizing them in a claim of establishing an original setting, but by faithfully hearing the intent of the literature that has already been shaped to confront its hearers with the divine imperative. Canon is the proof that the biblical material has been collected and preserved, not for antiquarian reasons, but as a result of its nature as an eternal Word of God addressed to each generation.

e. Any attempt to write a theology of the prophets that disregards the canonical shaping, whether in a search for the prophets' *verba ipsissima* or in a pursuit after prophetic self-understanding, can only end up with a formulation that has little to do with the prophets of the OT.

f. Much of the problem of understanding the NT's use of the OT prophets lies in the failure to take seriously the canonical perspective held in common by both Jews and Christians of the first century A.D.[96]

Childs concludes his article by rejecting the title of canonical criticism for the approach he proposes, since it is confusing; it seems like it is an instrument of or another step in historical-critical methodology. In fact, with the passing of time, that term would come to be reserved for the trend of the historical study of the formation of the canon, led by J. A. Sanders,[97] while the movement initiated by Childs would be known as the "canonical approach or method".

---

[96] It is worth quoting Childs' observation about this: "It is quite impossible to read the Old Testament prophets through the eyes of Duhm and Hölscher and yet understand what the New Testament is hearing in the Old!" (ibid., 54).

[97] Cf. J. A. Sanders, *Torah and Canon* (Philadelphia, 1972); *Canon and Community: A Guide to Canonical Criticism* (Philadelphia, 1984); *From Sacred Story to Sacred Text: Canon as Paradigm* (Philadelphia, 1987); "Stability and Fluidity in Text and Canon", in *Tradition of the Text: Studies Offered to Dominique Barthélemy in Celebration of His 70th Birthday*, ed. G. J. Norton and S. Pisano, OBO 109 (Freiburg and Göttingen, 1991), 203–17; "Canon as Dialogue", in *The Bible at Qumran: Text, Shape, and Interpretation*, ed. P. W. Flint, SDSSRL (Grand Rapids and Cambridge, 2001), 7–26; "The Modern History of the Qumran Psalms Scroll and Its Relation to Canon Criticism", in *Emanuel: Studies in Hebrew Bible, Septuagint and Dead Sea Scrolls in Honor of Emanuel Tov*, ed. S. M. Paul, R. A. Kraft, L. H. Schiffman, and W. W. Fields, VT. S 94 (Leiden and Boston, 2003), 393–411.

B. The Social Sciences Reading

As we have seen, methodological concern and hermeneutical reflection constitute one of the fundamental elements of the trend led by Childs. This same concern is found in the presuppositions of the approach to Scripture from the social sciences, although the position with respect to the texts, the interpretive criteria, and the results that the two trends obtain are radically different.

One of the most representative authors of the trend that studies the biblical texts from the social sciences is Ferdinand Deist (who died prematurely in 1997). In an article published in 1989, after analyzing the "change of paradigm" situation in which the exegesis of the prophetic books found itself, marked by the crisis in the "dominant paradigm", he dared to propose an "alternative paradigm" centered on the application of sociological and anthropological models to biblical texts.[98]

It is worth taking the time to comment on this article, not only because it presents a new interpretive model, but because it radically criticizes not only the dominant paradigm (understood as the interpretation that arose with Wellhausen) but all interpretation that aspires to call itself theological. In this sense, Deist's position, which we will later see in other authors, presents itself as a thorough challenge to ecclesiastical exegesis (whatever the denomination) and especially to the Catholic variety. Up until this point, the different interpretations, from the beginning of critical exegesis almost a century and a half ago, had operated in a *believing* context, even if it was that of the liberal Protestantism of the late nineteenth and early twentieth centuries, in which faith was reduced to a vague rational religiosity inspired by Christian ethics. For all those authors, the Bible was a *normative* text, however one might understand the *inspiration* that made it *canonical*. The trend at which we are now looking raised doubts about all these categories.

In Deist's view, the critical study of the prophetic books was from the beginning characterized by the search for the original words of the prophets (*ipsissima verba*), which had to be set in a framework within the true history of Israel and the Israelite religion. The historical-critical

---

[98] F. E. Deist, "The Prophets: Are We Heading for a Paradigm Switch?" in *Prophet und Prophetenbuch: Festschrift für Otto Kaiser zum 65. Geburtstag*, ed. V. Fritz, K.-F. Pohlmann, and H.-C. Schmitt, BZAW 185 (Berlin, 1989), 1–18.

method, in its different variations, has been at the service of this end. The prophets, from this perspective, and especially since the *lex post prophetas* thesis burst onto the scene, were seen as the creators of the religion of Israel (ethical monotheism). This high consideration for the prophets, observed Deist, was typically Christian, as can be seen by the different weight they have in the Christian NT (34 percent of the OT quotes) and in the Jewish Mishnah (11 percent of the OT quotes).[99]

The search for the *ipsissima verba* of the prophets and the emphasis on their uniqueness were a result, Deist goes on to say, of romantic historiography, which strove to find the original sources and to place each character and each phenomenon in the setting of its unique circumstances.[100] That these concerns should continue being dominant until our day was due to a series of postulates of classic historical criticism (by nature diachronic) that in this case coincide with those of the supporters of synchronic study. Deist lists three:[101]

a. "The Christian theological community continued to proceed from the premiss of the uniqueness of either ancient Israelite or Christian religion, or of both, so that the search for the 'unique' (revelation) in the Old Testament tradition remained a relevant undertaking."

b. "The idealistic philosophy underlying historical-critical hermeneutics remained the philosophical basis of even the critics of historical criticism: the (divinely inspired, and hence a priori and unique) intellectual world" continued to be "viewed as the force that steered history".

c. The concept of texts "inherent in historical-critical methodology, and according to which texts are *reflections* of reality, thought processes and/or deposits of meaning, remained the basis of biblical research".

On this point, Deist shows himself to be radical, since he considers that both the defenders of the historical-critical method and its detractors, or those who support a synchronic approach to the text, are on the same side, sharing the same ideological coordinates. The polemic

---

[99] Cf. ibid., 3.

[100] On the criticism that Deist makes of classical historiography, cf. F. E. Deist, "The Problem of History in Old Testament Theology", *OTWSA* 24 (1981): 23–39.

[101] Cf. Deist, "Prophets", 4–5.

about historical-critical methods only goes so far as to discuss procedural matters, while leaving untouched the question shared by everyone about the interest in the meaning inherent in the text. A paradigm that wants to be called new, as Deist later explains, is distinguished by the fact that it raises new and different questions about the text.

Deist next lists the factors that, in his opinion, have contributed to undermine the dominant paradigm:[102]

a. *The appearance of new data that cannot be adequately explained on the basis of the presuppositions of the dominant model.* First, archeological finds showed that the phenomenon of prophecy was widespread throughout the Middle East and called into question the uniqueness of OT prophecy. The dominant paradigm tried to use the results of archeology to confirm the information in the text, and thus it made use of the prophets of Mesopotamia (professional or "cult" prophets) to explain the phenomenon of false prophecy. It portrayed the prophets as "God's ambassadors", lonely men without followers, and this preserved the uniqueness of prophecy in Israel. But this picture of the prophet as a lonely man seemed to be a construction without sociological foundation, since no idea can survive without the aid of a support group. Some other "patches" were proposed, but the paradigm could not stand up to the "stubbornness" of the new data. Second, historical-critical scholarship continued undermining its own foundations by placing a large part of the redaction of the prophetic books in the exile or later, so that the "originality" of these writings began to be considered doubtful.

b. *The assumptions of the academic world changed, with the result that the premises of the dominant model were seriously called into question.* Up until this point exegetical research sank its roots into the idealist philosophy that considered the spirit to be the driving force of human evolution. However, the rise of the social sciences[103] in the academic realm con-

---

[102] Cf. ibid., 5–14.

[103] It is obligatory to cite as a distant antecedent of this discipline the work of M. Weber, *Das Antike Judentum* (Tübingen, 1921), which even then was directly applied to the interpretation of the Bible. To learn about the work of other authors (W. Robertson Smith, É. Durkheim, A. Causse) who pioneered the application of this new science to Scripture, see C. E. Carter and C. L. Meyers, eds., *Community, Identity and Ideology: Social Science Approaches to the Hebrew Bible* (Winona Lake, 1996).

tributed to the questioning of the dominant model of rationality. Materialism entered the scene as an alternative model. Is it the spirit or rather matter that guides human processes? Must we think in terms of human freedom or rather in terms of determinism? This change of models was decisively affected by decolonization, which started in the 1960s and caused the so-called "Third World" to arise, with its characteristic socioeconomic problems. This circumstance was what favored the emergence of liberation theology, with its Marxist-materialist orientation, which holds that it is not ideas that shape a people's sociopolitical destiny; rather, it is socio-political realities that shape ideas (ideologies). The student movements of '68, the rejection of the hegemony of liberal capitalism over the Third World, and the devastating effects of that capitalism on nature contributed to bringing the model of received rationality to a point of crisis and to proposing a new model.

c. *New questions have appeared that cannot be dealt with or answered by the instruments of the dominant model.* The very results of historical-critical scholarship have raised a series of questions that are disturbing. If the words that can truly be attributed to the prophet are few, if it is not possible to reconstruct the oral tradition on the basis of the texts, if the distinction between true prophet and false prophet is only possible *ex eventu* and must be attributed to the Deuteronomistic editors, what then was a prophet? What was his role in society? What role did he play in the formation of the religion of Israel? In what sense can he be considered unique? For Deist, these historical questions cannot be effectively answered if one does not have a clear idea about the societies in which the prophets lived and in which the prophetic texts were produced. Nor can the dominant model answer these questions, because it does not look at the prophetic phenomenon or its texts from the point of view of social realities. In Deist's opinion, the rise of the canonical approach to the texts (or the synchronic approach in general) has to do with a situation of collapse in the face of questions without answers, which were sidestepped by resorting to a level of reading that dispensed with them.

d. *The champions of the dominant model slowly passed from the scene, and a new generation of scholars (who grew up under different circumstances) took its place.* Starting in the 1960s, the exegesis of the OT, until then dominated by the German academic world, began to become "internationalized", especially with the contributions of the American, English-speaking world, which was much more pragmatic and less tied to philosophical presuppositions and interested in the application of the social and anthropological sciences to biblical studies. Moreover, the authors of the great world views, composed within the framework of the classic paradigm, had already passed away, and no others of their stature had arisen. For Deist, it was significant that in recent years (for him this was the second part of the seventies and all of the eighties) no *History of Israel* or *Theology of the Old Testament* had been written that offered anything new or that even claimed simply to be comprehensive.[104]

The radicalness of the criticism Deist directs at the dominant model and, through it, at a whole way of approaching the Bible is seen in one of the questions directed at this model: If the prophets and their message have been reinterpreted for decades within the framework of the thought categories typical of the West (characteristic of the dominant model), how can their words and actions continue challenging the Western world?

---

[104] Today it would be necessary to correct this evaluation of Deist's, since after the publication of his article (1989), numerous and important contributions to the history of Israel and the theology of the OT have appeared. For the theology of the OT, see H. D. Preuss, *Theologie des Alten Testaments* (Stuttgart, 1991); Childs, *Biblical Theology of the Old and New Testaments*; A. H. J. Gunneweg, *Biblische Theologie des Alten Testaments: Eine Religionsgeschichte Israels in biblisch-theologischer Sicht* (Stuttgart, 1993); O. Kaiser, *Der Gott des Alten Testaments: Wesen und Wirken: Theologie des Alten Testaments* (Göttingen, 1993); J. Schreiner, *Theologie des Alten Testaments* (Würzburg, 1995); W. Brueggemann, *Theology of the Old Testament: Testimony, Dispute, Advocacy* (Minneapolis, 1997); M. Nobile, *Teologia dell'Antico Testamento* (Turin, 1998); P. R. House, *Old Testament Theology* (Downers Grove, 1998); R. Rendtorff, *Theologie des Alten Testaments: Ein kanonischer Entwurf* (Neukirchen-Vluyn, 1999); E. S. Gerstenberger, *Theologien im Alten Testament: Pluralität und Synkretismus alttestamentlichen Gottesglaubens* (Stuttgart, 2001); C. H. H. Scobie, *The Ways of Our God: An Approach to Biblical Theology* (Grand Rapids, 2003); W. Herrmann, *Theologie des Alten Testaments: Geschichte und Bedeutung des israelitisch-jüdischen Glaubens* (Stuttgart, 2004). A lengthy commentary on the theologies of the OT published before 1999 can be found in J. Barr, *The Concept of Biblical Theology: An Old Testament Perspective* (Minneapolis, 1999). For the history of Israel, cf. R. Albertz, *Religionsgeschichte Israels in alttestamentlicher Zeit* (Göttingen, 1992); H. Jagersma, *A History of Israel to Bar Kochba* (London, 1994); T. L. Thompson, *Early History of the Israelite People* (Leiden, 1994); I. Finkelstein and N. A. Silberman, *The Bible Unearthed: Archeology's New Vision of Ancient Israel and the Origin of Its Sacred Texts* (New York, 2001); M. Liverani, *Oltre la Bibbia: Storia antica di Israele* (Rome and Bari, 2003).

The second part of Deist's article is devoted to presenting the paradigm he calls *alternative*.[105] In his opinion, this paradigm, based on new presuppositions, is still "under construction". The questions this paradigm addresses are those that arise from a different experience of reality, from a new view of the world, and from an alternative model of rationality. Here are some examples: What was the Israelite society of the eighth, seventh, and sixth centuries B.C. like? What social model could best describe those societies? What were the social conditions under which the people lived? From what social stratum did the prophet come? Was there a social institution by the name of "prophet"? If so, what role did it play in the society? What attitude did the prophet have toward political hegemony, oppression, or ideology? What was the content of his ideology? These questions have to do with the social forces that produced that phenomenon we know as "prophet" and with the ideological nature of his oracles.

From these questions arise others that radically question the dominant model: Was prophecy really a unique phenomenon? Was the basic concern of the prophets related to religious questions as theoretical as monotheism or with concepts such as the covenant? What was the reflection in society of words like "justice", "righteousness", "sin", "iniquity", and so on, in the era of prophets like Amos, Isaiah, and Jeremiah? Since these questions have to do with the societies and social structures of OT times and with the socioeconomic life of those days, we should employ strategies that are new (and thus different from those used by the dominant model) to answer. These new strategies constitute a new paradigm.

However, this alternative paradigm does not arise only as a response to the new questions. An important role in its appearance has been played by the new direction that archeology has taken in recent decades. The "new archeology", as opposed to the old variety, has emancipated itself from biblical exegesis, which it used to serve by providing "footnotes" to the text of the OT. The new Syro-Palestinian archeology is interested in social, economic, and political systems, in their changes, in the forces that provoke them, and in daily life in those societies. The application of one social model or another to the data that archeology

---

[105] Deist, "Prophets", 14–18.

supplies gives us an adequate answer to the new questions that have just been listed.

Starting in the eighties, the presence of the alternative paradigm is additionally attested by a growing body of literature that interprets the OT from the point of view of sociology and anthropology, precisely by responding to the new questions already mentioned.

Deist finishes his article by predicting a kind of "personality change" in the prophets if they are studied from the new point of view. This will lead, in his opinion, not only to rethinking the nature of ancient prophecy, but also to rethinking the "prophetic task" of the Church in modern society, a role that until now had been modeled only on the romantic figure of the prophet that the dominant paradigm created.

Deist's article was written before the fall of the Berlin Wall, and thus we might have been left with some doubt about whether the new ideological circumstances were going to neutralize the alternative paradigm or whether, on the contrary, they were going to strengthen it. In Deist's case, the "fall of ideologies" (among which was included the materialist-Marxist model) did not affect his radical approach, and the proof of this were his later publications, especially his work published posthumously.[106]

But the clearest proof that the "alternative paradigm" remains standing is given in an article by Charles E. Carter published in 1999.[107] In it he reviews the attempts to apply the social sciences to the Hebrew Bible in recent decades, and, in fact, no change in this tendency has been observed since 1989; on the contrary, one could speak, rather, of growth in it.[108] Most of this article, after giving the background of the social sciences in their application to the Bible, is devoted to laying out the most important contributions of this discipline in the last thirty years. Thus, it goes through contributions on subjects as varied

---

[106] F. E. Deist, *The Material Culture of the Bible: An Introduction*, BS 70 (Sheffield, 2000).

[107] C. E. Carter, "Opening Windows onto Biblical Worlds: Applying the Social Sciences to Hebrew Scripture", in *The Face of Old Testament Studies: A Survey of Contemporary Approaches*, ed. D. W. Baker and B. T. Arnold (Grand Rapids, 1999), 421–51.

[108] Proof of it could be the presence up to the present day, in the annual meetings of the Society of Biblical Literature (which gathers most North American exegetes and scholars from other countries), of a section called "The Social Sciences and the Interpretation of Hebrew Scripture".

as the model of society that best describes ancient Israel, the theories about the manner of the settlement of Israel in Canaan, the political and social causes that provoke the transition from a tribal society to a monarchy, the current models that can be applied to prophets (such as shamanism or spiritual possession in contemporary tribal societies), the role of women in Israelite culture and its religion, the study of the sociology and psychology of the community in the exile, production models or subsistence strategies in ancient Israel.

But the part that is most interesting for our reflection here is the last one, in which Carter asks himself why the academic community of evangelical (and thus Protestant) origin has generally shown itself[109] to be quite reluctant to adopt the new methodology in its biblical studies.[110] In these pages we find an attempt to make the new model (which calls into question the biblical fundamentals of the Christian faith) compatible with belonging to a "traditional" Church that still holds to part of Christian dogma. Although the discussion concentrates on the Evangelical Church, in the background he openly poses the problem of the role of faith in the interpretation of Scripture, to which I will return in the next chapter.

In Carter's opinion, there are three reasons that explain the attitude of caution that characterizes many evangelical scholars with regard to the new model:

a. *A theological commitment to the uniqueness of biblical Israel coupled with a desire to avoid cultural and religious relativism.* The greatest concern may stem from the tendency of the social sciences to view human culture on a continuum, which would stand in stark contrast to the wish for uniqueness that the election of Israel implies for the history of salvation. The sacred writers assert the radical difference between the faith of Israel and that of the pagan nations. To the data that Scripture itself gives us are added, according to Carter, the presuppositions that some evangelicals add to it, such as plenary inspiration and inerrancy. This author goes on to say that these theological presuppositions are not necessarily incompatible with sociological or anthropological theories,

---

[109] Carter in fact differentiates between the American evangelical community (more conservative) and the British one (more open to the new methods).

[110] Carter, "Opening Windows", 442–48.

in spite of the fact that some authors use them to reject any theological commitment.

b. *A hesitation to apply cross-cultural parallels to the biblical world and an attempt to avoid reading modern world views into ancient Israel.* Again, Carter affirms the compatibility (specifically, the *complementarity*) of the results of the social sciences applied to Scripture with the content of the biblical traditions. Even so, he wonders whether it is legitimate to complement the biblical narrative with the modern models from the social sciences and if by doing this one necessarily undermines the commitment of the exegete to Scripture as the Word of God.

c. *A concern that social science criticism may diminish the more legitimate aspects of biblical interpretation.* For the evangelical community, the ultimate aim of all of the methods used by scholars is the interpretation of Scripture for (in favor of) the community of faith. For this reason, biblical exegesis (establishing the original meaning of the text) and hermeneutics (proposing a contemporary meaning of that text) are both *theological* tasks. Scripture is not a dead document but a *living* one, capable of transforming the lives of people, communities, and even whole cultures. Those who think this way logically look with distrust upon a whole stream of scholars who advocate the use of the social sciences in the interpretive task as an alternative to theologically oriented (believing or confessional) research. Carter presents two clear examples of this stream: *The Bible without Theology*,[111] by Robert Oden, and *In Search of "Ancient Israel"*,[112] by Philip Davies. In both works, their authors suggest that biblical scholarship has for too long been subject to "theological agendas" that render such study tendentious or biased by nature. Further, they suggest that for critical scholarship to be truly objective, it must extract itself from any theological commitment.[113]

---

[111] R. A. Oden, *The Bible without Theology: The Theological Tradition and Alternatives to It* (San Francisco, 1987).

[112] P. R. Davies, *In Search of "Ancient Israel"*, JSOT.S 148 (Sheffield, 1992).

[113] The most extreme position is that of H. Avalos, who proclaims the end of biblical studies. He believes that the academic world that studies the Bible is conditioned by religious interests and therefore incapable of judging objectively. If it did so, it would recognize that the ideological world of the Bible finds itself in contradiction with our modern thinking. The Bible is therefore irrelevant in our world (and even dangerous), and it should be abandoned. Only the

As Carter himself points out, this is just "the most recent volley in the long-standing tension between theologically oriented studies and a supposedly more 'neutral' religious studies approach to Scripture". This has widened the gap that already existed between the study of the Bible practiced in seminaries, which is more theological, and the more "independent" study done at universities.

In spite of this panorama, Carter claims that the social sciences are by no means anti-theological and that they need not be peripheral in theologically oriented study. In fact, Carter devotes the final line of his article to offering some examples of the work of evangelical scholars who make use of the resources of the social sciences to feed into their biblical exegesis.[114]

I will finish this section devoted to the use of the social sciences in the interpretation of the prophets by presenting another exegetical tendency that, while it does not formally belong to this trend, in fact winds up laying a foundation for it or justifying it. It is *Ideologiekritik*, or ideological criticism. One of its best representatives is Robert P. Carroll, well known in the field of studies of the prophets for his commentary on the book of Jeremiah,[115] who in various contributions has developed the meaning of this trend.[116] Here I will limit myself to one of the latest ones, which he wrote precisely in memory of Deist[117] and which attempts "to clarify further my own thinking on the relation of ideology and *Ideologiekritik* to Bible and Biblical Studies".[118]

---

interests of religious communities and their economic backing support a kind of study that turns out to be anachronistic (H. Avalos, *The End of Biblical Studies* [New York, 2007]).

[114] Carter, "Opening Windows", 447–48.

[115] R. P. Carroll, *Jeremiah: A Commentary* (London, 1986).

[116] Cf. R. P. Carroll, "On Representation in the Bible: An *Ideologiekritik* Approach", *JNSL* 20 (1994): 1–15; "An Infinity of Traces: On Making an Inventory of Our Ideological Holdings: An Introduction to *Ideologiekritik*", *JNSL* 21 (1995): 25–43; "Jeremiah, Intertextuality and *Ideologiekritik*", *JNSL* 22 (1996): 15–34; *Wolf in the Sheepfold: The Bible as Problematic for Theology* (London, 1997). For a general idea about this trend, see the following works, which gather diverse contributions: E. Castelli et al., *The Postmodern Bible* (New Haven and London, 1995), and S. Žižek, ed., *Mapping Ideology* (London and New York, 1994).

[117] R. P. Carroll, "Biblical Idolatry: *Ideologiekritik*, Biblical Studies and the Problematics of Ideology", *JNSL* 24 (1998): 101–14.

[118] Ibid., 102.

Carroll begins by recognizing that the application of *Ideologiekritik* to biblical studies is controversial precisely because not everyone accepts that there is in the Bible a thing that can be called "ideology". By its nature, *Ideologiekritik* is based on a hermeneutics of *suspicion*, while ecclesiastical communities and theologians prefer a hermeneutics of *trust*.[119] In fact, the latter conceive of ideology as a modern product, typical of the societies that sprang from the rationalist Enlightenment and, thus, alien to ancient societies. In Carroll's opinion, those theologians would be willing to apply *Ideologiekritik* to the results of modern exegesis but not to the writers who produced the Bible. The English author, on the other hand, states that ideology "is everywhere and in everything. It is the natural condition of our existence. It is the medium in which we live and move and have our being. It is all pervasive, like the air we breathe."[120]

In contrast to the exegetes who approach the Bible as a "collection of religious texts that must be read in a confessional manner", Carroll prefers an alternative approach that treats the Bible as "a collection of ideological documents". "Whether ideology", Carroll explains, "is to be detected in the writings themselves (as text) or as being inscribed in the text by the ideologues who wrote it or in the reading communities that first canonized and then transmitted the Bible down through the centuries as a foundational sacred text or in contemporary reading communities and/or among their teachers and preachers is a moot point."[121] Carroll makes his own choice when he states that he *prefers* to read the Bible *"as if* it participated in the ideological operations of second temple power politics".[122]

Under these conditions, scholars seek in the Bible the elements of a system of thought and/or praxis or an ideology in which the writers constructed their view of the world and their notion of how to operate in it. This view of the world is displayed in a *mega-account* that incorporates poetry, prophecy, and sapiential observations. As if foreseeing

---

[119] Cf. ibid., 103. In this same sense, cf. R. P. Carroll, "Whose Prophet? Whose History? Whose Social Reality? Troubling the Interpretative Community Again: Notes Towards a Response to T. W. Overholt's Critique", *JSOT* 48 (1990): 33–49.

[120] Ibid., 104.

[121] Ibid.

[122] Ibid.

some objections, Carroll observes that in many of those accounts it is possible that there is little or no ideology. But he also observes that *Ideologiekritik* has more to do with the activity of collecting and organizing texts than with the anonymous authors behind each textual unit. In fact, he goes so far as to state, "Between these implied canonizers and the writers of the text a great abyss is fixed."[123]

In the specific analysis of the biblical texts, Carroll coins the term "ideolatry" to refer to the ideology that is behind the final form of the (Hebrew) Bible. By this he means to affirm that it is the worship of an idea, specifically worship of the idea of Yahweh as God, which has dominated the construction of the Bible as we know it today. Anticipating the more than probable perplexity of his readers, Carroll recognizes that he prefers to use the term "ideology" in place of the one that classic scholars or theologians would use, namely, "theology". While the classic scholars spoke of Yahwist theology, Carroll speaks of Yahwist ideology or, rather, ideolatry:

> Also, it seems to me that theologians working on the Bible have a great tendency to yield to the temptation to treat the human words used by human writers to express their ideas, beliefs, feelings about 'god' as if these words were somehow not human words but 'divine words' delivered to the writers from outside the human sphere (the myth and ideology of inspiration). This is to confuse the 'works of men's hands' (the biblical writings themselves) with whatever transcendental reference may be assigned to them. In other words, this is idolatry plain and simple or, to use the biblical trope, 'the works of men's hands'.[124]

A practical example of the difference between ideological criticism and the theological approach is the position that is held in contrast to the Catholic principle of the unity of Scripture. Carroll states that when a writer uses the sign "God", it cannot simply be assumed, or dogmatically declared, that that sign is the same as (or equivalent to) all the other signs used for "God" by the rest of the writers of the Bible:

> The dogma that everything written by all the biblical writers using the various signs for 'god', whether treated as a common noun or a proper

---

[123] Ibid., 106.
[124] Ibid., 107.

name, somehow adds up to a coherent, consistent, let alone systematic, ideology of god seems to me to be part of an ideology of reading the Bible determined by extrabiblical dogmatic systems and not a statement of fact or one capable of demonstration from the biblical texts themselves.[125]

In view of the plurality the Bible itself shows, Carroll thinks the most suitable approach to it is the one that respects that plurality. So he concludes by stating:

> I prefer to take the pluralist approach to reading the Bible than to priv-ilege one particular ideology because pluralist readings protect readers from becoming entangled in biblical ideology.[126]

In the following chapter, when I deal with the question of the moral exercise of freedom by the exegete,[127] I will have occasion to carry out a critical evaluation of the trend that studies the prophets from the social sciences, the most significant authors of which I have just presented.

VII. Conclusions

The history of the interpretation of the prophets is another of the al-ready classic pages of modern exegesis. It has some points in common with that other page studied in the previous chapter, that of the for-mation of the Pentateuch. First of all, they have a common origin. The leitmotif that triggers both studies is summarized in the phrase *lex post prophetas*. On this fundamental principle Wellhausen constructs his documentary hypothesis, and on this principle one begins to under-stand the leading role of the prophets in the religion of Israel. They are the initiators of a pure religion, ethical monotheism, that only later will be betrayed by Jewish ritualism and legalism.

There are other points, though, that distinguish the character of the two studies. In the investigation of the prophets, philosophical and cultural presuppositions have had a more determinative weight than

---

[125] Ibid., 108.
[126] Ibid., 113.
[127] Chapter 3, II C.

they did in the discussion about the composition of the Pentateuch. In this latter page, literary discussion, on the basis of the text, its parts, and the stitches of its sutures, still plays a very important role. In fact, in the previous chapter a large part of the discussion concentrated on the weak points, from the point of view of literary methodology, of the documentary hypothesis. However, when discussing the nature and role of the prophet in the religious history of Israel, reference to the texts has been in a way secondary, and it could even be said that on occasion those texts have served as proof of a previously embraced theory.

To what causes can this difference be attributed? In the discussion about the figure of the prophet, the most original nature of the religion was at stake and, in the background, the true nature of Christianity. While the Jews betrayed the pure religion of the prophets, Christ, the heir to their ethical monotheism, was betrayed by the Church. The liberal Protestantism of the late nineteenth and early twentieth centuries saw in these figures the possibility of claiming a religiosity free of the ties of dogma. The trigger for all this investigation was a hypothesis rather than a fact: the Law is later than the prophets; the founder and creative element of the religion of Israel was the prophets, not the Law. It is very significant that Wellhausen said that when he first heard that hypothesis, he was already inwardly prepared to receive it. It is not surprising, therefore, that more space has been devoted in this second chapter to the philosophical and cultural presuppositions that hide behind the image of the prophet that has been transmitted since the end of the nineteenth century.

Also, in the direction the studies have taken in the last thirty years, investigation of the prophets has separated itself from that which concentrated on the Pentateuch. In the latter, criticism of the dominant model was done with the instruments of the model itself, literary criticism (Rendtorff). In a way, the claim of synchronic reading (Clines) is also made in the name of literary criticism: the final form of the text is a fact of the object of study that cannot be skipped over. In the case of recent studies on the prophets, the criticism of the dominant model is made on the basis of some presuppositions that are radically different from the previous ones. It is evident in the case of studies based on the social sciences that they call into question the theological method itself (which starts with faith, whatever kind it may be).

But the same can be said of the canonical method that Childs backs, which, in contrast to Clines, has a whole methodological approach (in this case starting with faith) that challenges the presuppositions of the usual biblical interpretation.

I have wanted to leave for the next chapter the discussion these two new models introduce. Precisely because they openly pose the methodological and hermeneutical problem, they will serve as a framework to deal with the characteristic dimensions of the Catholic interpretation of the OT.

Characteristic Dimensions of the
Catholic Interpretation of the Old Testament

In this third chapter I will go on to ask, in a positive sense, about the dimensions that characterize a suitable interpretation of Scripture, now that in the preceding chapters I have carried out a diachronic reading of the results of exegesis in two fields: the study of the composition of the Pentateuch and critical investigation of the prophets. This reading has helped to uncover the philosophical and cultural presuppositions of critical exegesis that have led, in many cases, to interpretive models with serious defects, incapable of doing justice to the object of study. The data from that discussion, together with the problems posed by the new interpretive trends in each field, will be the framework that will now make it possible, in this new chapter, to deal with the characteristic dimensions of the Catholic interpretation of the OT. Although I am concerned specifically with the study of the OT, I treat it as part of Sacred Scripture, for which reason the principles that govern its interpretation are the same ones that apply to the whole Bible, and therefore I frequently refer to it as a collection. Throughout this chapter I will make reference to the Dogmatic Constitution on Divine Revelation, *Dei Verbum*, which in section 12 states how Sacred Scripture should be interpreted.

I. The Nature of Revelation and the Two
Methodological Dimensions of Exegesis

In the introduction to this investigation, I began with the words of Pope Benedict XVI in which he recalled (referring to DV 12) the need to consider in exegesis the two methodological levels that do justice to the nature of Scripture: the historical-critical and the theological. It is time to return to this guideline about method.

But before doing so, we should reflect on the very nature of the object of our study: Scripture. It can properly be said of it that it is the *written and inspired witness to revelation.*[1] Scripture *is not* revelation but, rather, attests to it,[2] albeit in a privileged (inspired) manner. On this point, the actual structure of *Dei Verbum* is very illustrative. Indeed, in the first chapter, titled *Revelation Itself*, which presents the nature and object of revelation (DV 2–4), faith as the appropriate response to this revelation (DV 5), as well as the truths revealed (DV 6), Scripture is not mentioned at any time. Only in the second chapter, devoted to *Handing on Divine Revelation*, is the role of Scripture and tradition introduced, specifically because of their function in this "handing on". It is therefore clear that the whole of Scripture refers, through its witness, to the historical revelation that reaches its peak in Jesus Christ.

Moreover, the witness we find in Scripture is not just any kind of witness. It is a *written* witness, and in this sense it is distinct from the oral traditions or the institutions that lie within the great channel of

---

[1] Cf. the use of the term *testimonium* (with regard to the revelation in Jesus Christ) applied to the New Testament in DV 17–19. For its part, the document *The Interpretation of the Bible in the Church*, by the PBC, in the chapter devoted to the characteristic dimensions of Catholic interpretation, says, "What characterizes Catholic exegesis is that it deliberately places itself within the living tradition of the Church, whose first concern is fidelity to the *revelation attested* by the Bible" (italics mine). On the fortune of the category of "attestation", "witness", or "testimony" to define Scripture, see P. Sequeri, "La struttura testimoniale delle scritture sacre: Teologia del testo", in *La rivelazione attestata: La Bibbia fra Testo e Teologia: Raccolta di Studi in onore del Cardinale Carlo Maria Martini, Arcivescovo di Milano, per il suo LXX compleanno*, ed. G. Angelini (Milan, 1998), 3–27.

[2] "The biblical Word attests to Revelation, but does not contain it in the sense of absorbing it and turning it into a sort of thing that one could stick in one's pocket. The Bible attests to Revelation, but the concept of Revelation as such is broader" (J. Ratzinger, "Biblical Interpretation in Conflict: On the Foundations and the Itinerary of Exegesis Today", in *Opening Up the Scriptures: Joseph Ratzinger and the Foundations of Biblical Interpretation*, ed. José Granados, Carlos Granados, and Luis Sánchez-Navarro [Grand Rapids, 2008], 26). "Both Testaments, the Old and the New, fix their eyes on Jesus; both offer the same witness to him in alternating choruses, whose counterpoint is resolved in harmony. . . . Christians accept this testimony and put their faith in Christ. They do not see in Scripture revelation, exactly, but its instrument, its vehicle, its attestation" (H. de Lubac, "Comentario al preámbulo y al capítulo primero", in *La Revelación divina: Comentarios a la constitución dogmática "Dei Verbum"*, ed. H. de Lubac, B. D. Dupuy et al. [Madrid, 1970], 357–58), 3rd ed. (Paris, 1983).

tradition (DV 7). In addition, it is an *inspired* witness, and therefore it is said of it that it is the Word of God and that it has God as its author, although by virtue of the law of the Incarnation the authorship can also be attributed to the sacred writer. Inspiration ensures the truth of the written witness, endowing the text with a normative or canonical character.

Returning to the guideline about method—the methodological need for exegesis to consider the historical-critical and theological levels at the same time—we can now better understand why this guideline does not arise as a principle external to the object of exegesis, the biblical text.[3] Scripture, by its nature, attests to revelation that must be received with faith (DV 5). In fact, Scripture itself, by virtue of its character as a witness, is a work or expression of faith, which in turn is an appropriate response of man to revelation, a response supported by revelation itself. At the same time, by virtue of its character as inspired, Scripture is a witness of the Holy Spirit, accessible, once again, only through faith.[4]

The dichotomy that could arise between Scripture as the Word of God—and thus as the witness of the Holy Spirit—and Scripture as a reflection of faith on the historical revelation is brought back to unity only if one considers that "divine revelation has been received into the womb of human faith, a faith effected by the grace of revelation itself."[5] Therefore the problem consists of the right understanding of the act of faith. The historical event of revelation claims to be incisive in history itself and in the lives of men. That is, it claims to be *significant*, and it is when it is received with faith.

Thus it is especially clear that the witness that reaches us in the books of Scripture is an achievement of faith, and, since this is fruitful because of the action of the Holy Spirit, the written work that springs from it becomes a normative witness to revelation. Man's response, in his free decision to adhere to the event of divine self-communication, thus

---

[3] I return in the following paragraphs to some reflections I have already offered elsewhere. See I. Carbajosa, "Il Testamento divino offerto alla libertà umana", *Oasis* 7 (2008): 17–21.

[4] In this context, one can well understand the statement of DV 12 that "Holy Scripture must be read and interpreted in the same spirit in which it was written."

[5] H. U. von Balthasar, *The Glory of the Lord: A Theological Aesthetics*, vol. 1: *Seeing the Form* (San Francisco, 1982), 536.

becomes an instrument of this very self-communication (inasmuch as it achieves in faith the objective forms of tradition and Scripture) and at the same time a condition of the evidence and the significant character of the event itself.[6]

In this sense exegesis, in order to approach its object in an appropriate manner, must be based on faith. And this requires that its very method must possess, from the beginning, a theological dimension that corresponds to the nature of Scripture and of the event to which it attests—the self-communication of God in history.

Moreover, this divine self-communication, that is, revelation, indeed happens in history, in space and time, thus triggering the same dynamic as every event located in history. "This plan of revelation is realized by deeds and words having an inner unity" (DV 2) that offer themselves to human interpretation like every deed and like every word. In turn, Scripture, as a written witness to this revelation, is submitted to the material conditions of all literary works. The Word of God has become a human word in an admirable gesture of divine condescension: "For the words of God, expressed in human language, have been made like human discourse, just as the word of the eternal Father, when He took to Himself the flesh of human weakness, was in every way made like men" (DV 13). Because of this dynamic of the Incarnation, so characteristic of revelation, Scripture is subject to a necessary historical analysis (textual, literary, linguistic, and so on). The historical-critical dimension of the exegetical method is required, therefore, by the very nature of the object studied.

It is important to observe that the two methodological levels (historical-critical and theological) of which the Pope speaks can be distinguished but not separated without grave harm for interpretation. Benedict XVI himself, who in the Synod on the Word of God underlined the need to distinguish and affirm two levels, is the one who has noticed the risk of separating them, by incorporating in his post-synodal exhortation a concern that was not in his speech in the synodal hall:

In this regard we should mention the serious risk nowadays of a dualistic approach to sacred Scripture. To distinguish two levels of approach to the

---

[6] Cf. A. Scola, *Chi è la Chiesa? Una chiave antropologica e sacramentale per l'ecclesiologia* (Brescia, 2005), 118–27; A. Scola, *Questioni de antropología teológica* (Rome, 1997), 163–71.

Bible does not in any way mean to separate or oppose them, nor simply to juxtapose them. They exist only in reciprocity. Unfortunately, a sterile separation sometimes creates a barrier between exegesis and theology, and this "occurs even at the highest academic levels".[7]

Precisely because of this, and to contribute to the understanding of the unity of exegetical method, from here on I will use the term *dimensions* instead of *levels*. To speak of the "historical-critical and theological dimensions" of the exegetical method likewise takes into account the Pope's concern and has the advantage, from the terminological point of view, of making more comprehensible how the two levels can be distinguished without being separated.

Both methodological dimensions, distinct but not separate, are necessary to gain access to the object.[8] These are not dimensions that can be added up or superimposed or that even complement one another. The separation of the two dimensions or, seen from another point of view, the difficulty (theoretical and practical) in understanding that they form an indivisible unit has constituted the heart of the problem of exegesis for more than two hundred years, as we have had occasion to see in the introduction to this investigation and as we will see below,

---

[7] *Verbum Domini* 35.

[8] Ricoeur speaks of two moments of the comprehension of a text in a single process, moments that are held together by the requirement of meaning in the text itself: "Therefore, far from the objective and the existential being contraries . . . it must be said that the meaning of the text holds these two moments closely together. It is the objectivity of the text, understood as content—bearer of meaning and demand for meaning—that begins the existential movement of appropriation. Without such a conception of meaning, of its objectivity and even of its ideality, no textual criticism is possible. Therefore, the semantic moment, the moment of objective meaning, must precede the existential moment, the moment of personal decision, in a hermeneutics concerned with doing justice to both the objectivity of meaning and the historicity of personal decision. In this respect the problem Bultmann posed is the exact inverse of the problem which contemporary structuralist theories pose. The structuralist theories have taken the 'language' side, whereas Bultmann has taken the 'speaking' side. But we now need an instrument of thought for apprehending the connection between language and speaking, the conversion of system into event. More than any other discipline that deals with 'signs,' exegesis requires such an instrument of thought. If there is no objective meaning then the text no longer says anything at all; without existential appropriation, what the text does say is no longer living speech. The task of a theory of interpretation is to combine in a single process these two moments of comprehension" (P. Ricoeur, *The Conflict of Interpretations: Essays in Hermeneutics* [Evanston, 1974], 397–98).

in relation to the document *The Interpretation of the Bible in the Church*, by the PBC, and the principles contained in DV 12.[9]

Without claiming to solve the problem in these notes for reflection, I will try to offer some keys for understanding the indivisible unity of the hermeneutical process. Scripture is a single object or reality accessible through a single path made up of the two dimensions required by the nature of the object. As attested revelation, Scripture cannot be reduced to a methodologically accessible *text* (historical-critical dimension) that does not question freedom (theological dimension). As a witness to revelation, Scripture preserves the nature of an event that is happening here and now, challenging my freedom. To this characteristic of the historical witness to revelation, following the Magisterium of the Church, the name "sacramental" can be given.[10] G. Colombo, going into this dimension in depth, speaks of a "symbolic structure" of revelation.[11]

This same terminology could be used to speak of the nature of the witness to revelation that is Scripture, which offers itself to the interpreter with a *symbolic* character. To be faithful to the nature of Scripture, the exegete, like the believer, must put his freedom at risk in the face of the written witness. Only this freedom (faith) is capable of handling the "symbolic structure" with which the truth gives itself in the witness (revelation).

From the Greek *symbolon* (root *sym-ballō*), the term *symbol* alludes to the identity that arises from the act of gathering or joining the fragments of a previously broken object to facilitate the mutual recognition of those who were taking care of the parts. Only the union of the fragments generates a complete, new *form*, which, in turn, generates the mutual recognition of those who had remained strangers. The sym-

---

[9] Cf. chapter 3, III B.

[10] The encyclical *Fides et ratio* speaks of *ratio sacramentalis* of revelation (FR 13). Previously, the dogmatic constitution *Sacrosanctum Concilium* had spoken of *fidei sacramenta* ("sacraments of faith": SC 59).

[11] Cf. G. Colombo, "Grazia e libertà nell'atto di fede", in *Noi crediamo: Per una teologia dell'atto di fede*, ed. R. Fisichella (Rome, 1993), 39–57. A. Scola follows Colombo in this terminology (cf. Scola, *Chi è la Chiesa?*, 118–20). Cf. also the use that Von Balthasar makes of this terminology when he discusses the form-sign relationship in Jesus Christ (Von Balthasar, *Glory*, 1:198–218).

bolic structure of the historical event of salvation (an event in history is the Alpha and the Omega of history), paradigmatically present in the *hypostatic* union that is realized in Christ (human nature and divine nature in a single person), is preserved in Scripture.[12]

It can thus be understood why the historical-critical and theological dimensions require each other in the exegetical task. They do so by virtue of the nature of their object, not by virtue of a moral demand or a pious effort. Indeed, it should not be forgotten that the method of approaching an object is imposed by the object itself.[13] The essence of Scripture, the witness to revelation, by virtue of its symbolic structure, will not be reached by means of a historical method in which no part is played, from the beginning (constituting the very method), by faith, as human freedom, generated and sustained by grace, which responds to the call of the witness, generated and sustained by grace.

The dynamic of the involvement of human freedom in knowledge, on the basis of a witness or testimony, has been well described by Hans Urs von Balthasar. It is worth quoting him at length:

> Now, the freedom of spirit in its self-communication, which is not annulled even in its act of revealing itself, implies a new and specific attitude also in the spirit that receives this communication . . . As soon as the communication becomes free . . . the verification of the relation between content and expression no longer comes immediately under the purview of the knower's judgment. The freedom of the one revealing stands in the way. The word that he has pronounced is no longer a mere expression of the internal word but a *testimony*. The speaker establishes an equation between the content and the form of his utterance. The equation cannot be checked over from the outside; the speaker vouches for the correctness

---

[12] "The Gospels were written by men who were among the first to have the faith and wanted to share it with others. Having known in faith who Jesus is, they could see and make others see the traces of his mystery in all his earthly life. . . . His deeds, miracles, and words all revealed that 'in him the whole fullness of deity dwells bodily' [*Col* 2:9]. His humanity appeared as 'sacrament,' that is, the sign and instrument, of his divinity and of the salvation he brings: what was visible in his earthly life leads to the invisible mystery of his divine sonship and redemptive mission" (*Catechism of the Catholic Church*, 2nd ed., 515).

[13] "The sovereign stipulation of the scientific method holds that an object is grasped, not with a 'general method', but rather with the 'method corresponding to the object' " (R. Guardini, "Holy Scripture and the Science of Faith", trans. Scott G. Hefelfinger, *Letter and Spirit* 6 [2010]): 412.

of the equation. In vouching for this as a person, he creates for the receiver a substitute for its missing ability to verify. The declaration of the truth thus becomes a kind of deposition, and as such it implies the ethical characteristic of truthfulness. By the same token, there is a corresponding *faith* on the part of the receiver. Without this faith, any exchange of truth between free entities is unthinkable.[14]

A historical-critical study of Scripture that dispenses with faith (or incorporates it methodologically only at a later time) will certainly be able to arrive at knowledge about the historical dimension of revelation. But it will not arrive at the *meaning* of the events and words it studies.[15] It will do no good to say that faith can be added at a later time: the symbolic structure of revelation and its written witness does not make it possible for the final image to be arrived at (to be recognizable) by two parallel means whose results (obtained independently) are added up at the end. It is not possible to *deduce* the final identity or image from the careful, separate study of each of the parts of the *symbol*, since this is only arrived at in the union of the two pieces. This union constitutes the starting point of the object, because only this union has before it the true object of study.

It will be my task now to show how the two methodological dimensions can be maintained in an indivisible unity in the study of the OT. For this purpose, I will start with the data and considerations accumulated in the two preceding chapters, especially about the new proposals for interpretation that contain many elements of hermeneutical reflection. Some of these recent proposals will make it possible to travel the negative path: to show how the exclusion of faith as an integral part of the method leads to partial results that are not capable of exhaustively accounting for the total object of study.

---

[14] H. U. von Balthasar, *Theo-Logic*, vol. 1: *The Truth of the World* (San Francisco, 2000), 96.

[15] "The proper essence of the holy text remains cut off, in the strictest sense of the word, as long as the adequate disposition is not present—that is, faith. The one considering the holy text in a merely historical way does not see the proper object at all. He sees only the external appearances, psychological contexts, philological and cultural meanings of the word" (Guardini, "Holy Scripture", 419).

II. The Theological Dimension of the Method: Faith, the Appropriate Presupposition for Biblical Interpretation

An essential presupposition of the Enlightenment, in its application to the study of Scripture, is that faith is an element that gets in the way of objective knowledge, for which reason it should be excluded from the method we use to study the Bible. We already saw in the second chapter that Spinoza was one of the first who, as early as the middle of the seventeenth century, gave voice to this hermeneutical presupposition, when he stated that "the method of interpreting Scripture, does not differ from the [correct] method of interpreting nature", for which reason the exegete, in his study, should not permit the presence of "other criteria or data for interpreting Scripture and discussing its contents than what is drawn from Scripture itself and its history".[16]

We have had occasion to see, by way of our diachronic look at the results of exegesis over the last two centuries, how this principle—the exclusion of faith from the method—has shaped a large part of biblical interpretation, especially its main branch, the studies based on the historical-critical method. One of the virtues of that diachronic look was precisely that of being able to draw lessons from the history of exegesis. And a first lesson is that the exclusion of faith has not produced the advantage of a greater "objectivity" in the knowledge of the Bible. On the contrary, paradoxically the study of Scripture, "freed" from Christian—or Jewish—dogma, has built on other philosophical presuppositions that in fact have clearly conditioned, as we have had occasion to see, the results of exegesis. In reality, we have witnessed a transfer of presuppositions: to the degree that faith, as a basic presupposition of biblical interpretation for many centuries, has been withdrawn, other presuppositions have taken its place.

Almost 350 years after Spinoza, we can say that his project for an objective study of Scripture, following the method of the natural sciences, has not been realized.[17] In fact, the second half of the twentieth

---

[16] B. Spinoza, *Theological-Political Treatise* (Cambridge, 2007), 98.

[17] *Pace* Ska, who states almost exactly the opposite: "All in all, we are surely for the most part disciples of Spinoza and our reading of the Bible supports and confirms his views in many ways. On other points, we have gone further and this is quite normal" (J.-L. Ska, "Old and New

century, which was enormously fruitful in hermeneutical reflection, has shown that it is pure naïveté to claim to be free of the presuppositions or prejudices with which one sets out to gain knowledge. Furthermore, and this is one of the great contributions of contemporary hermeneutics, "prejudices" or "prior understandings" play a role that must be recognized in the process of gaining knowledge.[18]

But is objectivity, then, impossible? In the introduction to this work, I started with the *desideratum* of Ratzinger that historical-critical exegesis should do a diachronic reading of its own results, so that it could recognize the "interference" in its task of philosophical presuppositions of a widely varying nature. Historical exegesis, said Ratzinger, should distance itself "from the impression of quasi-scientific certainty with which it has largely been accustomed to present its interpretations".[19]

Even before Ratzinger, in 1928 the great German theologian Romano Guardini realized that the question about objectivity in exegesis had long been invalidated by the desire to apply the method of the natural sciences to a human, and specifically religious, expression inscribed in history, as Scripture is. Since the way to approach an object is imposed by the object itself, the method of knowing that must be applied to a human, historical, literary, or religious phenomenon cannot be the same as the one applied to a phenomenon of the world of matter:

> Realms of being . . . are qualitatively diverse, not deriving from one another. . . . There is no . . . knowing that could be directed in a uniform way upon a chemical reaction, a mechanical apparatus, the growth process of a plant, the development of an animal, a human stirring of emotion, the formation of a concept, an ethical decision, a philosophical problem of essence, the religious phenomenon of prayer. A largely dominant way

Perspectives in Old Testament Research", in *The Exegesis of the Pentateuch: Exegetical Studies and Basic Questions*, ed. J.-L. Ska, FAT 66 [Tübingen, 2009], 266).

[18] "The very teachers of the historical method never manage to rid themselves entirely of the prejudices of their time, their social environment, their nationality, and so on. Is this a defect? Even if it were, I believe that it would be the task of philosophy to study why this defect accompanies every human undertaking. In other words, I consider it scientific to recognize *what is*, rather than to start with what should and could be. In this sense I attempt to get beyond the notion of method that is characteristic of modern science (which, on the other hand, preserves its limited validity) and to install as a principle what *always* happens" (H. G. Gadamer, "Hermeneutik und Historismus", *PhR* 9 [1962]: 248–49).

[19] Ratzinger, "Biblical Interpretation in Conflict", 8.

of thinking thinks so. But such a knowledge simply does not exist! The supposition is false and to tolerate it at all reveals a spiritual feebleness!

In the face of such a will to know, the essential element within the various realms of objects closes itself off. If this essential dimension is to be apprehended, then knowing must be living. The ontological particularity of things must correspond to a noetic particularity of the act of knowing.[20]

The current of thought of which Guardini is speaking is the one responsible for wanting to introduce a single method of gaining knowledge (the scientific one, or the method of the natural sciences) about all realities, by which it in fact deforms or reduces both the subject of the knowledge and its object:

> [All reality] is leveled into a general schema of intellectualistic cognition, in which an abstract, homogeneous cognitive apparatus, the subject, stands before an object, which is just as homogeneous in its abstract objectivity, whether we are dealing with a stone or a plant or a person. And this disposition has been dogmatized in the name of being scientific according to that science which stems from comprehending mechanical things.[21]

The desire to apply the method proper for knowledge of the natural sciences to Scripture contains a double naïveté that is, in reality, a double disloyalty: one with regard to the object of knowledge and another with regard to the subject who knows. With regard to the object of knowledge, one cannot try to reduce all of reality to the single field of mechanical objects, to which a single mode of gaining knowledge is applied, the one characteristic of the natural sciences.[22] The object we want to know, Scripture, is the written witness to an event set in history, which has to do with the religious dimension of man. The method of knowing that is characteristic of the natural sciences cannot be applied to this object quite simply because this method does not correspond to the object of interest to us.

---

[20] Guardini, "Holy Scripture", 403.

[21] Ibid., 46–47.

[22] The distinction that Kant makes between "phenomenon" (the realm of what is understandable through reason, marked by space, time, and causality) and "noumenon" (of which we do not have sensible intuition but only ideas and which, therefore, cannot be cognizable) is behind this desire to reduce the field of knowledge to sensible objects (cf. I. Kant, *Critique of Pure Reason* [Cambridge, 1998], 338–65).

Moreover, with regard to the subject, it is naïve to think that the ideal position for him when gaining knowledge is "neutrality" or indifference, "affective" non-involvement with the object being studied. In the first place, this neutrality is not found even in the field of scientific investigation, and, in fact, there is no reason why it should be the most appropriate position. The history of science is full of examples that illustrate this point: neither is the investigator "neutral" in relation to the object, nor is neutrality the most appropriate condition for gaining scientific knowledge.[23] But in addition, in the range of human cognitive experience, there is a long series of objects that especially require the involvement of the subject to make an appropriate knowledge possible. Furthermore, these are realities that offer themselves (or unveil themselves) to the individual and his knowledge to the degree that he is involved in them. This is evident in the field of human relations, where the involvement of the subject with the object is fundamental, for example, to know whether I can trust a person, to know whether a person really loves me, or to discover whether a person is lying about a serious matter.

To these types of objects that require the involvement of the subject to be known belong all the realities that have to do with the individual's "fulfillment", with "salvation"; and of course, all religious realities. And it is obvious that this involvement will be necessary to know God. In this case, it is clear that knowledge is not possible unless the subject is actively engaged.[24] God, to whom the religious dimension of

---

[23] "A purely objective, unconcerned disposition towards the object remains barren. Only that disposition bears fruit which enacts the earnestness of committing oneself to the object. . . . When the subject perceiving values admits them into his lived experience, then it portends a threat to his world of values, closed in upon itself. But this happens only to the extent that he is receptive, committed, and earnest in knowing" (Guardini, "Holy Scripture", 408). With regard to the history of science and the epistemological problem of the natural sciences, cf. G. Gismondi, "Epistemologia", in *Dizionario Interdisciplinare di Scienza e Fede: Cultura scientifica, Filosofia e Teologia*, ed. G. Tanzella-Nitti and A. Strumia (Rome, 2002), 1:486–504, with extensive bibliography.

[24] "This too . . . is true of the question of God. There is no such thing as a mere observer. There is no such thing as pure objectivity. One can even say that the higher an object stands in human terms, the more it penetrates the center of individuality; and the more it engages the beholder's individuality, then the smaller the possibility of the mere distancing involved in pure objectivity. Thus, wherever an answer is presented as unemotionally objective, as a statement that finally goes beyond the prejudices of the pious and provides purely factual, scientific information, then it has to be said that the speaker has here fallen a victim to self-

every person makes reference, never presents himself as a fact to which I gain access by means of "objective" knowledge, like a book on the table is or the genealogical tree of a person. God is always "my God", my problem, because the religious problem, the problem of salvation, is "my problem".[25] Because of the fact that I am a human person, I am inside this problem, and I cannot know it except on the basis of my involvement in him.

What, then, is the appropriate position to know that object which is called "Scripture", that *written and inspired witness to revelation*? Since the Bible is a religious expression that makes reference to the problem of the salvation for which every man longs, the appropriate position before it is the religious attitude. This attitude will certainly be a condition for the possibility of a true knowledge of the Bible, but it will not be sufficient. The religious fact to which the OT and NT attest (and of which they are an expression) is entirely peculiar to them: it is the positive revelation in history, time, and space of God. A claim that is certainly unprecedented and that therefore requires a decision by the investigator; significantly, it is a claim that has to do with *his* religious problem and to which therefore he *must* respond.

The fact to which the OT and NT refer has not stayed anchored in its own era (as might have happened); rather, it has come through

---

deception. This kind of objectivity is quite simply denied to man. He cannot ask and exist as a mere observer. He who tries to be a mere observer experiences nothing. Even the reality 'God' can only impinge on the vision of him who enters into the experiment with God—the experiment that we call faith. Only by entering does one experience; only by cooperating in the experiment does one ask at all; and only he who asks receives an answer. . . . [T]he mere neutral curiosity of the mind that wants to remain uninvolved can never enable one to see —even in dealing with a human being, and much less in dealing with God. The experiment with God cannot take place without man" (J. Ratzinger, *Introduction to Christianity*, trans. J. R. Foster [San Francisco, 2004], 175–77).

[25] "Only when I take God as the salvation of my person does he enter into the reality that is possible, full, and decisive for me. Not when I say 'God'; but only when I say 'my God'" (Guardini, "Holy Scripture", 411). From the field of philosophy, X. Zubiri has been able to show lucidly the personal involvement of man in the knowledge of God: "Therefore, the presence of God in my substantive reality is not merely a real presence in itself. If it were just this, God would be but a mere object among others, perhaps the most sublime of all objects, but nothing more; and therefore the most that I could do would be to direct myself to Him. This is not the case. God is not an object, but precisely and formally the terminus of religation. I am not directed, but religated to Him. Therefore, God is not an object; prior to being an object and in order to be able to be one, He is fundament. He is foundational in my destination to be absolute" (X. Zubiri, *Man and God* [Lanham, 2009], 120).

time and presents itself with the same claim today as an announcement: God, the Mystery who has made all things, has chosen a people
through which to take salvation to everyone; when the fullness of time
came, he decided to communicate through his Son, made man for us;
in Christ, by means of the paschal mystery and the sending of the Holy
Spirit, people are reconciled with God and find new life. The investigator has to respond, not to a fact from the past, but to a present fact.
And that fact, because of the form in which it presents itself (and by
its very nature), requires a personal and critical verification, a personal
involvement: the exercise of verifying the correspondence between the
religious needs and the fact proclaimed in the terms proclaimed.[26]

In reality, anyone who would like to approach that object called the
Bible would find himself obliged to take a position concerning a present
fact, the Christian proclamation, the origin of which is written there.
And vice versa, whoever comes across the Christian proclamation today will have to take a position concerning what that proclamation
says about its origins, which are attested in Scripture.

The appropriate response to the positive revelation of God in Jesus
Christ is called faith. This is the appropriate presupposition for the correct interpretation of Scripture. In fact, faith can be defined as a "cognitive disposition"; more specifically, as the "cognitive disposition that
corresponds to the Word of God".[27] As was already seen in the previous point, this faith, as an appropriate response of man to revelation,
forms part of the very nature of revelation (DV 6), for "God's Word,
from the outset, wants to be fruitful in the fruitfulness of the believing
person. In the very form in which it addresses man, the Word of God
already wants to include the form of man's answer to God."[28] And it
has also been seen that one fruit of this faith is Scripture itself. Faith,
therefore, is at the origin of the object and presents itself as a basic
presupposition for the subject who wishes to know the object.[29]

---

[26] On the dynamic of verification (criteria of truth) or of the adaptation of the Christian
experience to human anthropological structure, cf. Scola, *Questioni di Antropologia Teologica*,
209–11; J. Prades, "La fe como gracia. Libertad de la fe", in *Diccionario de teología*, ed. C.
Izquierdo, J. Burggraf, and F. M. Arocana (Pamplona, 2006), 407–15.

[27] Guardini, "Holy Scripture", 418.

[28] Von Balthasar, *Glory*, 1:538.

[29] "Faith will always remain the presupposition, never to be superseded by knowledge, for
faith establishes the level at which this mystery is given" (Guardini, "Holy Scripture", 421).

I will return now to some of the characteristics that were listed about that particular cognitive attitude toward the object—the attitude called faith. They will help to draw a profile of the appropriate position for the exegete who approaches the OT as Scripture.

A. The Starting Point: A Unique Event in History

Faith forms part of the religious dynamic, a dynamic that in turn forms part of the natural structure of man, which is uncovered especially in contact with reality. The Christian faith, however (and something similar could be said of the faith of Israel), presents a dynamic that is quite particular with regard to the natural human religiosity that is at the origin of religious creativity.[30] Faith in its entirety has to do with a spatio-temporally situated fact that makes the claim to be *the* intervention of God in history "to reveal Himself and to make known to us the hidden purpose of His will" (DV 2). The starting point, therefore, is *outside* of men: a historical event that enters the domain of human knowledge like any other event and that requires an answer from them (*requires*: significantly, the event has to do with their religious dimension).

The Christian faith, therefore, is not deducible from the natural religiosity of people. It is an act that is essentially "dumped" onto a quite specific historical manifestation, which has a series of methodological implications of the highest importance. And these implications will be relevant for one's approach to Scripture, since it is an expression of

---

For this purpose it is worthwhile to quote at length the statement by H. R. Niebuhr: "This faith opens the way to knowledge. It removes the taboos which surround our intellectual life, making some subjects too holy to be inquired into and some too dangerous for us to venture into. Yet it grants reverence to the mind for which now no being is too low to be worthy of a loving curiosity. All knowledge becomes reverent and all being is open to inquiry. So long as we try to maintain faith in the gods, we fear to examine them too closely lest their relativity in goodness and in power become evident, as when Bible worshipers fear Biblical criticism, or democracy worshipers fear objective examination of democracy. But when man's faith is attached to the One, all relative beings may be received at his hands for nurture and for understanding. Understanding is not automatically given with faith; faith makes possible and demands the labor of the intellect that it may understand" (H. R. Niebuhr, *Radical Monotheism and Western Culture* [New York, 1960], 125–26).

[30] On the relationship between the Christian faith and the religious creativity of man, see the document by the International Theological Commission, *Christianity and the World Religions* (Vatican City, 1996).

faith (a written and inspired *witness*) that refers to the event that gives rise to faith itself.

Since the Christian faith cannot be traced back to a mere religiosity, the historical event on which it is based is an inescapable fact for all who want to understand the phenomena that spring from that same faith and even its very nature. But that historical event is not merely *available to* the interpreter; it does not present itself as an object that can be *understood* as physical objects are. It is an event that calls for verification in order to be known. It therefore demands the freedom of the interpreter. And the kind of verification needed is historical and at the same time religious. It entails a kind of imperative: "You *must* decide."[31] Significantly, the claim of that founding event requires an answer of everyone who approaches it: Is the history of Israel a place of the revelation of God or not? Is Jesus of Nazareth who he says he is or not? Can a point in history be the Alpha and the Omega of history? This is a claim that has to do with the *salvation* of men, with the fulfillment of their persons, with their religious dimension.

The verification, to be fair, must be done in accordance with the conditions that the object itself imposes. This means verifying what that reality says about itself. And the verification includes, and today it can no longer fail to include, the traces that event leaves in history, up until the present.[32] Interpreters cannot avoid responding because they consider the claim a fact from the past. If that were so, it would be necessary to decide about the truth of that moment in history. But

---

[31] "The lowest form of offense, that which, humanly speaking, is the least guilty, is to let the whole question about Christ remain undecided and to judge in this fashion: 'I do not presume to pass any judgment; I do not believe, but I pass no judgment.' That this is a form of offense escapes the attention of most men. The fact is that people have clean forgotten the Christian *'thou shalt.'* Therefore it is that they do not perceive that this is offense, this thing of treating Christ as a matter of indifference. The fact that Christ is preached to thee signifies that thou shalt have an opinion about Christ. The judgment that He is, or that He exists, or that He has existed, is the decision for the whole of existence. If Christ is preached to thee, it is offense to say, 'I will have no opinion about it'" (S. Kierkegaard, *Fear and Trembling and the Sickness unto Death*, trans. Walter Lowrie [1941; Garden City, New York, 1954], 260).

[32] One of the most recent trends in biblical exegesis is the one that bears the name *Wirkungs-geschichte*, or "History of the effects of the text", which studies the interpretation of a particular biblical text throughout history and the influence that text has had on theology and culture. Cf. Pontifical Biblical Commission, *The Interpretation of the Bible in the Church* (Vatican City, 1993), I, C 3.

that claim continues in history; it goes on being contemporary in that social body which is the Church.[33]

B. Reason Open to Reality

It is plain that a verification of this type presents itself as a challenge to modern reason. If the starting point is a fact in history, which continues to be present and requires verification, and not a mere piece of natural religiosity, reason will have to *open itself*, in accordance with its nature, to a piece of information it did not possess beforehand, from which something new may come, something *not deducible*. Throughout the preceding exposition, we have seen numerous examples of self-sufficient reason conceived as the *measure* of all things, which excludes a priori the gnoseological uniqueness of a point in history.[34] Put another way, the possibility is excluded that God, the absolute truth, can intervene in history by appointing a space and a time to which reason must submit itself by means of the dynamic of verification. While, as we have seen, Kant was the author who most clearly formulated this objection of modern reason,[35] a large part of the results of critical exegesis that we have analyzed are indebted to this principle.[36]

However, the priority of the event as a gnoseological principle is not opposed to, but rather fits well with, the true nature of reason, which is openness to reality. French philosopher Jean Guitton stated that "it is reasonable to submit reason to experience",[37] implicitly suggesting

---

[33] "The Teacher who expounds God's commandments, who invites others to follow him and gives the grace for a new life, is always present and at work in our midst, as he himself promised: 'Lo, I am with you always, to the close of the age' (Mt 28:20). Christ's relevance for people of all times is shown forth in his body, which is the Church. For this reason the Lord promised his disciples the Holy Spirit, who would 'bring to their remembrance' and teach them to understand his commandments (cf. Jn 14:26), and who would be the principle and constant source of a new life in the world (cf. Jn 3:5–8; Rom 8:1–13)" (*Veritatis Splendor* 25).

[34] A. Carrasco Rouco has shown the role that this type of reasoning has played in the various phases of the search for the historical Jesus (A. Carrasco Rouco, "La puesta en cuestión histórico-crítica del testimonio apostólico sobre Jesucristo", *RET* 61 [2001]: 207–31).

[35] Cf. chapter 2, IV.

[36] Cf. *Verbum Domini* 35.

[37] J. Guitton, *Nuevo arte de pensar* (Madrid, 2001), 85 (original French ed.: *Nouvel art de penser* [Paris: Aubier, 1946]).

that what is irrational is reason that wants to deduce from itself the explanation of reality, regardless of any encounter with it.

The OT offers us a clear example of this "open reason" necessary to know adequately. In the first book of Kings, we are presented with the figure of Solomon, the sage par excellence in Israel. In the third chapter, Solomon, conscious of his youth and inexperience and overwhelmed by the task of guiding a numerous people, addresses to God this beautiful request aimed at acquiring wisdom:

> "And now, O LORD my God, you have made your servant king in place of David my father, although I am but a little child; I do not know how to go out or come in. And your servant is in the midst of your people whom you have chosen, a great people, that cannot be numbered or counted for multitude. Give your servant therefore an understanding mind to govern your people, that I may discern between good and evil; for who is able to govern this great people of yours?" (1 Kings 3:7–9)

What Solomon asks for is an "understanding heart" (literally, "a heart that listens": *lēb šōmēaʿ*), that is, reason (according to the Semitic sense of the term *lēb*)[38] open to what comes from the outside, to the reality that desires to judge rightly, to understand adequately. In fact, farther on, the same book of Kings says that God, when he responds to Solomon's prayer, grants him "wisdom and understanding beyond measure, and *largeness of mind* (*rōḥab lēb*) like the sand on the seashore" (1 Kings 4:29). Commenting on Solomon's request, G. von Rad says:

> What he, the paradigm of the wise man, wished for himself was not the authoritative reason which reigns supreme over dead natural matter, the reason of modern consciousness, but an 'understanding' reason, a feeling for the truth which emanates from the world and addresses man.[39]

Another paradigmatic case that Scripture presents to us is that of the Jew Paul of Tarsus. In his story, it is evident that the event of the encounter with "Jesus of Nazareth" (cf. Acts 22:8), on the road to Dam-

---

[38] In the Hebrew vocabulary, "heart" indicates the seat of conscious life (memory, imagination, attention, intelligence, will, mind, intention, conscience, and so on) and not of feelings. Cf. L. Alonso Schökel, "leb", in *Diccionario bíblico hebreo-español*, ed. L. Alonso Schökel (Madrid, 1994), 380–84. Cf. also L. Köhler, W. Baumgartner, and J. J. Stamm, "leb", in *The Hebrew and Aramaic Lexicon of the Old Testament* (Leiden, 2001).

[39] G. von Rad, *Wisdom in Israel* (London, 1972), 296–97.

ascus, established a new principle of interpretation and knowledge.[40] And it is precisely in the interpretation of Scripture (in the case of Paul, the Old Testament) where this event turns out to be determinative. Indeed, Paul had received the education typical for a rabbi: at the feet of Gamaliel (cf. Acts 22:3) he had familiarized himself with all the techniques of reading Scripture. Without a doubt, of him it could be said that he was an "expert" in biblical exegesis. However, Paul states that he, like all Jews, had a veil on when reading the Old Testament:

> But their minds were hardened; for to this day, when they read the old covenant, that same veil remains unlifted, . . . Yes, to this day whenever Moses is read a veil lies over their minds. (2 Cor 3:14-15)

It was not going deeper in the Jewish "hermeneutical method" that made it possible for him to understand the OT; rather, it was an event that is set in space and time:

> . . . that same veil remains unlifted, . . . because only through Christ is it taken away. . . . [B]ut when a man turns to the Lord the veil is removed. (2 Cor 3:14, 16)

It was therefore the saving event of Christ, which had entered the life of Paul, that made it possible for him to understand the Old Testament. In this case it is evident that it was an event that expanded the limits of his reason, opening it to receive the principle, Christ, who explains all Scripture. In fact, all the preaching of the apostle showed the fruitfulness of this new principle in its application to the interpretation of Scripture. The principle entered his life as an event; it is not deducible. But once it entered, it had the (persuasive) power to explain reality in all its factors. Although it is *not deducible*, it is nevertheless a *reasonable* principle.[41]

---

[40] Cf. J. Carrón Pérez, *Acontecimiento y razón: Principio hermenéutico paulino y la interpretación moderna de la Escritura*, Sub 1 (Madrid, 2001).

[41] This is, in fact, the dynamic of faith, at once *grace-filled* and *reasonable*: "Once the gratuitous and surprising event of revelation has taken place, we find a no less surprising correspondence between man (with his constituent desires and questions) and this event. Therefore faith shows its credibility before the unbeliever, too. Between the event of revelation and the structure of humans, there is a continuity within a greater discontinuity. . . . The *rationality* of faith is expressed in its conformity or coherence with anthropological structure, which makes it possible to take it in its original sense of adaptation to the complete nature of man, which is precisely a rational nature" (Prades, "La fe como gracia", 407).

Benedict XVI has lucidly identified the origin of the secularized hermeneutics of the Bible in a closed reason:

> Indeed, the secularized hermeneutic of sacred Scripture is the product of reason's attempt structurally to exclude any possibility that God might enter into our lives and speak to us in human words. Here too, we need to urge a *broadening of the scope of reason*. In applying methods of historical analysis, no criteria should be adopted which would rule out in advance God's self-disclosure in human history. . . . It calls for a reason which, in its investigation of the historical elements present in the Bible, is marked by openness and does not reject *a priori* anything beyond its own terms of reference.[42]

The Pope's call to broaden the limits of reason is today more urgent than ever. Contrary to what many may think, the dualism that modern exegesis presents will be resolved, not with generic calls to greater devotion or "spirituality", but *by expanding the spaces of our rationality*.

C. *The Personal Involvement of the Exegete: His Moral Responsibility*

I have insisted on the fact that the whole of Scripture refers, by its nature, to a fact set in time and in space. Therefore, the category of witness is the one that best defines it. This is a piece of information that is of great importance in facilitating an adequate approach to the object. And it is a piece of information that imposes itself on the exegete and demands his freedom: he must make a decision in view of the claim that Scripture contains and that arrives in our day with the same force in the Christian experience. And the decision entails a risk. In fact, Ricoeur goes so far as to speak of a "bet" in the task of interpretation.[43] Here the personal involvement of the exegete comes into play. Significantly, an essential characteristic of the category of witness is that it requires one to exercise freedom in a moral manner. In order to interpret a witness, the involvement of the subject is necessary, and

---

[42] *Verbum Domini* 36.

[43] Cf. P. Ricoeur, "Le Sujet convoque à l'École des Récits de Vocation Prophétique", *RICP* 28 (1988): 83–99.

in the field of interest here this will always be a "moral" experience.[44] The reflections that have preceded this section, in this third chapter, have sufficiently shown the decisive role that the position of the interpreter plays in knowledge. In the type of knowledge of interest here, there is no "neutral" position. The exegete must decide.

In his apostolic exhortation *Verbum Domini*, Benedict XVI clearly highlights the role that the freedom of the exegete plays in the hermeneutical process:

> Here we see the reason why an authentic process of interpretation is never purely an intellectual process but also a lived one. . . . There is an inner drama in this process, since the passage [from letter to spirit] that takes place in the power of the Spirit inevitably engages each person's freedom.[45]

Now that we have reviewed the basic characteristics of the most appropriate position in relation to the object of our study, we are in a position to identify the general terms that define the moral responsibility of the exegete and to judge it specifically in its practical applications. Now is the time to begin to assess the results of the most recent exegesis.

I will anticipate one possible objection, the one that states that the relationship between the literary corpus we call the Bible and a particular religious tradition is a fact outside of Scripture itself, or one that can be passed over. This position has against it the very reality of Scripture. Without that religious tradition, the Bible would not have been born, much less transmitted whole down to our day. In fact, that corpus is transmitted by a believing community and comes to us in a particular context of interpretation. With rare exceptions, we approach the Bible starting with the interest that a believing community raises in us.

Moreover, we have seen that only contemporaneousness with that fact to which Scripture attests puts us in an adequate position to understand it. What is at stake in the position of the exegete in relation to that

---

[44] "The concept of witness, as it is developed in biblical exegesis, is hermeneutical in a twofold sense. First of all, in the sense that it *offers* to interpretation content to interpret. Beyond that, in the sense that it *requires* an interpretation" (P. Ricoeur, "L'Herméneutique du témoignage", in *Lectures 3: Aux Frontières de la philosophie*, ed. P. Ricoeur [Paris, 1994], 130).

[45] *Verbum Domini* 38.

fact is not simply the imperative of a series of necessary decisions prior to approaching an object that will scarcely impinge upon the knowledge of it (like someone who must necessarily decide which edition of a work he will use before he starts to read it). In fact, the decision in the face of the Christian claim (the one we can find in the NT and that the Church continues to proclaim) will determine the results of exegesis.

To illustrate this point, I will start to judge, on the basis of the criteria set out, some positions on the approach to the prophets from the social sciences, the model already presented in chapter 2.[46] The three authors studied, F. Deist, C. E. Carter, and R. P. Carroll, avoid the inevitable decision with relation to Christianity (or Judaism), which, however, is in itself a moral exercise of freedom that has its consequences in the results of the exegesis they propose.

Deist is, in this sense, radical. A basic presupposition of his exegesis is the a priori rejection of the uniqueness of ancient Israel and the Christian religion, a uniqueness on which biblical interpretation has been based for centuries, including that which followed the historical-critical method. In fact, his criticism of the latter method makes no reference to matters of procedure (choosing between a diachronic or synchronic approach) but, rather, refers to a fundamental issue: historical-critical exegesis still considers the text a *reflection* of reality, of a single reality that is what really interests it. The text is considered the way to gain access to it.

The kind of questions that the "new paradigm" based on the social sciences proposes shows quite clearly the a priori denial of the unique character of a point in history. What is of interest in this method is not *who* this or that prophet was or *what* he said, but questions like *what social model* best describes the Israelite society of that era or *what conditions* (economic, social, political) created a favorable environment for the emergence of a prophetic figure.[47] These are questions about social structures and the models that describe them as well as about the daily socioeconomic life of those eras.

---

[46] Unless otherwise stated, the references to the various authors are taken from the texts cited in chapter 2, VI B: "The Social Sciences Reading".

[47] Cf. F. E. Deist, "The Prophets: Are We Heading for a Paradigm Switch?", in *Prophet und Prophetenbuch: Festschrift für Otto Kaiser zum 65. Geburtstag*, ed. V. Fritz, K.-F. Pohlmann, and H.-C. Schmitt, BZAW 185 (Berlin, 1989), 14–15.

Carter describes very well the presupposition on which these types of studies rest: the social sciences conceive of human culture as a continuum.[48] This essential continuity is understood in a strong sense, within a materialistic ideology: cultural products are the result of the economic, social, and political determinants of each era. When these determinants are known, on the basis of "standard" models (in view of the essential continuity of all human culture), every historical contingency can be "explained" or "understood".

It is plain that, in fact, the possibility of *discontinuum* (or *unicum*) within the historical *continuum* is excluded, that is, the possibility that a contingent event, set in time and in space, could constitute the key to understanding all of history and even its meaning. Ultimately, this is the denial of the possibility that God could intervene in history. If such intervention were possible, it is evident that the point that received it, and the historical form it assumed, would be entirely novel from the epistemological and even phenomenological point of view.[49]

The denial of the uniqueness of a moment in history is a baseless a priori. Under the guise of "neutrality" or "objectivity", it is in fact a choice that involves a final act of disloyalty, which, we must not forget, is always a moral choice. It is necessary to understand both the background (a certain cultural context that is conducive to it) and the consequences (a certain type of exegesis) of this position. So I will review, in an orderly manner, the disloyalty and irresponsibility that this position entails as well as some factors that are at its origin and the consequences it brings.

---

[48] Cf. C. E. Carter, "Opening Windows onto Biblical Worlds: Applying the Social Sciences to Hebrew Scripture", in *The Face of Old Testament Studies: A Survey of Contemporary Approaches*, ed. D. W. Baker and B. T. Arnold (Grand Rapids, 1999), 443.

[49] "Although faith in the *logos*, the meaningfulness of being, corresponds perfectly with a tendency in the human reason, this second article of the Creed proclaims the absolutely staggering alliance of *logos* and *sarx*, of meaning and a single historical figure. The meaning that sustains all being has become flesh; that is, it has entered history and become one individual in it; it is no longer simply what encompasses and sustains history but a point in it. Accordingly the meaning of all being is first of all no longer to be found in the sweep of mind that rises above the individual, the limited, into the universal; it is no longer simply given in the world of ideas, which transcends the individual and is reflected in it only in a fragmentary fashion; it is to be found in the midst of time, in the countenance of one man" (Ratzinger, *Introduction to Christianity*, 193–94).

1. The Irresponsibility of a "Neutral" Position That Excludes Faith

How is it possible to recognize (or at least take into consideration) the uniqueness of a point in history if its exceptionality is not present in some way today and its claim does not actually challenge my freedom? Put another way, how can I accept a historical uniqueness that I cannot in some way verify today in the terms in which it presents itself? Indeed, only because that uniqueness has come down through history and offers itself to my freedom today is it possible to speak of the moral responsibility of the exegete in relation to the fact to which Scripture attests.

This reveals the irresponsibility of the position that claims to start from a "neutral" point of view with regard to the literary corpus that is Scripture and that therefore accuses the theological reading, which springs from faith, of being partial or tendentious. We have already seen how Carter identified this claim in some authors who start from the social sciences and state that in order for critical investigation to be truly objective it must be kept outside of any theological commitment. As Carter also emphasized, we are seeing "the most recent volley in the long-standing tension", typical of the late nineteenth and early twentieth centuries, "between theologically oriented studies and a supposedly more 'neutral' religious studies approach to Scripture".[50]

Why is this apparently "neutral" position morally irresponsible? Because it does not decide—does not take a position—with relation to the fact to which Scripture attests and which continues to be present today with all the force of the original claim, offering itself for verification.[51] Precisely because of this, "neutrality" is not the most appropriate position. And not only is it not appropriate (for only an involvement with the prolongation in time of the unique event makes it

---

[50] Another volley of that same tension is the debate that has been generated around the work *Religionsgeschichte Israels in alttestamentlicher Zeit* (1992), by Albertz, in which the German historian goes back to the point of view of the School of the History of Religions to deal with the history of Israel. According to this point of view, we should speak, not of the "history of Israel", but of the "history of the religion of Israel". This latter discipline would take the place of the theology of the Old Testament by denying the unity or consistency of its object of study (whether the OT or the "history of Israel"). Cf. the articles in the monographic volume of the *Jahrbuch für Biblische Theologie* 10 (1995) devoted to this discussion and titled *Religionsgeschichte Israels oder Theologie des Alten Testaments?*

[51] The Gospels illustrate this dynamic perfectly. In the presence of Jesus, in view of his claim, it was necessary to take a position. Whoever tried to avoid it in fact positioned themselves against him.

possible for me to understand it), but it is morally irresponsible: the exegete *must* decide. To avoid this decision is disloyalty to the event he sees before him and to his own religious problem, a position that additionally involves serious problems for knowledge, as we will see below.

Plainly, the problem of the claim of "neutrality" by some forms of exegesis is a hermeneutical problem that goes beyond the matter of *non-decision* with regard to the uniqueness of a point in history. Some of the factors have already been mentioned previously (concept of reason, relation to the object of knowledge, claim to objectivity, reduction of the method of knowing to the method of the natural sciences, concept of faith as interference), and others will be treated next (influence of the cultural context). Now my interest is to emphasize the irresponsibility that a position like this involves in relation to the Christian event present in history that offers itself for verification.

Moreover, the "neutrality" of which I am speaking is only apparent. When Carroll refers to ecclesiastical or theological interpretation as the "hermeneutics of trust" and contrasts it to the "hermeneutics of suspicion", it is clear that he considers the former *naïve* and the latter *critical*. Neutrality, in this case, would be a position that arises from suspicion, from doubt: all the texts are an expression of an ideology that wants to impose or justify itself, and it is the task of the exegete to go through the biblical account and uncover that ideology.

Carroll's position shows, in addition, the irresponsibility already alluded to in relation to the event to which Scripture attests and that comes down to us. The hermeneutics of trust, which is based on faith, is this by virtue of the decision of the exegete with relation to a present fact that has been judged *trustworthy* by means of the dynamic of verification, which is always critical. Plainly, this is the verification of a phenomenon that concerns the religious dimension of man, which has its own "critical" dynamic. And it is a verification that must begin with a non-deducible fact (the Christian claim) that has already put itself forward, offering itself to the freedom of the interpreter. The hermeneutics that springs from faith, and thus from trust, cannot for that reason be described as precritical or naïve. Rather, it corresponds to the nature of things: Scripture comes to me in a context of interpretation that offers itself for my consideration.

Because of all this, to prefer, as Carroll puts it, "the pluralist approach to reading the Bible" to "one particular ideology", for the reason that "pluralist readings protect readers from becoming entangled in biblical ideology", is a position that, on the contrary, could indeed be described as naïve because of its claim to neutrality, if it were not for the fact that the adjective that best suits it is *disloyal* to the object of study as it comes down to us.

2. Some Decisive Factors That Are Hidden behind the "Neutral" Position

To be fair about the issue with which we are concerned, the moral exercise of the responsibility of the exegete, we need to pay attention to some factors in the cultural environment in which we operate that, in fact, condition the position of the interpreter with relation to Scripture. With no desire to be exhaustive, I will concentrate on two factors that certainly determine our position with relation to reality: Kantian criticism of positive religion and censure or relativization of the religious dimension of man.[52]

When we studied the philosophical and cultural presuppositions that are hidden behind the view of the prophets shared by Wellhausen, Kuenen, and Gunkel, we had occasion to explain Kant's objection to the claim of the Christian event to have universal value.[53] In Kant's opinion, only pure religion (which for the authors cited represented the ethical and individual religion of the prophets of Israel), like mere rational faith, can have that claim, and not a positive, historical religion, bounded in time (like the religion of the Law in Israel or the Christianity of dogmas, accounts, rites, and law). Put another way, a historical event cannot be a necessary and universal truth. Now it is time to see how this objection of Kant's survives in the cultural milieu of today and conditions the correct approach to Scripture.

The concept of reason that the Enlightenment established and that has come down to our day, dictating the principles that every method of scientific knowledge must fulfill, includes the Kantian objection under the presupposition, in the words of G. E. Lessing (a contemporary of Kant), that "*contingent truths of history can never become the proof of necessary*

---

[52] On these matters, cf. J. Prades, "Un testigo eficaz: Benedicto XVI", in *Dios salve la razón*, ed. Benedicto XVI, G. Bueno et al. (Madrid, 2008), 7–27.

[53] Cf. chapter 2, IV.

truths of reason."[54] It is understandable, then, that a type of reason such as this should have difficulty taking seriously into consideration the Christian event as the Catholic Church proposes today, with all of it centered around the mysteries of the Incarnation, life, Passion, death, and Resurrection of Jesus Christ, strongly rooted in history, a history that is described as the history of salvation.[55]

A concept of reason like the one described can admit, sometimes just barely, the existence of God, the ultimate and universal principle, the order of the cosmos, but, as we already saw in chapter 2,[56] it is scandalized by Christian dogma: that God can become man or that a piece of bread can become the Body of Christ. Every supernatural revelation would remain outside the domain of the reasonable and could be rejected as impossible. Throughout the nineteenth century, the progressive imposition of the concept of enlightened reason was followed by a progressive abandonment of Christian dogma and defection from every Church that aspired to be faithful to its original nature.

Perhaps the author who best understood the influence of the Kantian revolution in the foundations of biblical criticism, and the consequences it entails, was Ernst Troeltsch. In an essay published in 1898, titled "On the Historical and Dogmatic Method in Theology",[57] Troeltsch formulated the three principles that uphold the "historical method":

---

[54] G. E. Lessing, "On the Proof of the Spirit and of Power", in *Philosophical and Theological Writings* (Cambridge, 2005), 85.

[55] "[T]he profession of faith [says] that the man Jesus, an individual executed in Palestine round about the year 30, the *Christus* (anointed, chosen) of God, indeed God's own Son, is the central and decisive point of all human history. It seems both presumptuous and foolish to assert that one single figure who is bound to disappear farther and farther into the mists of the past is the authoritative center of all history. . . . Yet at first this article of faith represents a stumbling block for human thinking. In this have we not fallen victim to an absolutely staggering kind of positivism? Can we cling at all to the straw of one single historical event? Can we dare to base our whole existence, indeed the whole of history, on the straw of one happening in the great sea of history? Such a notion, which even in itself is an adventurous one and seemed equally improbable to both ancient and Asiatic thought, is rendered still more difficult in the intellectual climate of modern times, or at any rate rendered difficult in a different way, by the fashion in which history is now dealt with by scholars: that is to say, by the historico-critical method" (Ratzinger, *Introduction to Christianity*, 193–95).

[56] Cf. chapter 2, IV.

[57] E. Troeltsch, *Gesammelte Schriften*, vol. 2, *Zur religiösen Lage, Religionsphilosophie und Ethik* (Tübingen, 1922), 729–53.

a. *Principle of criticism* or methodical doubt: According to this principle, our judgments about the past (and therefore, about history) cannot claim to reach *truth* but only a greater or lesser *probability*.

b. *Principle of analogy*: This is the basic criterion that in fact evaluates the greater or lesser probability of a historical report. According to this principle, what happens in our present experience serves as a criterion of probability for what could have happened in the past. A continuity in human experience is therefore assumed.

c. *Principle of correlation*: This assumes that all historical phenomena are interrelated in such a way that any change must correspond to a particular cause and imply a particular effect. The historical explanation of a phenomenon should be confined to the chain of known causes and effects.

The principle of analogy, which is at the heart of the historical method, starts with the Kantian objection: it assumes a historical continuity that shuts out the possibility that a historically unique occurrence, an *unicum*, exists.

Troeltsch was lucid not only in identifying the presuppositions of historical criticism but also in setting out its consequences. Indeed, in his opinion, these principles are incompatible with the dogmatic method of theology and, in general, with traditional Christian faith. Whoever utilizes the historical method, if he is consistent, will arrive at results that classical theology must necessarily reject. Troeltsch himself compares this method with the leaven that transforms the whole batch of dough and winds up breaking the mold of the theological method used until then.[58]

It is plain that accepting this incompatibility entails the establishment of the reason-faith split, for which reason the latter would be left with no other fate than to wander through the indeterminate space of devotion and of ideas with mythical garb. The space of knowledge would be on the side of reason, which operates using the historical method. The consequences for the Christian faith are extremely serious. Essential statements of the Creed, such as the divinity of Jesus Christ, his Incarnation and Resurrection, and certain elements that permeate

---

[58] Ibid., 730.

the Gospels, such as the miracles, could not be the object of historical knowledge. Moreover, they would not be plausible from the historical point of view if we heed the principle of analogy: in our present experience, Troeltsch would say, we do not see God as a factor of reality, we do not see dead people resurrected, nor do we witness the breaking of the causal chain by means of miracles.

We can now better contextualize the presupposition of exegesis based on the social sciences, which conceives of human culture as a *continuum*. In spite of the fact that these new methods claim to go *beyond* the historical-critical method (that is, to be more radical), in the area of the historical plausibility of the texts, they share with the latter the same principle of analogy: it is present experience that judges the past. That is why the denial of the uniqueness of a moment in history is an inescapable a priori for these methods.

If we do not want to find ourselves obliged to accept this presupposition, we must uncover the fallacy involved in the principle of analogy as it is utilized by the most classic historical criticism and by the methods based on the social sciences.[59]

To do this it is necessary to begin by defending the truth that this principle contains and that makes historical understanding possible: the criteria of historical judgment must *in some way* be present in one's experience. There is a basic continuity in human experience that makes it possible to take a look at the events of other eras and understand them, just as it makes it possible for the literature of other eras to be pleasing. But the application of the principle of analogy must be accompanied by an openness of reason to novelty and to the uniqueness of some events, both in the present and in the past. Without this openness, the principle of analogy leads to an insoluble dilemma that Ted Peters formulates in the following way:

---

[59] Cf. the criticism of Troeltsch's principle of analogy carried out by V. A. Harvey, *The Historian and the Believer: The Morality of Historical Knowledge and Christian Belief* (New York, 1966), 3–9, 14–19; W. Pannenberg, *Grundfragen systematischer Theologie: Gesammelte Aufsätze* (Göttingen, 1967), 45–57; M. Hengel, "Historische Methoden und theologische Auslegung des Neuen Testaments", *KuD* 19 (1973): 85–90; T. Peters, "The Use of Analogy in Historical Method", *CBQ* 35 (1973): 475–82; G. Maier, *Das Ende der historisch-kritischen Methode* (Wuppertal, 1974), 48; E. Krentz, *The Historical-Critical Method* (Philadelphia, 1975), 55–61; and W. J. Abraham, *Divine Revelation and the Limits of Historical Criticism* (Oxford, 1982), 92–115.

The problem is that the events upon which Christendom seems to rest (e.g., miracles, the resurrection of Jesus, etc.) are unique. But the historian who employs the principle of analogy precludes such uniqueness at the outset, i.e., he must assume that the events of the past, like all events, are analogous to those he experiences in the present.[60]

To apply the principle of analogy while having in the background (consciously or unconsciously) a positivist philosophy or an exaggerated anthropocentrism leads to a grave myopia in the historical realm.[61] It is naïve (perhaps one should say *irrational*) to claim that one's own present experience (normally understood as sensory experience) covers the whole range of what is possible.[62] In fact, the category of *possibility* forms part of the cognitive dynamic of our reason. By virtue of this category, which is present *in some way* in my experience since it is inherent in reason, I can consider reasonable an event in the present or the past that has not previously formed part of my horizon of knowledge. Does this mean that reason must admit, from the outset, just any explanatory hypothesis about events in the past? It is plain that this openness in knowledge is just one factor, although a decisive one, in historical knowledge, which must necessarily interact with other factors, such as multiple attestation or Troeltsch's own principle of correlation (which would make it necessary to show the effects of a hypothetical event in history).

Moreover, the principle of analogy puts all its weight on present experience as the place that provides the elements needed to judge

---

[60] Peters, "Use of Analogy", 475. Cf. Harvey, *Historian and the Believer*, 32. In the same sense, but without alluding to the principle of analogy, cf. T. A. Roberts, *History and Christian Apologetic* (London, 1960), 173–74.

[61] The major criticism that Wolfhart Pannenberg makes of the principle of analogy, as formulated by Troeltsch, is its "unnecessary anthropocentrism". Unnecessary in the sense that "the basic principle of the universal correspondence of all historical phenomena does not have an anthropocentric structure to begin with" (Pannenberg, *Grundfragen systematischer Theologie*, 46). The problem is that the principle, in the hermeneutical universe of Troeltsch, is closed to the comprehension of those peculiar, unique, or inhomogenous events (such as the irruption of the divine into history). That is, it is guilty of anthropocentrism (cf. Pannenberg, *Grundfragen systematischer Theologie*, 45–54).

[62] Cf. the examples that William J. Abraham gives of events that have been verified in history but should not be considered plausible because they find no analogy in our usual experience (Abraham, *Divine Revelation*, 101–4).

every past event. In this sense, and rightly so, a historical judgment will depend on the *quality* of the present experience of the interpreter who approaches the past. Precisely because of this, the elements already presented, which define faith as an appropriate presupposition of biblical interpretation, are revealed to be decisive: the starting point of a unique event in history that continues to be present today, reason open to reality, and the moral responsibility of the exegete.[63] In this sense, the experience of Lessing is paradigmatic, as he suffered in his own flesh the dilemma that the principle of analogy would pose later: in his present experience miracles do not take place, and therefore he cannot accept the miracles reported in Scripture as proofs of the Christian doctrines of the Gospels:

> Thus I do not deny for a moment that prophecies were fulfilled in Christ; I do not deny for a moment that Christ performed miracles. But since the truth of these miracles has ceased entirely to be proved by miracles still practicable today, and since they are merely reports of miracles (however undisputed and indisputable these reports may be), I do deny that they can and should bind me to the least faith in the other teachings of Christ. I accept these other teachings for other reasons.[64]

With extreme lucidity and disarming sincerity, Lessing identifies the ultimate problem that every exegete and every believer must face: the distance that lies between the unique events of the past and one's present experience:

> This, this is the broad and ugly ditch which I cannot get across, no matter how often and earnestly I have tried to make the leap. If anyone can help me over it, I beg and implore him to do so. He will earn a divine reward for this service.[65]

Once again, it is evident that there is a need for the unique event of revelation, to which Scripture attests, to continue being present in the experience of the exegete and the believer, so that it can expand

---

[63] Respectively, sections II A, II B, and II C of chapter 3.

[64] Lessing, "On the Proof of the Spirit and of Power", 86.

[65] Ibid., 87. In the opinion of G. Theissen, one of the most renowned scholars of the historical Jesus, "After over 200 years of historical critical scholarship the gulf has deepened, lengthened and widened" (G. Theissen, "Historical Scepticism and the Criteria of Jesus Research or My Attempt to Leap across Lessing's Yawning Gulf", *SJT* 49 [1996]: 148).

their reason and their freedom in order for them to understand what presents itself as the *unicum* of history.[66]

The ambiguity of the principle of analogy, as it is presented by Troeltsch and applied by historical criticism, together with the Kantian objection about positive religion (on which Troeltsch's principle of analogy feeds) have exercised a profound influence on biblical investigation and have come down to our day as a heavy inheritance that conditions in no small measure the position of some contemporary exegetes as they consider the Christian claim that the Church conveys.

In the cultural milieu of our era, another factor is additionally present that had barely made its appearance in the nineteenth century and that conditions the position of the exegete with respect to Scripture even more. Indeed, most of the European intellectuals of the nineteenth century (those who influenced the cultural context) were and considered themselves to be "religious" men. Without a doubt, this was true of all the figures we have studied in the history of both the investigation of the sources of the Pentateuch and in that of the prophets. They were men who recognized the religious dimension that was part of their make-up and who tried to order their own lives in accordance with the religious problem. All these figures are linked to some (Protestant) Christian confession, although in most cases they only recognized in Christ the highest example of human religiosity: the one who called God "Father". This made all of them still recognize in the history of Israel and in the Gospels a historical uniqueness, not in the sense that they attested to the intervention of God in history (and thus a normative moment), but in the sense that they were the highest positive expression (and certainly the one most in accordance with reason) of the religiosity of our civilization.

The twentieth century and, most likely, the last part of the nineteenth, however, were witness to the appearance of the phenomenon of agnosticism and atheism, especially in Europe. I cannot stop here to illustrate this process in its origins, its expressions, or its development.

---

[66] In fact, the prolongation in history of this revelation is implicit in the argument "of the spirit and of power" of Origen's *Contra Celso*, which is Lessing's starting point: "because of the prodigious miracles which may be proved by this argument among many others, *that traces of them still remain among those who live according to the will of the Word*" (cf. Lessing, "On the Proof of the Spirit and of Power", 83; italics mine).

Suffice it to say that it is a phenomenon that cannot be separated from the transition that the nineteenth century completed in so many consciences: from Christian dogma to the mere religiosity of Christian inspiration. *In fact*, the "children" of those sincerely religious intellectuals are today (in barely two or three generations) agnostics or atheists.

What is of interest here is not so much the phenomenology of agnosticism or atheism and their influence on present-day culture. Rather, I am seeking to describe the position of detachment or lack of commitment to the reality, in general, and to the human experience itself, in particular, that is hidden behind these cultural movements and that today determines, more than the movements in and of themselves, the position of the interpreter of Scripture. It is precisely this detachment in relation to reality that is at the root of the irreligiosity of modern reason, which represents the height of the process I am describing. This irreligiosity, in spite of being presented as a natural condition of reason, is a choice that denies basic dimensions of reason itself. It is, therefore, profoundly irrational. Indeed, the nature of reason is openness to total reality, in all its factors.[67] And it is in the "impact" with reality that that natural dynamism of man, which is religiosity, is awakened.

So then, one of the most acute "illnesses" of our era is the weakening of the nexus with reality[68] that facilitates, as in no other era in history, living disconnected and with one's back turned to it; but, to be sure, not without drastic consequences. This disloyalty to reality is especially evident when one faces the "religious problem". This is the heart of the second determining factor that is hidden behind the "neutral" position in relation to Scripture.

The trend that studies the Bible on the basis of the social sciences

---

[67] Ricoeur, faced with the modern separation between knowing and believing, between reason and faith, demands the use of "whole reason": "It is an incessant reform of thinking, but within the limits of reason alone. The 'conversion' of the philosopher is a conversion within philosophy and to philosophy according to its internal exigencies. If there is only one *logos*, the *logos* of Christ requires of me as a philosopher nothing else than a more complete and more perfect activation of reason; not more than reason, but *whole* reason. Let us repeat this phrase, whole reason; for it is this problem of the integrality of thinking which will prove to be the core of the whole problematic" (Ricoeur, *Conflict of Interpretations*, 403).

[68] "What is in crisis, it seems, is this myterious nexus that unites our being with reality, something so deep and fundamental that it is our innermost sustenance" (M. Zambrano, *Hacia un saber sobre el alma* [Madrid, 2000], 104).

represents a novelty in the history of the critical exegesis of the last two hundred years. Some of its authors not only approach Scripture outside of faith but consider the religious dimension, and its expression, a mere hermeneutical choice, an ideology, moreover, that deforms knowledge. But to consider the religious problem an ideology or merely one choice among others is an act of serious disloyalty toward the very structure of human experience and toward reality itself,[69] as we have already seen. Only an era like ours, in which the nexus with reality has been enormously weakened, can be witness to an "exegesis" like this.[70]

When Carroll speaks of the tendency theologians have "to treat the human words used by human writers to express their ideas, beliefs, feelings about 'god' as if these words were somehow not human words but 'divine words' delivered to the writers from outside the human sphere", he is doing no more than giving voice to the perception of reality that considers the religious dimension of man to be, not a constituent factor of his nature, but a certain ideological interpretation of his nature. That same perception would not consider the very existence of reality (the fact that being, and not nothing, exists) and the wonder it produces the origin of the religious position; religiosity is supposed to spring, not from the experience of contact with reality, but as a projection ideologically conformed to certain desires. "God" is supposed not to belong to the domain of what is real, of what is cognizable. Religious beliefs are supposed not to have any foundation *in re*. The mentality that is dominant today in a large part of the culture, especially European, tolerates them in the private domain, in the same

---

[69] In reality, the true (totalitarian) ideology is that which, by denying every religious dimension, claims to be merely the affirmation of reality as it actually appears. But that "reality", in turn, has broken its links to the real world and is not an object of experience. It remains in the hands of ideology. This is how Hannah Arendt describes this ideology: "Ideological thinking becomes emancipated from the reality that we perceive with our five senses, and insists on a 'truer' reality concealed behind all perceptible things. . . . The ideal subject of totalitarian rule is not the convinced Nazi or the convinced Communist, but people for whom the distinction between fact and fiction (i.e., the reality of experience), and the distinction between true and false (i.e., the standards of thought) no longer exist" (H. Arendt, *The Origins of Totalitarianism* [Cleveland, 1958] 470–71, 474).

[70] J. Barr studies Carroll's exegesis under the heading "Postmodernism" (cf. J. Barr, *History and Ideology in the Old Testament: Biblical Studies at the End of a Millennium: The Hensley Henson Lectures for 1997 Delivered to the University of Oxford* [Oxford, 2000], 141–62).

way as it is possible to tolerate a person "believing" things that do not exist in reality.

It is plain that, in a position such as the one described, reason is considered by nature to be atheistic and exclusive. Religiosity is not a "reasonable" dimension but, rather, irrational or non-rational, marginalized to the area of feeling or imagination. But as I have been saying, the postulate that atheistic reason, on which a large part of knowledge today is built, is not even close to having been proven; quite the contrary. This is a debate that our *intellectus fidei* necessarily has to enter.

It is very important to understand that the perception of reality about which I have been talking permeates our culture, because, *in fact*, it influences, as we have seen, the way many authors approach the Bible. And let us not think that this mentality affects only unbelieving people or those who do not belong to a Church. The perception of reality described is the one that "by default" dominates a large part of education and, certainly, most of the media, which shape the dominant mentality.[71] It is therefore critical to understand that it is this perception of reality, which excludes the religious dimension, and not the agnostic and atheist movements, that is found at the origin of a certain exegesis and in the cultural baggage of a large number of people who approach Scripture.

The two factors described so far have been presented as factors that in some way condition the moral exercise of the exegete's freedom. It is fair to make two observations in order to be able to understand this statement correctly. First, a conditioned moral responsibility does not cease to be properly called a responsibility, that is, a responsible exercise of one's own freedom in relation to reality (in the case of the exegete, Scripture and the Christian event that the Church conveys). These conditioning factors that are breathed in the atmosphere do not ultimately annul the freedom of the exegete, who preserves his moral ability to make decisions in relation to his own experience and in relation to the Christian claim that reaches him in a proposal. Secondly, however, it would be very harmful for the fruitful interpretation of Scripture not

---

[71] On the cultural context that dominates the West and on its influence on the Church, see A. MacIntyre, *After Virtue: A Study in Moral Theory*, 3rd ed. (Notre Dame, 2007); F. J. Martínez Fernández, *Más allá de la razón secular: Algunos retos contemporáneos para la vida y el pensamiento de la Iglesia, vistos desde Occidente*, Cuadernos 1 (Granada, 2008).

to take into account these factors that in fact determine our position in relation to reality, usually unconsciously, including the reading of the Bible. Any solution to the problem of the crisis of exegesis must take into account the determinative role of the factors mentioned, just as it in fact has to take into account the other philosophical and cultural presuppositions we have been able to study so far. Needless to say, all education in the correct approach to Scripture must be conscious of that cultural atmosphere which has a decisive effect on knowledge, if it does not want to be deceived.

3. Consequences of the "Neutral" Position

Finally, I will describe the consequences of a position that denies a priori the uniqueness of the Christian event in the interpretation of Scripture under the guise of "neutrality". These consequences can be easily identified by studying the results of the interpretation that follows the model of the social sciences.

If one denies the historical *discontinuum* to which Scripture attests (and which is worthy of consideration by virtue of its effects and its permanence in time) and a priori affirms a *continuum* of human culture, the interpreter will approach the biblical past on the basis of the coordinates of his present, which he judges to be paradigmatic of all time. In order to be able to study and interpret a past on the basis of our experiences in the present (the place where we take a "snapshot" of the *continuum*), the social sciences devise models or structures, throwing questions at the past that are considered "pertinent".

In this way the approach from the social sciences projects onto Scripture, and onto the phenomena it describes, social, political, economic, and ideological models that "work" in the present. It is not hard to imagine the violence this action does to the text. The basic consequence of this approach is that the text "rebels" against a reduction of this kind: the models that are imposed on it do not manage to explain it exhaustively. An approach that makes the claim of being "neutral" is revealed, by any reckoning, to be "partial".[72]

---

[72] This is how the document *The Interpretation of the Bible in the Church*, by the PBC, describes the risks of the sociological approach to Scripture: "If the work of sociology consists in the study of currently existing societies, one can expect difficulty when seeking to apply its methods to historical societies belonging to a very distant past. . . . Moreover, the sociologi-

The inadequacy of the model in explaining the phenomenon described in Scripture is not hard to understand. The model is not "neutral", and neither is the *continuum* in fact a continuum. The models or structures created to interpret phenomena and societies of the past are not at all "neutral" (nor can they be); in the case being studied here, they are all indebted to a dialectic and Marxist view of history and its evolution. The questions judged "pertinent", which we saw in chapter 2 when analyzing the reading from the social sciences[73] and which are directed at ancient societies, are very expressive in this sense. I refer the reader to that chapter to verify this point.

Moreover, the presupposition that human culture appears as a *continuum* hides, under a certain attractiveness, a final fallacy, as I have previously shown.[74] Certainly, in history and in the human condition, there is a *continuum* that forms the basis for the existence of historical, social, and anthropological science. But in the context of interest here, this *continuum* is understood as a determinism that leaves no room for factors that cannot be foreseen, starting with human freedom. Nevertheless, historical processes and the societies that figure in them always play with that imponderable, human freedom, which governs all alike. That a historical process is driven by economic interests or by surprising generosity is not something that can be determined a priori, and history is full of examples of imponderable factors that condition the course of peoples. When Deist proposes an approach to Scripture based on a certain social model, he is well aware of what he is doing and what is at stake. Significantly, he explicitly rejects understanding the development of history on the basis of ideas and spirit (as German idealism did, and also most of the German exegesis we have studied) and proposes a new model of rationality based on materialism, in which matter and not spirit guides human processes and in which determinism and not human freedom dominates historical processes.

---

cal method does tend to pay rather more attention to the economic and institutional aspects of human life than to its personal and religious dimensions" (I D 1).

[73] Chapter 2, VI B.

[74] Chapter 3, II C 2.

III. The Historical Dimension of
the Interpretation of Scripture

Now that I have dealt with the theological dimension of the interpretation of Scripture, a determinant in one's approach to it, I will move on to study that other aspect of its nature which likewise determines the method: its historical dimension.

But before doing that, it is worthwhile to draw attention to something that has already come to light during the study of the theological dimension of exegesis and that will again manifest itself even more clearly in the study of its historical dimension. I am referring to the impossibility of separating the two fields, an idea for which I argued at the beginning of this chapter. The two dimensions can be distinguished and, therefore, studied in their specific natures, as we are doing, but always as integral parts of the one approach to Scripture in which the two are not juxtaposed but interwoven from the beginning.

Precisely for this reason, it should not be surprising that next, when describing the historical dimension of the interpretation of Scripture, I have to go back over the hermeneutical choices of the exegete and the relationship between the methods of literary analysis and faith as basic presuppositions of this interpretation. In the same way, in the preceding section, the study of the theological dimension of exegesis has had to face questions of historicity, epistemology, philosophy, and cultural context.

A. The Need for a Historical and Literary Study of Scripture

Both in the introduction to this book and at the beginning of this chapter, I underlined the need for a historical and literary study of Scripture that corresponds to an essential part of its very nature: a literary corpus that attests to a historical event. We are at the heart of the Catholic genius: the revelation of God takes place in history; it is offered to man at coordinates of time and space, in the fragility and nearness of apparently contingent deeds and words that must be received and interpreted. In the present chapter,[75] I recalled how DV 13 inserts Scripture

---

[75] Cf. chapter 3, I.

into that same dynamic of divine condescension by drawing a parallel between the mystery of the Incarnation (the Word of God becomes human flesh) and that other great mystery by which the words of God are expressed in human words.

By this same dynamic, the Bible is found at the opposite pole from the religious literature gathered under the name "Qur'an", which is conceived by the Muslim world to be the literal transcription of an "uncreated" Qur'an that is found beside God and that "descended" and was delivered to Muhammad.[76] Islam (at least in its dominant branch) does not entertain the possibility of a historical or literary study of the Qur'an because it does not believe there was any human participation in its composition.

The Church, on the contrary, and before her Judaism, has always argued for the active role of the *sacred writer* in the composition of the sacred books, so much so that in many cases tradition and the biblical manuscripts themselves have transmitted the name of the human author to whom each work is attributed. God is the *author* of Scripture by way of the *inspiration* that the Holy Spirit exercises in the sacred writer, who can also properly be called the author.[77] By virtue of this dynamic, Scripture offers itself for historical and literary study as a fruitful and necessary way of understanding it.

Ever since ancient times, the Christian interpretation of Scripture, and specifically of the Old Testament, paid attention to the study of the *history* and the *letter* as an integral part of an adequate reading. While the Antiochean School made the literal meaning and historical typology the password of its interpretation, we cannot forget that the founder of the Alexandrian exegetical school, Origen, could well be considered the father of the textual criticism of the Old Testament because of his attention to the text in his magnum opus, the *Hexapla*. Among the

---

[76] Cf. A. T. Welch, R. Paret, and J. D. Pearson, "Ḳur'ān", in *Encyclopédie de l'Islam: Nouvelle édition*, ed. P. Bearman, T. Bianquis, C. E. Bosworth, E. van Donzel, and W. P. Heinrichs (Leiden, 1960–2005), 5:401–35; M. Arkoun, "Corano", in *Dizionario del Corano*, ed. V.A. (Milan, 2007), 175–80; D. Gril, "Rivelazione e ispirazione", in *Dizionario del Corano*, 724–30. A complete and multidisciplinary study of the Qur'an is found in J. D. McAuliffe, ed., *Encyclopaedia of the Qur'ān* (Leiden, 2001–2006), 6 vols.

[77] "In composing the sacred books, God chose men and while employed by Him they made use of their powers and abilities, so that with Him acting in them and through them, they, as true authors, consigned to writing everything and only those things which He wanted" (DV 11).

Latin Fathers, Saint Jerome stands out for his attraction to the "original text" of the Old Testament, which would be shown in his *Hebraica Veritas* principle, which was of so much influence in the West and in the Latin Church by way of his translation of the Vulgate.

This attention to the historical and literary aspects of Scripture, on the basis of its nature, has been established in the first two paragraphs of DV 12.[78] The first of them serves as the foundation from which the second is derived. Precisely because in Sacred Scripture God speaks through men in human fashion, it is necessary to investigate the intention of the sacred writer (cf. DV 12a). And in order to discover that intention, one must give attention to the "literary forms" in which each sacred writer expresses himself, considering the circumstances of his time and culture, that is, the "customary and characteristic styles of feeling, speaking and narrating which prevailed at the time of the sacred writer" as well as "the patterns men normally employed at that period in their everyday dealings with one another" (DV 12b).

B. The Historical-Critical Method: Lights and Shadows

Although the dogmatic constitution of the Second Vatican Council does not explicitly mention the historical-critical method, this is the universally recognized method to deal with the task that DV 12a–b requires of the interpreter of Scripture. So much so that, as we already saw in the introduction, the document *The Interpretation of the Bible in the Church*, by the PBC, which shows the common feeling of Catholic exegetes, describes it as "the indispensable method for the scientific study of the meaning of ancient texts".[79]

---

[78] For a careful study of DV 12, see P. Grelot, "La inspiración de la Sagrada Escritura y su interpretación: Comentario al capítulo III", in De Lubac and Dupuy, *Revelación divina*, 2:15–58; J. Gnilka, "Die biblische Exegese im Lichte des Dekretes über die göttliche Offenbarung (Dei Verbum)", *MThZ* 36 (1985): 5–19; M. A. Molina Palma, *La interpretación de la Escritura en el Espíritu: Estudio histórico y teológico de un principio hermenéutico de la constitución 'Dei Verbum'*, 12 (Burgos, 1987); L. Alonso Schökel, "Interpretación de la Sagrada Escritura", in *La Palabra de Dios en la historia de los hombres: Comentario temático a la constitución "Dei Verbum" del Vaticano II sobre la Divina Revelación*, ed. L. Alonso Schökel and A. M. Artola (Bilbao, 1991), 385–417; H. Hoping, "Theologischer Kommentar zur Dogmatischen Konstitution über die göttliche Offenbarung *Dei Verbum*", in *Herders Theologischer Kommentar zum Zweiten Vatikanischen Konzil*, ed. P. Hünermann and B.-J. Hilberath (Freiburg, Basel, and Vienna, 2005), 3:695–831.

[79] PBC, *The Interpretation of the Bible in the Church* I A. For a thorough assessment of this doc-

This same document, when it has to give a value judgment on the historical-critical method "at the present stage of its development", and anticipating the criticisms to which it is subjected, states, "It is a method which, when used in an objective manner, implies of itself no a priori. If its use is accompanied by a priori principles, that is not something pertaining to the method itself, but to certain hermeneutical choices which govern the interpretation and can be tendentious."[80] It then recognizes that, in other eras, the method "separated itself from faith and at times even opposed it" but that, once it "was freed from external prejudices, it led to a more precise understanding of the truth of sacred Scripture". In the view of this document, "For a long time now scholars have ceased combining the method with a philosophical system."

I cannot avoid making some observations about these statements in the PBC document on the basis of the study carried out in the first and second chapters on the philosophical and cultural presuppositions of the exegesis of the Pentateuch and the prophets and, in the present chapter, on the indivisible unity of the two methodological dimensions of exegesis. Now I can verify what I said at the beginning of this section: when we study the historical dimension of biblical interpretation, we must necessarily return to theological and, more generally, hermeneutical questions. Thus, Ratzinger's observation, already included in the introduction, is confirmed: "The debate about modern exegesis is not at its core a debate among historians, but among philosophers."[81]

All the authors we have studied throughout the first two chapters used the historical-critical method. In all of them—we were able to see this especially in those who supported the dominant paradigms —the method was made up of prejudices that seriously affected the knowledge of Scripture and the results of exegesis. Even so, it could be thought that the PBC document considers the authors studied to be part of that era in which the method had not yet been freed from "external prejudices".[82] However, the overall impression after having

---

ument, see R. Vignolo, "Metodi, ermeneutica, statuto del testo biblico: Riflessioni a partire da L'interpretazione della Bibbia nella Chiesa (1993)", in Angelini, Rivelazione attestata, 29–97.

[80] PBC, The Interpretation of the Bible in the Church I A 4.

[81] Ratzinger, "Biblical Interpretation in Conflict", 19.

[82] In this study we have seen that recent exegesis that is governed by the methods of the

studied the recent developments in exegesis in the two fields that have been the object of our attention is that the historical-critical method, in its practical achievements, has not managed to unburden itself of those prejudices even today.

Moreover, the very idea of a "neutral" method freed of prejudices is at the very least naïve and, more seriously, reveals a separate conception of method and faith that establishes at the outset an insurmountable division between exegesis and theology. We thus find ourselves looking at yet another example (in this case, of a certain degree of importance, in view of the nature of the document) perceptible in exegesis today of the difficulty of bringing back into unity the two methodological dimensions that do justice to the nature of Scripture: the historical-critical one and that of faith. Already at the beginning of this chapter, we confronted this difficulty, showing how a historical method that dispenses with faith (in which faith is not involved from the beginning, shaping the method) or incorporates it only at a later time methodologically will not reach the essence of Scripture.[83]

Angelo Bertuletti is one of the authors who has most lucidly been able to see the dualism hidden in the statements of the document. It is worth quoting him at length. When commenting on this document's statement that the historical-critical method does not in and of itself imply any a prioris and that if its use is accompanied by such a prioris "that is not something pertaining to the method itself, but to certain hermeneutical choices which govern the interpretation and can be tendentious", the Lombard theologian says:

> Beyond this statement, which is surprisingly categorical in character, the principle conditions the whole approach of the Instruction, which treats the methodological aspect and the theological interpretation separately. . . . It is therefore not surprising that the part devoted to Catholic interpretation does not benefit from the journey through criticism. In it, the traditional concept is again proposed without any appreciable connection to the methodological problem. . . . The Instruction, although it professes neutrality of method, recognizes that this cannot be maintained in the process of theological application. . . . Methodological investiga-

---

social sciences is loaded with prejudices. The document of the Pontifical Biblical Commission, though, considers it to be, not within the historical-critical method, but rather part of the "approach through the human sciences".

[83] Cf. chapter 3, I.

tion cannot be separated from theological intelligence because the text, which is the condition that makes both of these possible, is the result of an operation in which both methodological and theological factors have always been mutually determined.[84]

Bertuletti observes that the old idea of an autonomous rationality that dictates its own laws, so much a part of all nineteenth-century exegesis, which seemed to have been abandoned in the twentieth on account of the hermeneutical debate, can and does persist in the separate conception of method.[85] Indeed, the second half of the twentieth century seemed to have decreed the end of the positivist ideal, which claimed to reach the truth through methodical science. In a parallel fashion, it seemed that exegesis—and this is how the PBC document understands it—had unburdened itself of the philosophical and cultural prejudices that permeated its methods. Now the method—the historical-critical method—careful not to admit "impurities", declares its neutrality and, on top of that, shows itself willing (or at least not especially hostile) to welcome a second level, a posteriori, of theological interpretation.

However, Bertuletti states, the old prejudice of autonomous rationality that is set up as a criterion of meaning continues to be present if "the abandonment of the identification of truth and method is not followed by a substantial revision of the method's concept of 'separation'. If this is maintained, it serves as a channel for the prejudice whose end has been decreed. The area of meaning that cannot be brought back to the method continues to be understood as 'external' to critical investigation."[86] This separate conception of the method, which is at the origin of the exegesis (scientific)-theology (dogmatic) dualism and which today is presented in a much more subtle manner, almost unnoticed, entails two serious, closely related consequences.

---

[84] A. Bertuletti, "Esegesi biblica e teologia sistematica", in Angelini, *Rivelazione attestata*, 134–39. The confirmation of that same dualism in the document serves, according to G. Borgonovo, to explain the difficulties that the notion of inspiration is experiencing today, the solution to which, in his opinion, is bound up with overcoming that dualism. Cf. G. Borgonovo, "Una proposta di rilettura dell'ispirazione biblica dopo gli apporti della Form- e della Redaktionsgeschichte", in *L'Interpretazione della Bibbia nella Chiesa: Atti del Simposio promosso dalla Congregazione per la Dottrina della Fede: Roma, settembre 1999*, ed. P. Grech, J. N. Aletti, M. Ouellet, and H. Simian-Yofre, Atti e Documenti 11 (Vatican City, 2001), 41–63.

[85] Cf. Bertuletti, "Esegesi biblica", 134.

[86] Ibid., 134.

On the one hand, the historical method, which is necessary to deal with the nature of the object, will continually be fueled by a series of hermeneutical choices, but now they will be much more unconscious than before, once the neutrality of the approach is proclaimed and the old prejudices are identified and injected.[87] Roberto Vignolo, commenting on the document being considered, observes that "in fact, the hermeneutical process begins as early as the very choice and even the devising of the method. . . . Hermeneutics does not arrive at the table of Scripture (or, in fact, of any text) as the dessert on a menu that has already previously been methodologically set."[88]

On the other hand, insistence on the neutrality of the method displaces faith to a later interpretive time, subsequent to the "technical" operations of approaching the text. This implies not only that, as we have seen, it will be other hermeneutical choices and not faith that make up the method, but that the interpretive activity entrusted to faith will always be conceived—and it cannot be otherwise—as an addition, as something optional.[89] The exegete will work in an objective or "scientific" manner on a methodologically accessible text, and only at a later time will he himself, or the theologian, be able to add a *spiritual* or *full* sense on the basis of faith. In the end, we are still looking at the same split between the critical level and the dogmatic level that we have already discovered in D. F. Strauss more than a century and a half ago.[90]

The PBC document, following the articulation of DV 12, affirms in its structure the two methodological dimensions that the study of Scripture requires. In fact, the first part, devoted to methods, is followed by two more, devoted to matters of hermeneutics and the dimensions of Catholic interpretation. In this sense, the document illus-

---

[87] Cf., in this sense, E. Nathan, "Truth and Prejudice: A Theological Reflection on Biblical Exegesis", *EThL* 83 (2007): 281–318.

[88] Vignolo, "Metodi, ermeneutica, statuto", 94.

[89] "The historical-critical approach, which makes use of the text to reconstruct the experience behind the text, does not avoid the illusion of an early datum that is supposed to be accessible regardless of the shape the text gives it. Precisely because it reduces the text to the history of its tradition, it does not recognize the relevance of the process of shaping the meaning the text indicates as a condition for access to theological truth. Thus it breaks the unity between theological truth and history, of which the originality of biblical faith consists" (Bertuletti, "Esegesi biblica", 146).

[90] Cf. introduction.

trates the current exegetical panorama very well: after accepting the limits of the exegesis of other eras, and their devastating consequences for theology, it ever more clearly recognizes the need to arrive at an interpretation of Scripture that is theological, based on faith. But the affirmation of both tasks, critical and theological study, does not hide the inability to bring them back to unity. And, obviously, this inability has its consequences in the results of exegesis.

Gabino Uríbarri, along the same lines as Bertuletti and on the basis of the PBC document, goes so far as to speak of a "schizophrenia" in current exegesis, which has its origin in the juxtaposition of methodology and hermeneutics that do not manage to join together correctly:

> The [Pontifical Biblical] Commission itself, in its presentation of such a broad and complete panorama, after discussion and study, also shows the real situation of exegesis, in which scientific method and theological hermeneutics are placed in a juxtaposed or paratactic manner instead of a conjoined or syntactic one. The confirmation of this, repeated time and again, proves that much work is still needed to be able to integrate what DV 12 asks of exegesis. The same juxtaposition of criteria in DV has been maintained in the usual practice of exegetical work. . . . If exegesis maintains a schizophrenia or, to put it more mildly, a juxtaposition between *methodology* and *hermeneutics*, as I suggest usually happens today, I very much doubt that the study of Scripture can really become the soul of theology, for this study is at grave risk of lacking a theological soul.[91]

In reality, the juxtaposition of methodology and hermeneutics, as Uríbarri rightly points out, is already found in the consecutive presentation of the two in DV 12b and DV 12c, without the conciliar document indicating how exactly to join them.[92] This is so much the case

---

[91] G. Uríbarri, "Para una nueva racionalidad de la exégesis: Diagnóstico y propuesta", *EstBib* 65 (2007): 283–84. Cf., in the same sense, G. Uríbarri, "Exégesis científica y teología dogmática: Materiales para un diálogo", *EstBib* 64 (2006): 547–78.

[92] Cardinal Ratzinger himself seems to imply this when he says that "while this situation is not the fault of the Second Vatican Council, the Council was also unable to prevent it. The Constitution on Divine Revelation attempted to hold the two sides of interpretation —historical 'explanation' and holistic 'understanding'—in a balanced relation. . . . Now, I am personally convinced that a careful reading of the *whole* text of *Dei Verbum* can identify the essential elements needed for a synthesis between the historical method and theological 'hermeneutics,' but the coherence between them does not simply lie ready to hand" (Ratzinger, "Biblical Interpretation in Conflict", 5–7). In this article, Ratzinger refers to the exposition that Gnilka gives on DV 12: "Die biblische Exegese".

that Norbert Lohfink speaks of a "terra incognita" or "unknown territory" in DV 12—one in which critical methodology and theological hermeneutics live together.[93] To arrive at the point of being able to join harmoniously the critical and theological dimensions of the single biblical interpretation is, without any doubt, the central problem of exegesis today.

To illustrate the presence of hermeneutical choices in the first stages of the historical method, I will now devote some attention to two areas of the critical study of the Old Testament: textual criticism and literary criticism. Specifically, I will concentrate on the question of the *original text* that textual criticism seeks to reconstruct and on the literary discussion about the *diachronic* or *synchronic* study of a book.

C. *Textual Criticism and the Search for the "Original" Text of the Old Testament*

Precisely because of the dynamic of divine condescension, alluded to in DV 13, by which the words of God are expressed in human tongues, an essential task of the exegete will be to know the languages in which those divine words have come down to us: Hebrew, Aramaic, and Greek. When we refer to divine words in the context of Scripture, we are referring to written words, words that need a medium (papyrus, parchment), a material (ink), and, above all, the activity of the copyists so that it can be transmitted and come down to us in full. But the copyists who for centuries have copied and transmitted the text have introduced changes in it, consciously or unconsciously (errors), as is demonstrated by the huge quantity of textual variants that each book of the Bible holds. Because of all this, the very first task of the exegete is textual criticism: on the basis of the ancient manuscripts that have come down to us (in an original language or in translation), to try to go back to the "original" text.

But textual criticism, before it starts to work on a particular book, needs to answer a basic question: Which text is to be reconstructed? What is the "original" text? This is a question that is not at all abstract. Let us take as an example the book of Jeremiah. What is the

[93] Cf. N. Lohfink, "Der weisse Fleck, in *Dei Verbum*, Artikel 12", *TThZ* 101 (1992): 20–35.

text we should reconstruct? The Hebrew text that is behind (*Vorlage*) the Greek of the *Septuagint* (LXX) and that is partially attested by Qumran manuscripts 4Q Jer[b] and 4Q Jer[d] or the proto-Masoretic text, that is, the Hebrew consonantal text from which the Masoretic manuscripts derive and that is also attested in Qumran (4Q Jer[c])? The two texts differ considerably. The Greek text of the LXX in Jeremiah is one sixth shorter than the Masoretic text (MT). It is missing not only words or short phrases here and there but paragraphs and whole sections. In addition, the Greek text has differences in the order of some sections or of entire chapters. The oracles against the nations are located in the middle of the book, while in the MT they are found at the end (and with a different order of oracles in relation to the LXX).

Almost all the authors agree that the Hebrew *Vorlage* of the LXX in Jeremiah is an earlier text than the one found in the MT. It would represent a "first edition" of the Hebrew text that began to be copied and transmitted and that, in time, was translated into Greek. The proto-Masoretic text, for its part, would represent a later stage, a "second edition" that involved major redactional labor on the previous text. What is the "original" text that should be reconstructed? Emmanuel Tov, a Jewish exegete and one of the great figures of textual criticism of the OT, is inclined to reconstruct the proto-Masoretic text. The reason he gives, though (and he does not hide it), is not of a "critical" nature: textual criticism seeks to reconstruct the most original state of "that literary composition which has been accepted as binding (authoritative) by Jewish tradition, since textual criticism is concerned with the literary compositions contained in the traditional Hebrew Bible".[94] It is plain that Tov puts his technical skill at the service of a hermeneutical choice, which has as its subject Jewish tradition, which canonizes not only a particular book, but a particular textual form of that book.

---

[94] This statement is found in the first edition of Tov's *Textual Criticism of the Hebrew Bible* ([Minneapolis, Assen, and Maastricht, 1992], 177) and disappears in the second edition, in which the Jewish scholar seeks to tone down the definition in view of the witness of a short Hebrew text of Jeremiah in Qumran. Even so, in this second edition as well he privileges the textual form of the Masoretic tradition because it is the one the Jewish community transmits: "That corpus [the Hebrew Scriptures] contains the Holy Writings of the Jewish people, and the decisions that were made within this religious community also determine to a great extent the approach of the scholarly world towards the text" (E. Tov, *Textual Criticism of the Hebrew Bible*, 2nd ed. [Minneapolis and Assen, 2001], 179).

This example illustrates very well the difficulty in defining, especially in some cases, the boundary between literary criticism and textual criticism. In Tov's view, the textual form attested by 4Q Jer[b] and 4Q Jer[d] and by the Greek text of the LXX would belong to the intermediate stages of the literary formation of the book of Jeremiah. Literary criticism would concern itself with this. It is obvious that the Greek-speaking Eastern Church would not think the same thing, since it has always read and venerated the text of the LXX. While the Latin Catholic Church reads the long text of Jeremiah in the liturgy, this is due to the hermeneutical choices that guided Saint Jerome in his translation of the Vulgate (on the basis of the *Hebraica Veritas* principle).

If we set aside the case of Jeremiah, which is so unique, we can ask ourselves about another book, that of Psalms, which has no great differences with regard to its length and content in its manuscripts and versions.[95] Even so, the textual variants in details are very abundant and problematic.

Since in the case of the Psalter we do not, strictly speaking, have another "edition" prior to the one attested by the MT (as in the case of the book of Jeremiah), we could think that the text that should be read—and even before that, reconstructed—is the proto-Masoretic one. Once again, this criterion for choosing the text, while apparently "aseptic" (based on a critical tendency favoring what is "original"), hides clear hermeneutical choices. Above all, it reflects the choice of the text that was "stabilized" and "canonized" by the Pharisees, the only current from the rich variety of Judaism in the first century A.D. that survived the destruction of the temple (A.D. 70) and the Bar Kokhba revolt (A.D. 135).[96] But in addition, this choice casts aside other possi-

---

[95] With the exception of Psalm 151, which appears only in the Greek version of the LXX and in Qumran Hebrew manuscript 11QPs[a]. This latter manuscript could be another exception, because it contains previously unknown compositions that are intercalated between the psalms, arranged in an order different from the usual one. However, it is not clear that this is an actual edition of the Psalter. Cf. J. A. Sanders, *The Psalms Scroll of Qumrân Cave 11*, DJD IV (Oxford, 1965); U. Dahmen, "Psalmentext und Psalmensammlung: Eine Auseinandersetzung mit P. W. Flint", in *Die Handschriftenfunde vom Toten Meer und der Text der Hebräischen Bibel*, ed. U. Dahmen, A. Lange, and H. Lichtenberg (Neukirchen-Vluyn, 2000); U. Dahmen, *Psalmen- und Psalter-Rezeption im Frühjudentum: Reconstruktion, Textbestand, Struktur und Pragmatik der Psalmenrolle 11QPs[a] aus Qumran*, STDJ 49 (Leiden and Boston, 2003).

[96] In the opinion of Childs, a Protestant, this text "stabilized" by the Jewish community of the late first century A.D. would be the "canonical" text that the textual critic should recon-

bilities that in fact were already present before A.D. 70 and that today continue to be offered to the freedom of the exegete. I will illustrate this with some examples.

Psalm 40 contains some differences between the MT and the LXX. The one that most interests me is found in verse 7. The Hebrew text says, "You do not want sacrifices or offerings, and instead *you have opened my ear*", while the Greek manuscript tradition attests this form: "You do not want sacrifices or offerings, and instead, *you have formed a body for me.*" From the point of view of textual criticism, it is not easy to tell which is the variant that has precedence in a hypothetical genealogical tree. To put it another way, it is hard to tell which is the original reading and which is the secondary one. Which form should we read? It would be very simplistic to turn to the *Hebraica Veritas* principle of Saint Jerome in order to privilege the reading of the MT, since the Greek translation of the LXX is a witness, in many cases, to a Hebrew text different from the MT. Let me present some new facts.

Psalm 40 plays a very important role in the theology of the letter to the Hebrews. When this NT writing presents the entrance of the Son into the world by means of the Incarnation, in dialogue with the Father, it turns to the Greek version of Psalm 40:7-9, which says, "You do not want sacrifices or offerings, and instead, *you have formed a body for me*. Burnt offerings and sacrifices for sin did not please you. Then I said, 'Behold I come—for of me it is written in the scroll of the book—to do, oh God, your will!'" (cf. Heb 10:5-7). This is not an isolated case in the NT. The Psalms are cited with great frequency, often forming the foundation of early Christian "theology". And in some cases, the textual form turned to is the Greek of the LXX, which differs from the current Hebrew of the MT.[97]

In this sense, the history of the two Psalters of the Vulgate, both

---

struct, holding the Masoretic text to be a privileged vehicle (see Childs, *Introduction to the Old Testament*, 97-106).

[97] *Pace* P. Grelot, who thinks that the Greek reading "body" did not exist in the manuscripts of the LXX before Christ. It would, rather, have been introduced in the great codices of the fourth century A.D. because of the influence of the reading of the letter to the Hebrews (Heb 10:5). However, the French exegete does not go beyond the mere hypothesis. In addition, he does not solve the problem but, rather, transfers it to the letter to the Hebrews: Why did its author modify the Psalm in such a radical way? Cf. P. Grelot, "Le texte du Psaume 39,7 dans la Septante", *RB* 108 (2001): 210-13.

translations of Saint Jerome, is very instructive. The first version of
the Psalms, known as the Gallican Psalter (or *iuxta LXX*), seems to be
rather a revision of the earlier Latin version, made from the Greek text
of the LXX. The second, known as the Psalter *iuxta Hebraeos*, would
be a new translation from an unvocalized Hebrew text very close to
the present MT. It is well known that in the Latin Vulgate version, the
books of the Hebrew Bible were translated directly from the Hebrew.
The rest (the so-called "deuterocanonical" ones) were translated from
the Greek. There is only one exception: the Psalms. Indeed, the Gallican Psalter, translated from the Greek of the LXX, eventually prevailed
in the Latin Church[98] and was the one that wound up dominant in
the manuscript tradition of the Vulgate, displacing the version done
from the Hebrew. What was the reason for this very notable exception? Without a doubt, the weight of this book in the liturgy, through
the daily prayer of the hours, and the weight that, in turn, this book
has in the New Testament (which often cites it in its Greek version)
must have influenced this choice that has its origin in the monasteries
of Ireland and then France.

It seems quite logical to think that those monks, who were familiar with the NT, should have preferred the Psalms translated from
the LXX, because of the weight they had in Christian theology. This
would have been the dynamic that led to the preference for the Gallican
Psalter above the *iuxta Hebraeos* in the codices of the Vulgate. And we
should not forget the role the Vulgate played in the delimitation of the
canon that the Council of Trent, in its polemic with Luther, decreed
in 1546. After listing the seventy-three sacred books, and to avoid any
ambiguity, it concluded: ". . . autem libros ipsos *integros cum omnibus
suis partibus*, prout in Ecclesia catholica legi consueverunt et *in veteri
vulgata latina editione habentur.*" In this way, in those books, recognized
both by Jews and by Catholic and Protestant Christians, where there
are textual differences that separate the different traditions, the Catholic
Church recognized as authoritative the choices made by the Vulgate.
It is clear that by the expression *integros cum omnibus suis partibus* Trent
had in mind the problem of the Greek additions to Daniel and Esther,
which it ratified as canonical. More debated may be the question of

---

[98] At least starting in the ninth century, with the liturgical reform of Alcuin of York (cf. B.
Fisher and R. Weber, eds., *Biblia Sacra iuxta Vulgatam Versionem*, 3rd ed. [Stuttgart, 1983], xxi).

whether Trent makes textual choices about the book of Jeremiah or the Psalter by following the Latin version of the Vulgate (the long— Hebrew—text of Jeremiah; the Greek text in the Psalms). But, *in fact*, today in the Latin Catholic liturgy, the long text of Jeremiah is read, and, with regard to the use of the Psalter, many translation choices come, through the Vulgate, from the Greek version. Here are some of them:

a. The numbering: In the current liturgy of the hours of the Latin rite, the Psalms continue to be numbered according to the Latin version of the Vulgate (Gallican Psalter), which in turn follows the Greek of the LXX.

b. In the current liturgical lectionaries, the divine name *Yahweh* is not used but, rather, *Lord* (*Dominus*), from the Greek *Kyrios*, which was the way the LXX translated this name.

c. In the current liturgical translation, in several cases the translation choices of the LXX are followed, by way of the Vulgate (Gallican Psalter), when the plural *'elohim*, "gods" appears. In Psalm 8 we read "you have made him little less than the *angels*" (following the interpretation of the LXX), while the Hebrew text says "you made him little less than the *gods*." The same thing happens in 97:7 (all his *angels* bow down before him) and 138:1 (before the *angels* I sing your praise).

What we learn from this episode of the Psalter is that hermeneutical choices are not made once the methodical or critical, supposedly "neutral", analysis is concluded; rather, they arise from the very beginning and, in fact, determine the method. In the case of Psalm 40, it is obvious that an event outside textual criticism, the event of Christ attested in the NT and recognized in experience as a key to the interpretation of Scripture (that is, of the OT), can become a criterion to fix the sacred text. Historical revelation is a process under construction until God pronounces his final word in Christ. In this sense, the NT embraces the OT as the Scripture that existed before and that *remains forever*, and, at the same time, delineates its outlines on the basis of its fulfillment. The revelation of Jesus Christ provides new intelligence about the historical process of the formation of all Scripture, including that providential moment which was the translation of the books of the OT into the lingua franca of the Mediterranean, Greek, a decisive factor for the expansion of the early Church.[99]

Thus, a hermeneutical choice, starting with a personal decision by the exegete, plays a part in the fixing of the sacred text, in this case Psalm 40. It is a hermeneutical choice to start from the proto-Masoretic text (which implies a decision in favor of Pharisaic Judaism of the first century A.D.), and it is a hermeneutical choice to start from the text of the LXX that the New Testament uses (which implies a decision in favor of the interpretation of the Christian community of the first century A.D.).

In reality, all that has been said so far about the textual dimension of Scripture could also be said about the canon of the sacred books. It is not a critical authority that provides us with the list of canonical books; rather, it is a believing community that delivers it to us.

D. Literary Criticism of the Old Testament: Diachrony and Synchrony

Attention to the historical dimension of Scripture has led, in the last two hundred years, to studying the biblical corpus from the literary point of view, as any literary work could be studied. As we previously saw, *Dei Verbum* has underlined the goodness of this intention on the basis of the nature of Scripture by encouraging the study of the condi-

---

[99] In the second half of the twentieth century, the discussion about the inspiration of the Greek version of the LXX was reopened, and in it some authors (especially French ones, and basically from the Dominican school) highlight the providential value of this version for theology and for the expansion of Christianity, which should lead to a reconsideration of the statute about this ancient translation. Cf. P. Benoit, "La Septante est-elle inspirée?", in *Vom Wort des Lebens: Festschrift für Max Meinertz*, ed. N. Adler (Münster, 1951), 41–49; P. Auvray, "Comment se pose le problème de l'inspiration des Septante", *RB* 59 (1952): 321–36; P. Benoit, "L'Inspiration des Septante d'après les Pères", in *L'Homme devant Dieu, mélanges offerts au Père Henri de Lubac*, vol. 1: *Exégèse et Patristique*, Théologie 56 (Paris, 1963), 169–87; P. Grelot, "Sur l'inspiration et la canonicité de la Septante", *ScEc* 16 (1964): 387–418; D. Barthélemy, "L'Ancien Testament a mûri à Alexandrie", *ThZ* 21 (1965): 358–70; D. Barthélemy, "La Place de la Septante dans l'Église", in *Aux grands carrefours de la révélation et de l'eségèse de l'Ancien Testament*, RechBib 8 (Paris, 1967), 13–28; A. Schenker, "L'Écriture sainte subsiste en plusieurs formes canoniques simultanées", in Grech et al., *Interpretazione della Bibbia*, 178–86.

tions of the time and culture of the author as well as the literary genres of his era in order to discover the intention of the sacred writer.

In the dominant trend of the historical-critical method, literary criticism has concentrated almost exclusively on a *diachronic* study of the sacred text, that is, an analysis of the historical processes of the production of the text that would make it possible to distinguish the smaller units that constitute it and the stages through which it passed until arriving at its final form. The first two chapters of this work have illustrated this sufficiently, both in the study of the sources of the Pentateuch and in the study of the prophets.

Now it is time to return to some questions that remained open in those chapters, especially in the parts devoted to recent developments. There I was able to describe the birth of a trend that, by criticizing some *defects* in the historical-critical method, demanded the *synchronic* study of the text. Clines, for the Pentateuch, and Childs, for the prophets, were presented as the clearest examples. Moreover, the discussion about the type of literary analysis to which the biblical text should be subjected will serve to illustrate the presence of hermeneutical choices at the very heart of the historical-critical method.

I will begin with attention to the *fact* of Scripture as part of the loyalty due to the dynamic of divine *condescension* that is manifested in the written witness to revelation. The composite nature of the biblical texts is a very important characteristic of them, which has been rightly highlighted in the history of critical exegesis. However, we have been able to confirm that in the literary analysis that distinguishes smaller units and sources, especially within the Pentateuch, criteria that were not merely literary but also ideological have been involved, criteria at the service of a certain view of the historical development of Israel, its theology, and its literature, outside of the text. In this way—and this is one of the most frequently recurring, and at the same time just, criticisms of the historical-critical method—the exegesis of the last two centuries has paid more attention to extremely hypothetical smaller units than to the text as we have received it. At this point, loyalty to the *fact* of Scripture ceases to be such. The last few decades have in fact shown that the model of the "documentary theory" was a corset that was too tight for the Pentateuch.

The same evolution of the literary criticism (not restricted to the Bible) that in the past forty years has gone from concentrating on historical explanation to privileging the study of the text as a synchronic entity, significant in and of itself,[100] has helped correct the unilateralness of the diachronic study of the biblical books. In fact, this same trend is the one that has favored the birth of the different variants of the synchronic approach to Scripture. If it is a matter of being loyal to Scripture, does it not correspond to the *fact* of Scripture to pay attention to the final form in which the text reaches us, the only form that has been transmitted and read for more than two millennia?

In welcoming this just contribution of the synchronic approach, the document *The Interpretation of the Bible in the Church*, when assessing the historical-critical method, says, "With respect to the inclusion in the method of a synchronic analysis of texts, we must recognize that we are dealing here with a legitimate operation, for it is the text in its final stage, rather than in its earlier editions, which is the expression of the Word of God."[101] With this comment, the PBC gives an invitation for the integration of the synchronic reading into the historical-critical method, as "the indispensable method for the scientific study of the meaning of ancient texts".[102] But by so doing, it implicitly recognizes the presence of a criterion that is not "scientific" (in the strictest sense), or even literary, but theological in the historical method itself: it is the final form that is an expression of the Word of God and not an intermediate or reconstructed stage. By virtue of inspiration, we call the text as it has been delivered to us "the Word of God".

This call for the integration of the diachronic and synchronic approaches in the historical-critical method is, however, far from being realized in exegetical practice. In fact, in the most usual versions of this

---

[100] To be fair, it would be necessary to go back to *Cours de linguistique générale* by F. de Saussure, published in 1916, which is what introduced the concern with synchrony into the field of linguistics. Also decisive in this direction are the contributions of Gadamer (see H. G. Gadamer, *Truth and method*, trans. J.Weinsheimer and D. G. Marshall, 2nd rev. ed. [New York, 2004]), and Ricoeur (see P. Ricoeur, "Ermeneutica filosofica ed ermeneutica biblica", in *Exegesis: Problèmes de méthode et exercises de lecture*, ed. F. Bovon and G. Rouiller [Neuchâtel, 1975]; "The Canon between the Text and the Community", in *Philosophical Hermeneutics and Biblical Exegesis*, ed. P. Pokorný and J. Roskovec, WUNT 153 [Tübingen, 2002], 7–26). In the biblical field, this movement is well represented by works such as R. Alter, *The Art of Biblical Narrative* (London, 1981), and F. Kermode, "The Argument about Canons", in *An Appetite for Poetry: Essays in Literary Interpretation*, ed. F. Kermode (London, 1989), 189–207.

[101] PBC, *The Interpretation of the Bible in the Church* I A 4.

[102] Ibid., I A.

method, the synchronic reading is conceived as a *later* step in which a theological criterion now plays a part but which is preceded by an "objective" or "scientific" study of the essence, which can (and should) exclude all believing hermeneutics. The PBC's own document, in spite of the note on which I am commenting, favors, as we have already seen, an understanding of this kind.

Even so, the document cited is lucid when, after welcoming synchronic reading, it warns of the danger of an "exclusive" utilization of it that passes over the history of the text:

> But diachronic study remains indispensable for making known the historical dynamism which animates sacred Scripture and for shedding light upon its rich complexity. . . . We must take care not to replace the historicizing tendency, for which the older historical-critical exegesis is open to criticism, with the opposite excess, that of neglecting history in favor of an exegesis which would be exclusively synchronic.[103]

Thus the two Gordian knots of tension between the diachronic and synchronic readings of Scripture are now placed before us. On the one hand, that of the value of the final text as the only normative and authoritative text (in contrast to hypothetical intermediate stages) and, on the other, that of the need not to censor history, including both the history of the formation of the text and the history to which the text attests (in contrast to a "fundamentalist" reading or a reading that reduces the Bible to literature without a historical referent).

To illustrate both matters, I will concentrate on a debate that stretched over a long period of time and that was quite fruitful for exegesis: the polemic between Childs (1924–2007) and James Barr (1924–2006) about the canonical method and the matter of synchronic and diachronic reading.[104] The debate originated in the late seventies when Childs started to become known for the application of the canonical method, especially with the publication of his work *Introduction to the Old Testament as Scripture* (1979).[105] Since then, and on several occasions,

---

[103] Ibid., I A 4.

[104] Ska alludes to a similar debate that Norbert Lohfink and Eckart Otto are holding at present, centered on the possibility (or lack thereof) of a synchronic reading of the Pentateuch (see Ska, "Old and New Perspectives", 250, n. 18).

[105] The works in which Childs expounds the basic principles of the canonical method have already been cited (cf. n. 86 in chapter 2). For our purpose it is interesting to add the responses

Barr has shown himself to be in disagreement with the overall lines of the method, and he has made this clear in a variety of publications.[106]

One of the central emphases of the new method backed by Childs is the claim that each of the sacred books should be read in the context of the whole literary corpus to which it belongs, that is, in the context of the canon, this latter understood as a list of books that are normative for the Church. This emphasis has had the virtue of recovering (or at least putting in the center of the discussion), for the heart of "scientific" exegesis, the principle of the *unity of Scripture* enunciated by DV 12c, a theological (though also literary) principle that was somewhat eclipsed in the decades that followed the Second Vatican Council by the historical study of the texts suggested by DV 12a–b. This principle reads as follows:

> But, since Holy Scripture must be read and interpreted in the sacred spirit in which it was written, *no less serious attention must be given to the content and unity of the whole of Scripture* if the meaning of the sacred texts is to be correctly worked out. The living tradition of the whole Church must be taken into account along with the harmony which exists between elements of the faith. (DV 12c)

As we have already had occasion to see in the second chapter, Childs' insistence on a reading within the canon is not only literary but also theological, and in this sense he likewise welcomes the principles of interpretation, gathered in DV 12c, that are within *tradition* and on the basis of the *analogy of faith*, that is, *the harmony that exists between elements of the faith*.[107] It is a particular believing community that has closed the

---

that Childs has given to the criticisms he has received from Barr: B. S. Childs, "Response to Reviewers", *JSOT* 16 (1980): 52–60; "A Response", *HBT* 2 (1980): 199–211; "Childs Versus Barr: Review of Barr, *Holy Scripture*", *Interp* 38 (1984): 66–70; "Critical Reflections on James Barr's Understanding of the Literal and the Allegorical", *JSOT* 46 (1990): 3–9.

[106] J. Barr, "Review Article of B. S. Childs, *Introduction to the Old Testament as Scripture*", *JSOT* 16 (1980): 12–23; *Holy Scripture* (especially chapter 4); "The Synchronic, the Diachronic and the Historical: A Triangular Relationship?" in *Synchronic or Diachronic? A Debate on Method in Old Testament Exegesis*, ed. J. C. de Moor, OTS 34 (Leiden, New York, and Cologne, 1995); *The Concept of Biblical Theology* (especially chapters 23 and 24). The journals *Journal for the Study of the Old Testament* and *Horizons in Biblical Theology* in 1980 each devoted monographic issues to discussing Childs' work *Introduction to the Old Testament as Scripture* (*JSOT* 16 [1980]; *HBT* 2 [1980]).

[107] Cf. especially the last chapter of his work: B. S. Childs, *Biblical Theology of the Old and New Testaments: Theological Reflection on the Christian Bible* (London, 1992), 719–26.

books and fixed the canon and that delivers the Scripture in a particular interpretive context.

But the notion of "canon", for Childs, is not limited to the idea of a list of normative books. Indeed, Childs calls the final form of a particular biblical book the "canonical form". Only that final form is canonical, because "it alone bears witness to the full history of revelation. . . . It is only in the final form of the biblical text in which the normative history has reached an end that the full effect of this revelatory history can be perceived."[108] Obviously, this insistence on the final form is a call to a synchronic reading of the biblical text made, on the one hand, in a polemical context in which the diachronic study of each book, in the framework of the historical-critical method, is considered the only one capable of adequately understanding the essence of Scripture. It is here where the discussion of interest to us comes in, in which such decisive matters are at stake as the value of the final form of a book and the value of the history that is found behind that book (both the history of its redaction and the history to which it makes reference).

Barr criticizes this second notion of canon because he considers that when "canon" is used to establish a certain type of exegesis based on the final form, this is not "a public, objective or legislative fact: it is only an opinion, a proposal, a method which might be good or not so good."[109] In fact, "a biblical book might be read as it stands, without consideration of previous sources or of the circumstances of origin, perhaps even without consideration even of the intention of the author. Such a reading is certainly conceivable and indeed possible, and I would not be against it in principle. There remains the question whether such a type of interpretation could be *theologically* binding and authoritative."[110] In his opinion, this type of reading would not be very theological, since it completely ignores the historical process that is behind the text and is responsible for it. This is because "Theology as a mode of understanding comes into existence only when one moves

---

[108] B. S. Childs, "The Canonical Shape of the Prophetic Literature", *Interp* 32 (1978): 47–48.

[109] J. Barr, *The Concept of Biblical Theology: An Old Testament Perspective* (Minneapolis, 1999), 394.

[110] J. Barr, *Holy Scripture: Canon, Authority, Criticism* (Oxford, 1983), 101.

out of the plane of the text itself and begins to ask about the extrinsic realities to which the text refers."[111]

The question Barr poses really is decisive, and even more so in the area of Judeo-Christian revelation: the question of history. He accuses Childs of being interested, not in history as such, but in a late interpretation of it, which would be the final text. In Barr's view, the nature of the history of salvation requires that one pose the question of the "original": the *original event* that forms the basis for an account, the *original text* that is hidden in the folds of the final text, the successive *stages* that are *at the origin* of the final formulation of a law, or the different religious or theological *conceptions* that are *at the origin* of a final, presumably consistent, image of God.

In Barr's opinion, the canonical method has replaced the word "original", and the search connected with it, with its opposite, "final".[112] And this is wrong, not because what is early and original must be what is authentic and normative, but because what is early was, in its day, the text, and it was, therefore, canonical. Speaking of the freedom that the exegete or preacher must have when he is working, not on the final form, but on a prior stage of the text, he says:

> He is free to expound the creation story of Genesis 1 without tying it by links of meaning to the quite different story of chapter 2; he is free to expound the pericopes that represent Amos's original message without being forced to integrate them with the quite different message of the book's conclusion. . . . This is not because what is early and original is authentic and therefore authoritative. What is earlier *was* the text at one time, it was thus 'canonical', if we must call it so, in the biblical period itself. The portion which represents the 'earlier' text is still a legitimate and meaningful pericope of holy scripture. What the Yahwist meant in Gen. 2 is a valid and proper meaning of scripture, and so is what P meant in Gen. 1. . . .
>
> Thus, the earlier text is not, because it is earlier, automatically superior to the later; but the later, just because it was final, is certainly not superior to the earlier.[113]

---

[111] Ibid., 102.
[112] Cf. ibid., 77–78.
[113] Ibid., 92–93.

In Barr's opinion, by privileging the final form of the text, we are setting up the late community that canonized the text,[114] a community that in many respects was "deteriorating" (it is the one that, with Ezra and Nehemiah, laid the foundations of Judaism that reinterpreted all previous history), as an arbiter of Scripture.[115]

Do the canonical method, and Childs at its head, really scorn the history behind the text? That is not what Childs himself argues for. In his view, the Church has always insisted on "relating the text to the reality to which the text pointed", because, in fact, the text does not have an "authority separated from the reality of which it speaks".[116] He even uses the category of witness, in the manner in which I have been employing it in this work, to describe the nature of Scripture: "The role of the Bible is not being understood simply as a cultural expression of ancient peoples, but as a testimony pointing beyond itself to a divine reality to which it bears witness."[117]

A clear proof that Childs does not approach the text while setting aside its historical reference is the criticism that he has, in recent years, directed against the new methods of literary analysis applied to the Bible (narrative, rhetorical, and semiotic analysis). While in the seventies the birth of these methods, centered on the final form of the text, was presented as a dike against the dominant diachronic study that sought to reconstruct history, time has shown that the new methods were potentially as destructive as the trend they were seeking to correct:

---

[114] "Prime theological authority is thus given to the generations of the redactors and canonizers" (Barr, "Review Article of B. S. Childs, *Introduction*", 16).

[115] Cf. Barr, *Holy Scripture*, 93–94. Barr has a striking note where he tries to tone down his own statement that Scripture was fixed, that it had reached an end point, because the tradition was deteriorating: "In the case of the Old Testament one must guard oneself against the notion that Judaism as such represents a deterioration vis-à-vis the Old Testament; but the proper avoidance of this danger should not lead us into closing our eyes to the possible presence of deterioration, as measured by the standards of the major central strata" (Barr, *Holy Scripture*, 94, n. 13).

[116] B. S. Childs, *Biblical Theology in Crisis* (Philadelphia, 1970), 103.

[117] Childs, *Biblical Theology of the Old and New*, 9. Cf. the criticism that Barr makes against the category of witness as it is utilized by Childs: "The use of the text 'as witness' is really a dogmatic argument rather than one that belongs to biblical studies" (J. Barr, "The Synchronic, the Diachronic and the Historical", 14).

The threat lies in divorcing the Bible when seen as literature from its theological reality to which scripture bears witness. When the focus of the analysis lies in the 'imaginative construal' of the reader, the text is robbed of all determinative meaning within various theories of reader response. The effect is to render the biblical text mute for theology and to deconstruct its tradition in a way equally destructive as the nineteenth-century historicists.[118]

It is thus plain that Childs does not represent a type of approach to the Bible that takes it as just any literary work without a historical referent on which it depends. But Childs does not understand history as a process in which all moments and all expressions have the same value. Not all the moments or all the religious expressions of the history of Israel have the same normative value for us. And it is precisely here where the canon plays a basic role as a final (and authoritative) criterion for judgment:

But to take canon seriously is also to take seriously the critical function which it exercises in respect to the earlier stages of the literature's formation. . . . To work with the final stage of the text is not to lose the historical dimension, but rather it is to provide a critical theological judgment regarding the process.[119]

Only the final form of a book can be said to be canonical, in the sense that the full image that it transmits is normative for our faith. And that final form exercises a particular judgment about all the stages of the historical process that has Israel as its main figure. In fact, it emphasizes certain elements and diminishes the importance of others. Certainly, the biblical text reflects a history of encounter between God and his people. The canon serves "to describe this unique relationship and to define the scope of this history by establishing an end to the process. It assigns a special quality to this particular segment of history which is deemed normative for all future generations of this community of

---

[118] Childs, *Biblical Theology of the Old and New*, 723. Cf. also ibid., 205–6. In this, Childs would be in agreement with Barr, who makes this comment about the new synchronic methods: "I myself heard one of the leading practitioners of literary reading say that one of the advantages of his approach was that no clergyman or rabbi would ever raise any objection to it, since it made no connection, whether favourable or unfavourable, with religious concerns" (Barr, "The Synchronic, the Diachronic and the Historical", 11).

[119] Childs, "Canonical Shape", 48.

faith."[120] In reality, only that form has the complete (and therefore true) image of the history of revelation. It is evident that, in the history of revelation, the historical segment that covers the years of the life of Christ and the first ones of the Church has a decisive role. The event of Christ and the written witness linked to it, the NT, in fact become the authoritative interpreters of the whole history of Israel and its written witness, the OT.

Barr, on the contrary, seems to work backward, seeking a history that is difficult if not impossible to reconstruct, a history that is sought outside of the (normative) interpretation of that history which the final text offers us. In many cases this history is not only sought "outside of" the witness that the final form of it gives us, but it is sought in "dialectic with" this witness, conceiving the history of the redaction as a process governed by the struggle between different conceptions of God, of Israel, of the Law, of history, and of its main actors. Without any need to resort to the most extreme form of this historical search, the approach through the social sciences, we have seen how a good part of the studies that seek to reconstruct the "ideological" history of Israel (and the literary forms linked to it) project onto the biblical corpus a scheme that is indebted to modern categories—a scheme against which the text rebels.

Moreover, responding to Barr's criticisms, Childs points out that when he insists that the received text should be the object of the interpretation, he does not mean that the interpreter has to consider the final form an immovable stone. In fact, that final form should function as the starting point of exegesis, but the exegete "still has the responsibility of seeking to discern the kerygmatic shaping of the text as the vehicle for its witness within the whole composition".[121] The growth process of a text, with its different kerygmatic contributions, should be appreciated and judged on the basis of the final form.[122]

If this final image is privileged, it is for no other reason than because it is received as canonical, as the Word of God. On the contrary, if new criteria are sought to reorganize the material in a different manner, we can discuss the new image or images that result, but what is evident

---

[120] Ibid., 47.

[121] Childs, "Childs Versus Barr: Review of Barr, *Holy Scripture*", 68.

[122] Cf. the function Childs assigns to the diachronic study of a text in Childs, *Biblical Theology of the Old and New*, 216–17.

is that those images will never be normative for any believing community. In fact, "The usual critical methodology of restoring an original historical setting often involves stripping away the very elements which constitute the canonical shape. Little wonder that once the text has been anchored in the historical past by 'decanonizing' it, the interpreter has difficulty applying it to a modern religious context!"[123]

How is it possible to bring back to unity the tension, which this discussion makes it possible to glimpse, between the final form of the text and the history that underlies it? Once again, it is clear that we face a hermeneutical problem that goes beyond the "technical" abilities of the exegete to penetrate in his interpretive choices. I will return to some of the questions I tackled at the beginning of this chapter, which can help us clarify the problem.

I described Scripture as the *written and inspired witness to revelation*. From an understanding like this one is derived the absolute dependence ("referentiality")[124] of Scripture in relation to the event of divine self-giving that is realized in history. The very structure of *Dei Verbum* shows this clearly by situating Scripture, not in the first chapter, devoted to the *nature* of revelation, but in the second, devoted to its *transmission*. This said, it is necessary to remember that revelation, which happened in history, has wanted to transmit itself through, among other channels, a written (and thus fixed) and inspired (and thus truthful) witness that in fact interprets in an authoritative (and canonical) way the historical contingency that is the *form* of revelation.

The events through which revelation takes place in history are not *neutral* events.[125] When they happened, they were events that were offered for interpretation by men who received—or failed to receive—revelation. The appropriate way to receive revelation is the one that revelation supports: with faith, which forms part of the very nature of

---

[123] Childs, "Canonical Shape", 49.

[124] *Referentiality* is a technical term introduced by Barr himself into the exegetical discussion (cf. Barr, *Concept of Biblical Theology*, 416).

[125] This is the area of the debate, which began in the nineteenth century, about the distinction between *Historie* and *Geschichte*, which aims to disconnect actual historical events, the object of scientific study, from their interpretation. Cf. M. Kähler, *Die sogenannte historische Jesus und der geschichtliche biblische Christus* (Leipzig, 1892); G. Wobbermin, *Geschichte und Historie: Über die Notwendigkeit in der Religionswissenschaft zwischen Geschichte und Historie strenger zu unterscheiden, als gewöhnlich geschieht* (Tübingen, 1911).

revelation.[126] Since then, the historical event of revelation has come down to us as an *interpreted event*, in the forms of tradition and of Scripture. The form of knowledge that is faith witnesses to us about the events and words in which revelation is offered to men, and that witness reaches into the meaning of those same events and words.

In this sense, the only written, authoritative witness is the one we find in the books of the Bible, which have come down to us in a particular form that is already closed, considered inspired, and, therefore, canonical.[127] The image those books transmit, the only normative one, is *necessarily* linked, as a result of literary consistency, to the final form of each book. It is about a particular book, which comes down to us with a particular literary structure (content, order, arrangement of pericopes, connections between them, introduction and conclusion, and so on), that it is said: It is the Word of God. But in this case, *final form* and *history* are intrinsically linked by the inspired character of biblical witness: the image (or account) offered of the only history in which revelation is expressed is true.[128]

As we can see, the problem of inspiration and its relation to the different strata of the book and its final form arises in this context. In most of the books of the OT, it is evident that the process of redaction has been long and that more than one author / redactor / sacred writer

---

[126] " 'The obedience of faith' (Rom. 13:26; see 1:5; 2 Cor. 10:5–6) 'is to be given to God who reveals, an obedience by which man commits his whole self freely to God, offering the full submission of intellect and will to God who reveals,' and freely assenting to the truth revealed by Him. To make this act of faith, the grace of God and the interior help of the Holy Spirit must precede and assist, moving the heart and turning it to God, opening the eyes of the mind and giving 'joy and ease to everyone in assenting to the truth and believing it.' To bring about an ever deeper understanding of revelation the same Holy Spirit constantly brings faith to completion by His gifts" (*Dei Verbum* 5).

[127] "The canonical approach rightly reacts against placing an exaggerated value upon what is supposed to be original and early, as if this alone were authentic. Inspired Scripture is precisely Scripture in that it has been recognized by the Church as the rule of faith. Hence the significance, in this light, of both the final form in which each of the books of the Bible appears and of the complete whole which all together make up as canon. Each individual book only becomes biblical in the light of the canon as a whole" (PBC, *The Interpretation of the Bible in the Church* I C 1).

[128] "Therefore, since everything asserted by the inspired authors or sacred writers must be held to be asserted by the Holy Spirit, it follows that the books of Scripture must be acknowledged as teaching solidly, faithfully and without error that truth which God wanted put into sacred writings for the sake of salvation" (*Dei Verbum* 11).

has participated in the process. From the point of view of the theory of inspiration, is only the final redactor of the book inspired? The problem is that in many cases that final redactor is not responsible for more than a miniscule part of the book: sometimes he has done no more than put some texts in order, link them together with some redactional fine-tuning, add a beginning, and close with an ending. If the inspiration came only upon the one who wrote the last word, we would be leaving out of it a large part of the text (as well as its authors), which would come to be inspired because of the final action of the redactor. This position would come dangerously close to what the First Vatican Council condemned when it censured the reduction of inspiration to a kind of final *imprimatur* of the authority of the Church (under the influence of the Holy Spirit), which in the present case would be linked to the activity of the final redactor (as it were, an "ecclesiastical censor"):

> These [books of the OT and NT] the Church holds to be sacred and canonical, not because, having been carefully composed by mere human industry, they were afterward approved by her authority or merely because they contain revelation with no admixture of error, but because, having been written by the inspiration of the Holy Spirit, they have God for their author and have been delivered as such to the Church herself.[129]

Precisely because the sacred books were "written by the inspiration of the Holy Spirit", it seems logical to extend inspiration to each and every one of the authors who have participated in the formation of a book. The content of the different parts, sources, or documents that come together in a book should be in some way under the action of inspiration, if we do not want to reduce it to a mere "consequent inspiration", which would make a written work "composed by mere human industry"[130] become divine by a subsequent approval carried out as a result of the action of the Holy Spirit. In this way, divine *authorship* would be emptied of content. So, how should this inspiration be understood?

---

[129] Dogmatic Constitution *Dei Filius* (H 3006).

[130] This is the formulation of D. B. Haneberg, which appears to be the target of the condemnation by Vatican I: "It is possible that some Scripture was first put together by human industry alone and that, only because of having been brought into the canon, has been elevated to be the Word of God and, also because of this, has been made inspired (*inspiratio subsequens*)" (see D. B. Haneberg, *Versuch einer Geschichte der biblischen Offenbarung* [Regensburg, 1850]).

Norbert Lohfink turned his attention to this problem some time ago now, and his solution seems appropriate to me, because he assesses all the issues at stake in a very balanced way:

> If a book has been composed little by little, it is necessary to speak of many inspired authors. The inspiration of those individuals would not be applicable as early as their immediate work, in itself, but would characterize it as soon as it was ordained by God, in its tenor and meaning, for the definitive biblical book. . . . The inspiration of the many who have collaborated in a biblical writing would have to be considered as a unique whole, and, consequently, it would produce its effect of inerrancy a single time, at the moment of the final result of this collaboration.[131]

By accepting the inspired character of the different authors, and thus that of the content they produce, Lohfink subordinates the inspiring activity to the final form of the text, the canonical form, the only *form* of it that can properly be said to be inspired. In this way he argues for the divine authorship of the whole book, extending inspiration to all its stages, but, at the same time, he warns against the temptation to consider prior *forms* or *strata* of the book inspired, ones that are no longer within our grasp (the tradition or redaction of the book has not wanted to preserve them) and that literary criticism could (at least hypothetically) try to recover. History has shown us with sufficient clarity that in many cases, the "previous forms" recovered by literary criticism never existed and that the criteria to arrive at them were frequently incorrect (and not very literary). Fortunately, the Church never fell into the temptation to canonize or declare inspired the J, E, P, and D "documents" of the hypothesis backed by Wellhausen, nor does she do so now with the hypothetical Q document of the Gospels.[132]

By associating all the activity of inspiration with the definitive biblical book, Lohfink, assessing all the stages, recognizes the decisive and definitive role of that final stage which shapes all the material, a stage that, in fact, highlights certain elements and diminishes the importance of others, guiding it all in a certain direction, the one that comes to

---

[131] N. Lohfink, "Il problema dell'inerranzia", in *La verità della Bibbia nel dibattito attuale*, ed. V.A., (Brescia, 1968), 31.

[132] A "critical edition" of this "Q document" has even been published: J. M. Robinson, P. Hoffmann, and J. S. Kloppenborg, *The Critical Edition of Q: Synopsis Including the Gospels of Matthew and Luke, Mark and Thomas* (Louvain, 2000).

light in the synchronic reading of the final form. The big question, therefore, comes back to the acceptance or non-acceptance of a segment of history with sufficient authority to give a definitive shape to the books of the Bible and even to reinterpret those same books or the material received in a certain direction. The community that declares those books normative (whether Judaism or the Christianity of the first to second centuries A.D.), which is living in another segment of history that turns out to be decisive, is canonizing a certain image of revelation, the one contained in the final form of each book and of the whole biblical corpus.

The pull toward history contained in the very nature of Scripture has, in addition, another center of attraction in the present itself, as we have already seen at the beginning of this chapter. Indeed, the event of the self-giving of God in history is prolonged in time and space and reaches us today by means of a very particular historical form that is the Church. In fact, Childs has always linked the normative value of the canon to the authority of an ecclesiastical community in which this canon has its origin, a community that, in turn, continues advancing it today. To the accusation that Barr addresses to him, that insistence on the canon is a case of begging the question and that it indicates nothing that should be the primary factor for the interpretation of the Bible or that ought to be preferred to other criteria,[133] Childs responds:

> In my judgement, the acceptance of the canon as normative does not function initially as a derivative of reasoned argument. The canon is the deposit of the religious community's sacred tradition which one receives as a member of that body. The acknowledgment of a normative rule functions confessionally as a testimony to one's beliefs. Earlier attempts to ascribe to the Hebrew canon special qualities of excellence, as if it had the best text, or reflected a superior form of literature, or possessed a unique claim to historicity, seem to have been misplaced.[134]

---

[133] "Now what are the reasons why we should accept Childs' idea of the canon? Suppose we begin with a different opinion. Suppose we say that the canon, though significant, is not extremely important, that it is a third- or fourth-rank concept in the scheme of biblical theology; that it belongs to a world later than the biblical situation and that the actual biblical period, rather than the later world of the canonization, should be our interpretative basis . . . —suppose we begin with these conceptions, what reason does Childs offer us why we should abandon them and adopt his in exchange?" (Barr, "Review Article of B. S. Childs, *Introduction*", 14).

[134] B. S. Childs, "Response to Reviewers", 56. In fact, this is one of the main differences

As Childs very well recognizes, what is really at stake is "the classic theological problem of the proper relation of faith to reason". And Childs opts for a harmonious relationship when he states that, although the "testimony of faith and not reason establishes the canon", "there is an internal logic of faith within the framework of the confession."[135]

The reference to history, therefore, is pulled in two directions: toward the canon and toward the Church, which is the contemporary historical form that carries on through time the event of Christ, the true interpreter of Scripture. The content and unity of the whole of Scripture, the living tradition of the whole Church, and the harmony that exists between elements of the faith, the three criteria for the reading of the Bible enumerated in DV 12c, are contained here. Without this double tension, the nexus with history becomes vague, and even more so the farther away we get from the original events. And the search for history, disconnected from the two points of tension described, far from being "independent" or "neutral", remains connected, as we have seen, to images that are projected from the present.

In the context of all that has been said, we can now answer Clines' question that we left hanging at the end of the first chapter. This author, arguing for the synchronic reading, considered whether it served any purpose to have a theory about the origins of the Pentateuch. Now that we have understood how it is possible to integrate the value of history with the value of the final text, we can respond decisively that *it is useful* to have a theory about the origins of the Pentateuch, on the condition that it is a *good* theory, which, as we have seen, is none too

---

between Childs and Barr when considering the interpretive value of the canon. From Childs' position is derived the concept that outside its immanence in the life of a faith community (which brings with it the acceptance of a critical authority outside of oneself, a hermeneutical principle beyond one's own opinion), it is difficult to argue for the interpretive value of the canon beyond its literary value (books that come down to us together, in the same binding). In fact, Barr accepts (or considers inevitable) a datum extrinsic to the text that would have a hermeneutical valence, a "clearly worked-out theological system", like the one that Augustine or Calvin used to interpret Scripture. The problem is that, in Barr's view, those external entities would be subject to criticism and change over time. In fact, the biblical investigation of the last two centuries can be said to have introduced new critical authorities of a historical type. These external critical authorities, far from confirming the authority of the canon and the final form of each book, have brought to light the contradictions that the redactors and canonizers let slip in, thus inviting an alternative reading (cf. Barr, "Review Article of B. S. Childs, *Introduction*", 16–18).

[135] Childs, "Response to Reviewers", 56.

easy. Diachrony and synchrony should not be conceived of as alternate or opposite approaches. The very nature of Scripture requires both readings.

The critical function that the final form exercises with regard to the early stages of literary formation (in Childs' words) helps to situate both approaches correctly. In fact, a serious study of the process of redaction of a book can help clarify the normative theological judgment that the final form exercises on the intermediate steps. A clear example may be that of the first three chapters of Genesis. The literary study of these chapters not only helps us identify two different accounts, but it makes it possible for us, on the basis of comparative literature, to find Israel choosing certain narrative molds in its cultural setting (creation by word and by work), and not others (creation by war or by sexual contact), to express its convictions and articulating both narratives based on some essential theological demands: a single good creative principle, not two in tension (good and evil), the goodness of the creation (as opposed to the conception of matter as something negative), the creation of man and woman in the image of God, the mystery of the man-woman correspondence, the origin of evil linked to human freedom, and so on.

The silent revolution that Clines foresaw (a gradual transfer of the interest of exegetes toward other matters unrelated to the origins of the Pentateuch) could take place in the not too distant future. But it would not be welcome if it led one to forget about the historical dimension of Scripture. As Childs rightly observed when he saw the evolution of some methods of literary analysis that are based on the synchronic reading, an approach that sets aside the reference of the text to an objective reality can be as destructive as that of the historicism of the twentieth century.

Finally, the polemic between Childs and Barr has helped us to understand better in what sense the final form, understood as the canonical form, does not set aside history, which is so decisive for Christianity. History is always interpreted history, which comes down to us by way of a witness. Scripture and tradition, correctly connected in the terms used in DV 9,[136] authoritatively interpret (informing part of

---

[136] "Hence there exists a close connection and communication between sacred tradition and Sacred Scripture. For both of them, flowing from the same divine wellspring, in a certain way

the same movement of the Holy Spirit) the historical contingency in which divine revelation is produced. In this sense, it is worth noting that historicism and fundamentalism agree on the same exaltation of the origin at the expense of the text. Historicism denies the critical and interpretive function that the final form of the text exercises on all the original history, and it sets off on the adventure of recovering it outside of this text[137] (as we have seen, not only outside of it, but sometimes also in polemic with it). Fundamentalism, for its part, under the guise of respect for the received book, violates the literary and testimonial nature of the writing by claiming, through a *literal* reading, that the text and the original history coincide, as if the text were a kind of direct record of what happened.[138] In reality, in both cases, both history and text are lost.

---

merge into a unity and tend toward the same end. For Sacred Scripture is the word of God inasmuch as it is consigned to writing under the inspiration of the divine Spirit, while sacred tradition takes the word of God entrusted by Christ the Lord and the Holy Spirit to the Apostles and hands it on to their successors in its full purity, so that led by the light of the Spirit of truth, they may in proclaiming it preserve this word of God faithfully, explain it, and make it more widely known. Consequently it is not from Sacred Scripture alone that the Church draws her certainty about everything which has been revealed. Therefore both sacred tradition and Sacred Scripture are to be accepted and venerated with the same sense of loyalty and reverence" (*Dei Verbum* 9).

[137] "Historicism tends to accept as reality 'historical' phenomena (in the critical sense of the word), or if not explicitly as reality or as the substitute for reality itself, at least as the measure of what can be scientifically known. Any other source will be considered 'extra-historical' (in the full realist sense of the word); no account need be taken of such things, since one can never hope to know about real history except through these channels" (M. Blondel, *History and Dogma*, in *The Letter on Apologetics and History and Dogma* [Grand Rapids, 1995], 228.)

[138] "[Fundamentalism] refuses to admit that the inspired Word of God has been expressed in human language and that this Word has been expressed, under divine inspiration, by human authors possessed of limited capacities and resources. For this reason, it tends to treat the biblical text as if it had been dictated word for word by the Spirit. It fails to recognize that the Word of God has been formulated in language and expression conditioned by various periods. It pays no attention to the literary forms and to the human ways of thinking to be found in the biblical texts, many of which are the result of a process extending over long periods of time and bearing the mark of very diverse historical situations. Fundamentalism also places undue stress upon the inerrancy of certain details in the biblical texts, especially in what concerns historical events or supposedly scientific truth. It often historicizes material which from the start never claimed to be historical. It considers historical everything that is reported or recounted with verbs in the past tense, failing to take the necessary account of the possibility of symbolic or figurative meaning" (PBC, *The Interpretation of the Bible in the Church* I. F).

IV. The Reading of the Old Testament
from the Perspective of the New

As the final point of this chapter, I will deal with a matter that could well be considered a *testing ground* of biblical interpretation: the relationship between the Old and New Testaments. In their ways of dealing with this matter (how to articulate this relationship), the basic presuppositions that govern every method of exegesis are brought to bear, especially the problem of whether a historical event can be the criterion for the interpretation of a previous literary corpus, a subject in which the moral responsibility of the interpreter is also brought to bear.

This matter is by no means of secondary importance. There is a kind of position that is not infrequent among Christian exegetes, including Catholics, or at least it has not been in the last few decades. It is a position that, under the guise of *neutrality* or *objectivity*, dispenses with the NT and, more generally, with the event of Christ in the interpretation and presentation of the OT. The Christian interpretation of the OT is conceived as a later stage of the method, so that in the initial objective analysis we should be able to agree with the Jewish interpretation. Even without this last piece of naïveté (considering the Jewish interpretation the *natural interpretation of the OT*), to which we will return, the position described hides several infidelities and contradictions that, in one way or another, have already been uncovered in this chapter but with which we should deal in this new context.

For this purpose, and to deal with the broader and more decisive matter of the right OT-NT relationship, I will make use, as I did in the previous section, of a polemic among exegetes that has come up twice, the first time in the thirties and the second, very recently, in the nineties (both in the past century). In 1934, W. E. Vischer published a work titled *The Witness of the Old Testament to Christ*,[139] which provoked a sharp debate, especially in controversy-wracked Germany immediately prior to the Second World War. Indeed, Vischer was a

---

[139] W. E. Vischer, *Das Christuszeugnis des Alten Testaments*, vol. I: *Das Gesetz* (Zurich, 1934), trans. A. B. Crabtree as *The Witness of the Old Testament of Christ*, vol. 1, *The Pentateuch* (London: Lutterworth Press, 1949).

witness to the marginalization that the OT was suffering in Protestant theology and, in general, in the Christian culture of the mighty Germany. The anti-Semitism of that era obviously played a fundamental role,[140] although there were other factors that had been preparing the ground for some time.[141] To underline the importance of the OT for Christianity itself, Vischer conceived the project of showing how the books of the Old Covenant, one by one, give "witness of Christ" (*Christuszeugnis*).

Vischer's work had the undoubted virtue of provoking a discussion that centered on the OT and its relationship with the NT and with Christianity in general. His way of dealing with the problem, though, was very questionable, for it resorted to a quasi-allegorical reading of the OT, so that, in his opinion, the Christian eye could see a witness of Christ in any detail. In fact, Vischer goes on to say, we would not understand a single word of the whole Bible if we did not find Jesus Christ in the OT:

The stories of the lives of all those men [of the OT] is part of his [Jesus'] story. This is why the books are written with so little interest in the

---

[140] It suffices to read these lines from the encyclical *Mit brennender Sorge* that Pius XI addressed to the German bishops, when he was worried about the paths that national socialism was starting down: "Nothing but ignorance and pride could blind one to the treasures hoarded in the Old Testament. Whoever wishes to see banished from church and school the Biblical history and the wise doctrines of the Old Testament blasphemes the name of God, blasphemes the Almighty's plan of salvation, and makes limited and narrow human thought the judge of God's designs over the history of the world: he denies his faith in the true Christ, such as He appeared in the flesh, the Christ who took His human nature from a people that was to crucify Him; and he understands nothing of that universal tragedy of the Son of God who to His torturer's sacrilege opposed the divine and priestly sacrifice of His redeeming death, and made the new alliance the goal of the old alliance, its realization and its crown" (*Mit brennender Sorge* 15 [end]–16).

[141] Paradigmatic in this sense is Harnack's position with regard to the use of the OT in the life of the Church at the beginning of the twentieth century: "To reject the Old Testament in the second century was an error the Church rightly resisted; to maintain it in the sixteenth century was a destiny the Reformation could not escape; but still to preserve it in the nineteenth century as one of the canonical documents of Protestantism is the result of religious and ecclesiastical paralysis" (A. von Harnack, *Marcion: Das Evangelium vom fremden Gott* [Leipzig, 1920], XII and 217). Cf. I. Carbajosa, "La recuperación del Antiguo Testamento para la vida de la Iglesia: Estudio de *Dei Verbum* 14", in *Fuente de agua viva: Homenaje al profesor D. Enrique Farfán*, ed. J. Pascual Torró and J. M. Díaz Rodelas, SVal 55 (Valencia, 2007), 7–37.

biography of each character. What is written about them is written, in fact, as part of the biography of him through whom and for whom they live.[142]

Into the discussion that was provoked entered authors of the stature of Eichrodt, von Rad, Zimmerli, and Wolff, who uncovered the dangers of allegory and were careful to emphasize the need for starting with a historical-critical analysis in order to be serious about the witness of the OT.[143]

The echoes of that discussion were gradually muffled during the fifties until they died out, and a long period began in which the OT-NT relationship did not again appear as a central matter on the exegetical agenda. However, the last two decades have seen a new flourishing of studies about the relationship between the two Testaments, especially ones based on the phenomenon of the appeal to the OT in the NT.[144] Within this movement, although with a profile decidedly their own, can be included the studies of Childs that propose a Christian reading of the OT. It was logical that the leading mind of the canonical approach should end up proposing a reading of the OT in light of the whole canon and, therefore, in light of the NT.

Although as early as 1964 he published an article in which he argued explicitly for the role of the Christian faith in the interpretation of the

---

[142] W. E. Vischer, *Die Bedeutung des Alten Testament für das christliche Leben* (Zurich, 1938), 5.

[143] Cf. B. S. Childs, "Does the Old Testament Witness to Jesus Christ?" in *Evangelium—Schriftauslegung—Kirche: FS Peter Stuhlmacher*, ed. J. Ådna, S. J. Hafemann, and O. Hofius, (Göttingen, 1997), 57.

[144] See, as examples, E. E. Ellis, *The Old Testament in Early Christianity: Canon and Interpretation in the Light of Modern Research* (Tübingen, 1991); G. K. Beale, ed., *The Right Doctrine from the Wrong Texts? Essays on the Use of the Old Testament in the New* (Grand Rapids, 1994); S. Moyise, *The Old Testament in the Book of Revelation*, JSNT.S 115 (Sheffield, 1995); G. K. Beale, *John's Use of the Old Testament in Revelation*, JSNT.S 166 (Sheffield, 1998); C. A. Evans, "The Function of the Old Testament in the New", in *Introducing New Testament Interpretation*, ed. S. McKnight (Grand Rapids, 2000); R. Penna, "Appunti sul come e perchè il Nuovo Testamento si rapporta all'Antico", *Bib* 81 (2000): 95–104; S. Moyise, *The Old Testament in the New: An Introduction* (London and New York, 2001); M. J. J. Menken and S. Moyise, *The Psalms in the New Testament* (London, 2004); F. Belli, I. Carbajosa, C. Jódar Estrella, and L. Sánchez Navarro, *Vetus in Novo: El recurso a la Escritura en el Nuevo Testamento* (Madrid, 2006). In this last work there is abundant bibliography on this phenomenon. The very work *The Jewish People and Their Sacred Scriptures in the Christian Bible* (2001), by the PBC, can be seen as part of this renewed interest in the relationship between OT and NT.

OT,[145] it would be necessary to wait until 1992, after he had developed his canonical method and published his introductions to the OT[146] and the NT[147] and his theology of the OT,[148] for his systematic reflection on the unity of the Christian Bible to come out. It was precisely the publication of this last work, *Biblical Theology of the Old and New Testaments: Theological Reflection on the Christian Bible*,[149] that motivated the reopening of that old discussion about the witness of the OT. It was in this last work that Childs, returning to Vischer's expression, stated that the OT "bears witness to Jesus Christ".[150] Childs' statement which, in spite of its similarity in form, departs from that of Vischer in its justification, provoked the negative reaction of, among others, an authority in the field of the OT, Rendtorff, who paradoxically shared with Childs the same sensitivity toward the interpretation of Scripture in the context of the canon. Rendtorff's reaction was published in 1994,[151] and three years later, in 1997, Childs' response came out.[152] This exchange of opinions contains within it the elements essential to deal with the matter of the correct way to join the two Testaments together and, especially, the Christian reading of the OT.

Childs himself summarized in four points the reasons Rendtorff has for rejecting the claim that the OT gives witness to Christ:[153]

a. The Hebrew Scriptures maintain their integrity within the Christian Bible apart from the New Testament. This is a result of the form and function that the OT has in Christian revelation.

b. To say that the OT witnesses to Jesus Christ, and not generically to a messiah, is a dogmatic judgment that is divorced from historical

---

[145] B. S. Childs, "Interpretation in Faith: The Theological Responsibility of an Old Testament Commentary", *Interp* 18 (1964): 432–49.

[146] B. S. Childs, *Introduction to the Old Testament as Scripture* (Philadelphia, 1979).

[147] B. S. Childs, *The New Testament as Canon: An Introduction* (Valley Forge, 1984).

[148] B. S. Childs, *Old Testament Theology in a Canonical Context* (London, 1985).

[149] Childs, *Biblical Theology of the Old and New.*

[150] Cf. ibid., 477–80.

[151] R. Rendtorff, "Rezension Brevard S. Childs, *Biblical Theology of the Old and New Testaments: Theological Reflection on the Christian Bible*", in *Sünde und Gericht*, ed. J. Baldermann et al., JBTh 9 (Neukirchen-Vluyn, 1994), 359–69.

[152] Childs, "Does the Old Testament Witness to Jesus Christ?", 57–64.

[153] Cf. ibid., 59.

exegesis. This would mean subordinating exegesis to a prior dogmatic stance.

c. The role of a Christian biblical theology is to indicate the elements of both continuity and discontinuity between the two separate testaments without projecting New Testament theology back into the Old Testament. The attempt to relate the theologies of the two distinct testaments derives from the reflective activity of the Christian interpreter and cannot affect the historical sense of each set of texts. Therefore, "the Old Testament by itself is not *Christuszeugnis* [witness to Christ]." [154]

d. The final reason that Rendtorff lists has much to do with a personal position, quite understandable in an exegete in postwar Germany, which was awakening from the Nazi horror, observing the drastic consequences of anti-Semitism. [155] Indeed, Rendtorff has an exquisite respect for Jewish interpretation and for the pertinence of the Jewish reading of the Hebrew Bible. So much so that he shows special caution against attempts to Christianize the OT, to the point that on several occasions he has proposed replacing, in the Christian milieu, the name "Old Testament" with "Hebrew Bible" (for a Protestant, the Greek deuterocanonicals do not form part of the canon), "Scripture", or "First Testament". [156] As a consequence of this posture, he seeks an exegesis of the OT that can be shared by a Jew.

Childs articulates his response in two parts, adding to the last one a corollary about Jewish-Christian dialogue. In the first part he expounds the basic theological aspects that are at stake in this discussion, while in the second, the programmatic one, he distinguishes the three levels of reading of Scripture that make it possible for us to understand the degree to which we can say that the OT bears witness to Christ. I will now go into both parts.

---

[154] Rendtorff, "Rezension Brevard S. Childs, *Biblical Theology*", 365.

[155] Cf. R. Rendtorff, *Hat denn Gott sein Volk verstossen? Die evangelische Kirche und das Judentum seit 1945: Ein Kommentar*, ACJD 18 (Munich, 1989).

[156] Cf. R. Rendtorff, *Christen und Juden heute: Neue Einsichten und neue Aufgaben* (Neukirchen-Vluyn, 1998). Recently, Rendtorff has published some autobiographical reflections in which it comes out much more clearly how his theology and his biography go hand in hand: *Kontinuität im Widerspruch: Autobiographische Reflexionen* (Göttingen, 2007).

In the first part, Childs begins by specifying that the NT does not conceive of its central proclamation as mere historical continuity in relation to the OT. Childs is interested in emphasizing that in the NT itself an "ontological" plane (to use his words) is established that exegetes normally reject because they consider it an illegitimate intrusion from the field of philosophy. This ontological plane transcends the temporal sequence, although it does not annul it. Thus, the prologue of the Gospel of John presents Jesus Christ as the eternal Word who was together with God (Jn 1:1) from the beginning, while Colossians 1:15–16 states, "He is the image of the invisible God, the first-born of all creation; for in him all things were created." Jesus Christ is not only *after* historically but *at the origin* ontologically.

The second observation refers to the drastic separation between exegesis and theological reflection and, above all, to the characterization of each one. Normally the first is conceived as a historical and philological exercise, neutral and objective, that brings to light what the text says. The second, in contrast, is understood as a subsequent reflective activity, of a mainly speculative and, above all, subjective nature. Childs uncovers the falseness of these characterizations and claims that even Rendtorff (so attentive to the hermeneutical aspects of biblical exegesis) falls into this reduction when he insists that exegetical analysis should precede dogmatic considerations. In fact, Childs states, one already has certain theological presuppositions when one does exegesis. Although he does not cite Gadamer, he bases himself on the results of modern hermeneutics to argue that exegesis is not limited to discovering the grammatical meaning of a text but that by means of this, it should reach the essence. Thus, "explain" (*erklären*) and "understand" (*verstehen*) belong to the single activity of exegesis.

The third and final observation is intended to take care of Rendtorff's fear that turning to Jesus Christ as the essence of Scripture opens the door to an uncontrolled allegory, outside the control of historical-critical exegesis. Vischer's precedent was heavy in the air. To respond to this objection, Childs proposes considering the different levels of reading Scripture within a single method of interpretation that is capable of embracing all the dimensions of the text. To avoid misunderstandings, Childs specifies that his method does not in any way aspire to revive the medieval scheme of the four meanings, which, in his opinion, is very defective.

In the second part, Childs expounds the method mentioned above, presenting the three levels of reading the OT that the very nature of the text requires: historical, literary, and canonical. This is where he enters fully into the question of whether the OT gives witness to Christ or not. At the first level of reading, the historical one, it would not be right to introduce the person of Jesus Christ:

> If one is dealing seriously with the Old Testament genre of story as one legitimate form of its witness, then in this context to read back into the story the person of Jesus Christ, as Vischer did, or to interpret the various theophanies as the manifestation of the second person of the Trinity, is to distort this witness and to drown out the Old Testament's own voice. On the story level one cannot fuse promise and fulfillment.[157]

A second level of reading would be the literary one, which recognizes a single corpus (the Bible has come down to us bound into a single book) composed of two parts. At this level, the similarities and dissimilarities (continuity and discontinuity) of the two Testaments, the Old and the New, are analyzed. This is not an analysis in the style of the phenomenology of religions, which compares two groups of writings that belong to religious systems that are different but at the same time close. "Rather, it is an exegetical and theological enterprise which seeks to pursue a relationship of content", an enterprise in which "neither witness is absorbed by the other, nor are their contents fused."[158] At this level of reading, too, it would therefore not be legitimate to claim that the OT gives witness to Christ. In this way, Childs recognizes that Rendtorff is in part right, since he works at this level.

However, there is a third level of reading, the canonical one, a "third entrance to biblical exegesis which arises from the Christian confession that the church's Bible comprises a theological unity although its form combines two distinct sections, each with a unique voice".[159] Only at this third level can it be claimed that the OT gives witness to Jesus Christ. After arriving at this point, Childs is very interested in making clear what he is *not* talking about. He is not referring, at this third level, to a type of homiletic discourse that would come after rigorous exegetical analysis and that would subjectively unite the wit-

---

[157] Rendtorff, *Christen und Juden*, 61.
[158] Ibid.
[159] Ibid., 62.

ness of both Testaments in a uniformly Christian reading. In fact, classic critical exegesis offers no objection to this reading, since it makes no claim to objectivity; furthermore, it is offered as a kind of literary genre or creative game that is not based on rational arguments. Childs not only disconnects his third level from this homiletic reading, but he declares himself opposed to it, "because it shares all the assumptions and fatal weaknesses of classic Protestant theological liberalism".[160] If Childs does not speak of these kinds of "licenses" that exegesis allows for biblical theology, of what, then, does this "third entrance to biblical exegesis" consist?

> Rather, I am suggesting that confronting the subject matter of the two discrete witnesses of Scripture creates a necessity for the interpreter to try to understand the biblical text from the full knowledge of the subject matter gained from hearing the voices of both testaments. The interpreter now proceeds in a direction which moves from the reality itself back to the textual witness.[161]

In Childs' view, to say that the OT gives witness to Christ "is to move beyond the task of hearing the unique voice of the prophets' testimony to a coming royal figure".[162] The life, death, and Resurrection of Jesus Christ project a new light on the texts of both Testaments, which then give a unitary witness. Alluding to the fourth song of the servant of Yahweh (Is 53), Childs wonders whether it is possible to speak of Isaiah as the voice of Israel in the canon of the OT and at the same time to speak of his witness to Christ. And he answers by saying that not only is it possible, but it is even required for any serious Christian reflection. But this approach, says Childs, "is far removed from Vischer's in that its genre is confession not apologetics".[163]

It is at this point that Rendtorff comes into conflict with Childs, because he accuses him of imposing a dogmatic datum (external to the text) on his reading of the OT. Childs does indeed speak, at this third level, of a way of interpretation that "moves from the reality itself back to the textual witness", but he makes it very clear that it is the biblical text itself that obliges him to recognize that datum, because it

[160] Ibid.
[161] Ibid.
[162] Ibid.
[163] Ibid., 63.

"exerts theological pressure on the reader which demands that the reality which undergirds the two voices [OT and NT] not be held apart and left fragmented, but critically reunited".[164] In this way Scripture is not subordinated to dogma, because the datum, the essence, arises from the reading of both Testaments, from obedience to the canon.

That path which Childs describes "from the reality itself back to the textual witness" turns out to be decisive in order to be able to speak sensibly about a reading of the OT from the NT. The problem derives—and we have seen this in the discussion between Childs and Rendtorff—from how that path is conceived. In Rendtorff's view, it is an illegitimate path, since we subordinate exegesis to dogma. Childs, wishing to avoid this extreme, is not excessively clear in defining the terms of the path to which he himself alludes. In fact, it could be described, being consistent with his words, as the path "from the complete knowledge of the *content* (essence) that results from the hearing of both witnesses up to the written witness". But then the whole path seems to wander inside the reading, which is problematic. The problem is not so much whether the reality from which one starts is attested by Scripture—which is precisely what Childs wants to argue at all costs —but how one reaches that reality or how that reality reaches us. If it is reached through listening attentively to the voice of both Testaments, then Rendtorff's criticisms are understandable: we would be branding the Jewish reading as myopic (or deaf, using the simile of the voice), because it is not able to read beyond the end of its nose.

Now that we have arrived at this point, we could ask: Is this not the same accusation that Paul addressed to his Jewish brethren when he stated that "their minds were hardened" and that when they read Moses they have a veil over their hearts (= minds) (2 Cor 3:14–15)? Certainly the statement is clear, and it can and should be defended, but the very example of the apostle Paul helps us understand how (and how not) that veil is to fall. Indeed, immediately after speaking of the *veiled* reading of the OT, he states that "when a man *turns to the Lord* the veil is removed" (2 Cor 3:16), or, more synthetically, "only *through Christ* is it taken away" (cf. 2 Cor 3:14). What do the phrases *turn to the Lord* or *through Christ* mean for Paul? In his case, it is evident that the veil that he recognizes having had in his relationship to the OT

---

[164] Ibid., 62.

did not disappear because of a closer reading of those books or because of listening in an unprejudiced manner to the unanimous witness of the whole Jewish Scripture. In addition, we should keep in mind that we are talking, not about an uneducated man, but of a man versed in the Scriptures (cf. Acts 22:3; Phil 3:5), who in his letters demonstrates a great knowledge of the books of Israel and of the interpretive techniques of his era.

To the early Church and to every Jew who was willing to listen to him, it was obvious that the radical change in Paul came from an event, from a happening in his history, the encounter with "Jesus of Nazareth" (cf. Acts 22:8), on the way to Damascus. It is this event in the history of Paul, the encounter with the Risen One, that gives content to the expression "turn to the Lord", that is, convert. And it is that event which is behind the numerous occasions on which Paul makes use of the expression *"through Christ"*. The encounter with Jesus on the road to Damascus gave rise to a particular relationship between Paul and Christ, so that all of reality, reason, and feeling are lived *through Christ*.

The whole NT *attests* to this dynamic which we, in turn, can recognize in the present: it is the encounter with Christ that opens the understanding to comprehend the Scriptures. I will illustrate this with some passages.

The two disciples of Jesus who were going on the road to Emmaus on the first day of the week, after the crucifixion of their master, were burdened with skepticism (cf. Lk 24:13-35). It was not the reading of the Scriptures of Israel that lifted them out of that skepticism; it was a "chance" encounter with a man who reached them on the road that opened their understanding of those very Scriptures. It is noteworthy that Jesus (as later Paul would do with the Jews) censures the inability of his disciples to understand the sacred books of Israel: "O foolish men, and slow of heart to believe all that the prophets have spoken!" (Lk 24:25). But, in fact, the way they recognized that the Scriptures give witness to Christ is the explanation that he himself offered them: "And beginning with Moses and all the prophets, he interpreted to them in all the Scriptures the things concerning himself" (Lk 24:27). The proof that this was not an *extrinsic* or *forced* explanation is what happened in them while Jesus was speaking: "Did not our hearts burn within us while he talked to us on the road, while he opened to us the

Scriptures?" (Lk 24:32). Jesus' explanation "opened" (*dianoigō*, "open wide") the Scriptures to them; they recognized a surprising correspondence (described with the expression "hearts burn") between what the OT (the Scripture of that time) said and the events to which they had been witnesses while accompanying Jesus of Nazareth. Only then could they say, "truly we were foolish and slow of heart (= with slow, deficient reasoning) to understand what is clear in Scripture."

It was this same experience, which immediately afterward was repeated in the presence of all the apostles (44–45: "Then he said to them, 'These are my words which I spoke to you, while I was still with you, that everything written about me in the law of Moses and the prophets and the psalms must be fulfilled.' Then he opened their minds to understand the Scriptures."), that made his disciples able to bear witness in their preaching and their writings that Jesus was born, lived, suffered, died, and was resurrected *according to the Scriptures* (*kata tas graphas*).

Another truly illuminating episode is found narrated in the book of the Acts of the Apostles and, therefore, located in the period (which, in a way, is already our own) in which the risen Jesus ascended once and for all to heaven and stopped appearing to the disciples. It is the time of the Church. Chapter 8 presents us with an Ethiopian eunuch, a minister of Queen Candace, who is returning to his homeland after going on a pilgrimage to Jerusalem (Acts 8:26–39). As a devout proselyte, he is using the holy Scriptures of Israel, and, in fact, he is presented to us reading the prophet Isaiah, specifically the passage from the fourth song of the servant of Yahweh (Is 53). It is worth dwelling on the dialogue that takes place between this Ethiopian and Philip, the disciple of Jesus, who "moved by the Spirit" approaches his chariot:

> Philip ran to him, and heard him reading Isaiah the prophet, and asked, "Do you understand what you are reading?" And he said, "How can I, unless some one guides me?" And he invited Philip to come up and sit with him. Now the passage of the Scripture which he was reading was this:
>> "As a sheep led to the slaughter
>> or a lamb before its shearer is silent,
>> so he opens not his mouth.
>> In his humiliation justice was denied him.
>> Who can describe his generation?
>> For his life is taken up from the earth."

And the eunuch said to Philip, "Please, about whom does the prophet say this, about himself or about some one else?" Then Philip opened his mouth, and beginning with this Scripture he told him the good news of Jesus.

In this case we find ourselves with an episode of reading directly from the Scriptures of Israel. That all Scripture must be interpreted is seen by the question that the eunuch addressed to Philip about the identity of the mysterious servant. The passage was not transparent to him. What made the minister of Queen Candace come to understand the Scripture was not the reading of that very Scripture, but the encounter, again apparently "by chance", with Philip, who announced to him, testified to him, about an event: the life, death, and Resurrection of Jesus of Nazareth. And once again, the proof that that announcement and the interpretation of the OT that it carried with it were not extrinsic or forced was the eunuch's willingness to adhere to faith in Jesus, the Messiah, by asking for baptism ("And as they went along the road they came to some water, and the eunuch said, 'See, here is water! What is to prevent my being baptized?' " [Acts 8:36]), as well as the joy that sprang from this ("and went on his way rejoicing", [Acts 8:39]).

In this example, the understanding of Scripture on the part of the Ethiopian minister coincided with the recognition that the OT gives witness to Jesus Christ. Significantly, it starts from the episode of the servant of Yahweh, whose identity is revealed in the mystery of the Passion, death, and Resurrection of Jesus announced by Philip. Moreover, this case reveals very well the paradox that is found in that way of interpreting the OT which goes "from the reality itself to the written witness". On the one hand, what opens and unveils the Scripture is an event external to the reading of it (in the case of the episode being studied here, the encounter with Philip). On the other hand, that "external" event is previously attested in Scripture, in the OT (in the present case, the Ethiopian came to faith on the basis of the correspondence of an event, which was announced to him, with the authority of Scripture). It can thus be clearly seen that the witness of the OT is not *dispensable*, as if it could be eliminated once the event of Christ who comes to fulfill it has been manifested. It is the authority of the Scripture of Israel, normative for every Jew and every proselyte, that makes it possible for the eunuch to discover the correspondence between the Jesus who is announced to him and the promise that *is* the OT.

Saint Paul summarizes this paradox perfectly in his letter to the Romans when, in the context of a discussion concentrating on the Jewish people and their Law, he states: "But now the righteousness of God has been manifested apart from the law, although the law and the prophets bear witness to it, the righteousness of God through faith in Jesus Christ for all who believe" (Rom 3:21–22). The righteousness of God, which comes to us through faith in Jesus Christ, has been manifested apart from the Law (in its double dimension as legislation and Holy Scripture). It is not the fulfillment of the Law but faith in Jesus Christ, born in time, that gains us justification. However, and paradoxically, that righteousness of God, which is Jesus Christ (1 Cor 1:30), is attested by the Law and the prophets, that is, by the holy Scriptures of Israel.[165] And it is the case that the Law, as Scripture and holy promise, cannot *not* be fulfilled (cf. Hab 2:2–3; Mt 5:17–18).

On this path that we have followed through some passages of the NT, it has become evident that an adequate understanding of the OT, as prophecy of the fulfillment of Christ, is achieved only by means of the real encounter in history with the very event of Christ,[166] in his very person or through the living witness of his Church. Precisely because of this, it is important to underline that the encounter with Christ, which opens one's understanding to Scripture, as the apostles experienced it, cannot be replaced, *mutatis mutandis*, by the reading of the NT. The book of the Acts of the Apostles illustrates very well the form in which Christ remains in history: as an event, made of words and deeds, in the apostolic witness, raised up and sustained by the Spirit within the Church. It is not superfluous to recall that the Church lived for several decades without the NT. It is in this context that the NT should be received as a normative (inspired and canonical) witness of the event of Christ, an event that the Spirit continues to make present today, so that the promise of the Resurrected One is verified: "I am with you always, to the close of the age" (Mt 28:20).

Therefore, the claim that the OT reaches its fulfillment in the NT

---

[165] For the interpretation of this passage, cf. F. Belli, " 'Testimoniada por la Ley y los profetas'. Rom 3,21: Pablo y las Escrituras", *RevAg* 43 (2002): 413–26.

[166] Cf. Belli, Carbajosa, Jódar Estrella, and Sánchez Navarro, *Vetus in Novo*, 50–52.

does not turn out to be correct. The fulfillment of the hope and the promise of the OT is not carried out by another book, but by Christ, to whom the NT bears witness:

> But, above all, the Church reads the Old Testament in the light of the paschal mystery—the death and resurrection of Jesus Christ—who brings a radical newness and, with sovereign authority, gives a meaning to the Scriptures that is decisive and definitive (cf. *Dei Verbum*, 4). This new determination of meaning has become an integral element of Christian faith.[167]

To the contrary, the reduction of the event of Christ to his canonical witness in Scripture, outside of tradition (on the basis of the Lutheran principle *"sola Scriptura"*), is at the base of a certain type of problem in conceiving the relationships between the OT and the NT. Indeed, to say that one literary corpus "fulfills" another would be extremely difficult and, even if it were possible (we could think of the second part of a novel in which the intricate plot created in the first part is unveiled), that would not be the case of the OT-NT relationship in particular. Indeed, the notion of *fulfillment of Scripture*, as it is understood in the Christian faith (and is in fact seen in the NT), is greater than the static image of the *fulfillment of something that was written*. In this sense, the document the PBC published in 2001, *The Jewish People and Their Sacred Scriptures in the Christian Bible*, contains some very helpful observations:

> Christian faith recognises the fulfilment, in Christ, of the Scriptures and the hopes of Israel, but it does not understand this fulfilment as a literal one. Such a conception would be reductionist. In reality, in the mystery of Christ crucified and risen, fulfilment is brought about in a manner unforeseen. It includes transcendence. Jesus is not confined to playing an already fixed role—that of Messiah—but he confers, on the notions of Messiah and salvation, a fullness which could not have been imagined in advance; he fills them with a new reality; one can even speak in this connection of a "new creation" [2 Cor 5.17; Gal 6.15]. It would be wrong to consider the prophecies of the Old Testament as some kind of photographic anticipations of future events.[168]

---

[167] PBC, *The Interpretation of the Bible in the Church* I C 1. Cf. also section III A 2, "Relationships between the Old Testament and the New".

[168] Pontifical Biblical Commission, *The Jewish People and Their Sacred Scriptures in the Christian Bible* (Vatican City, 2001), §21.

Indeed, the fulfillment in Christ is presented as a *novelty*, and it has been perfectly attested as such in the NT. But the novelty and surprise reach their culmination, and we therefore speak of fulfillment and not of supersession, rupture, or negation, when once they take place they are shown to correspond mysteriously to the multi-century wait to which the OT attests.[169] Therefore it can be said that the OT gives witness to Christ; or once the novelty of Christ has taken place, it is possible to say, playing with the scene from Emmaus: "Oh, how foolish we were! How slow of heart to believe all that the prophets spoke!" (cf. Lk 24:25).

The experience of Jesus' disciples after the Resurrection, attested in the Acts of the Apostles, illustrates very well this double movement I am describing: from the event of Christ to the Scriptures, and from the Scriptures to Christ. Indeed, the apostles show that they are surprised that that to which they have been witnesses in time and space explains the Scriptures (the Passion of Christ illuminates the passages about the servant of Yahweh in Isaiah: Acts 8:26–39; the Resurrection of Christ gives meaning to the prophecy of Psalm 118:22, "The stone which the builders rejected has become the cornerstone": Acts 4:11–12). At the same time, they need to turn to the Scriptures to interpret the meaning of the events that they are experiencing and of which they are the main figures (Judas' betrayal is illuminated in the light of Psalm 109: Acts 1:15–20; the events of Pentecost are understood in the light of the prophecy of Joel: Acts 2:14–21; the alliance between Pilate and Herod starts to make sense on the basis of Psalm 2: Acts 4:25–28). Scripture (OT) and paschal event call to one another as words and deeds that are intrinsically united (cf. DV 2): "Scripture reveals the meaning of events and . . . events reveal the meaning of Scripture."[170]

Finally, to conclude this trip through the reading of the OT from the NT, I will go back to two matters that I only noted in passing at the beginning of this section and that can now be dealt with more clearly. The first one has to do with the moral responsibility of the Catholic exegete who interprets or teaches the OT. The interpretation of the OT outside of Christ or the NT, under the guise of objectiv-

---

[169] Cf. I. Carbajosa, "El Antiguo Testamento, realidad abierta", in *Entrar en lo Antiguo*, ed. I. Carbajosa and L. Sánchez Navarro, PD 16 (Madrid, 2007), 21–50.

[170] PBC, *The Interpretation of the Bible in the Church* III A 2.

ity or neutrality, involves an act of disloyalty. Christ is still presented today as an event that carries with it a certain reading of the OT in relation to which one *must* take a position. And one must do so because this implies a greater comprehension of the OT. To interpret the OT outside of Christ already implies a decision that *diminishes the importance of* the extent of the revelation of the Christian novelty. Christ's interpretation becomes *one* among others, with its rights. But as we have already seen in this very chapter, the event of Christ is directed at the person of the exegete as a radical novelty capable of expanding reason, throwing new light on all of reality. It is impossible to separate this personal experience from the exegetical task (the separation in fact exposes weakness in this experience).

Within this same matter, we could speak of a second act of disloyalty by the Catholic exegete who interprets the OT outside of Christ. It is disloyalty in relation to the witness of the NT. The passages in which Jesus himself or the sacred writers speak of the witness the OT gives of Christ are quite numerous. Once again, to read these (canonical and inspired) passages and not shape our interpretation of the OT in light of them implies weakness in one's Christian experience, a dualistic conception of the faith, which generates the drastic separation of (scientific) exegesis and (believing) theology:

> Philip found Nathanael, and said to him, "We have found him of whom Moses in the law and also the prophets wrote, Jesus of Nazareth, the son of Joseph." Nathanael said to him, "Can anything good come out of Nazareth?" Philip said to him, "Come and see." (Jn 1:45–46)

> You search the Scriptures, because you think that in them you have eternal life; and it is they that bear witness to me; yet you refuse to come to me that you may have life. . . . Do not think that I shall accuse you to the Father; it is Moses who accuses you, on whom you set your hope. If you believed Moses, you would believe me, for he wrote of me. But if you do not believe his writings, how will you believe my words? (Jn 5:39–40, 45–47)

> And he commanded us to preach to the people, and to testify that he is the one ordained by God to be judge of the living and the dead. To him all the prophets bear witness that every one who believes in him receives forgiveness of sins through his name. (Acts 10:42–43)

The second matter noted at the beginning of this section has to do with the commonplace that considers the natural, original, and objective interpretation of the OT to agree with the Jewish interpretation of it. In this way, the New Testament is perceived, consciously or unconsciously, as the book of another religion that has appropriated the Sacred Scriptures of the Hebrews for itself. I have branded this position as naïve because it implies an abysmal ignorance of the history of the formation of the OT and the history of Judaism, especially of the pluralistic Judaism of the first century A.D. The Jewish interpretation, and even its own canon of sacred books, is a very particular reading of the OT, the one practiced by the Pharisees, the only Jewish group that survived the destruction of the temple in 70 A.D. and the dramatic events that followed the Bar Kokhba revolt in A.D. 135. In this sense, it is a reading as legitimate, at first blush, as the one that could be made by that other Jewish "sect" that took the name of Christ. I will give the floor to a well-known Jewish exegete who can illustrate this point authoritatively (and who can by no means be suspected of favoring the Catholic position):

> The haggadic tendency makes of Scripture a literature which grew by accretion. This seems to me exactly the way in which literary reflection of a live religious tradition would grow. From the oral to the written, and from the book to canonicity, and from canon to midrash, represents a continuous process.
>
> In the first Christian century this midrash took two major turns (along with some minor ones). One midrash resulted in Mishna and Gemara, *The Midrash*, and the targumim; then Saboraim and the Gaonim and then philosophers, Aristotelian and neo-Platonic. The other resulted in Gospels and epistles, and ultimately a NT; there were in addition Apostles, Fathers, and Ante-Nicene Fathers, and Post-Nicene Fathers, and then philosophers, Aristotelian and neo-Platonic.[171]

To be sure, the Christian interpretation starts with a historical event that conditions its whole reading of the OT. But this is no less true of the Jewish reading, which implies a series of interpretive choices in the light of its own tradition, which was not the only one in the first century A.D. (we can think of the Sadducees, the Essenes, the Qumran community—whether or not it is associated with the Essenes—or the

---

[171] S. Sandmel, "The Haggada within Scripture", *JBL* 80 (1961): 122.

Zealots), including a particular position in relation to the Christian claim (one of rejection). When Catholic exegetes interpret the OT in the light of Christ (attested normatively in the NT), they are not doing anything different, from the methodological point of view, from what Jews do who interpret the OT from the Jewish oral tradition that finally crystalized in a second scripture: Mishnah, targumim, midrashim, Talmud, and so on. There is no *natural* or *objective* reading of the OT. Moreover, the reading that interests us is not that one, but a reading that does justice to what is attested there. And Christ, surprisingly (the exegete is the first one to experience the "surprise" of this reading and attest to it on the basis of his experience), fulfills the Scripture.

V. Conclusions

In this chapter I have described and discussed in depth the characteristic dimensions of Catholic exegesis in the framework of the two previous chapters, which have served to illustrate the basic problems of biblical interpretation.

My starting point was the very nature of Scripture, from which are derived the two dimensions that exegesis must bear in mind methodologically: the historical-critical and the theological. These two dimensions, of which Benedict XVI has reminded us, were already clearly expounded in DV 12. However, the great problem of modern exegesis is the drastic separation of the two dimensions or, to put it another way, the lack of understanding about the correct way to join them.

In order to understand this joining, I have tried to go back to the very nature of revelation, of faith as an appropriate response to it, and of Scripture as a written and inspired witness to it. From a correct understanding of these terms it follows that exegesis, as interpretation of Scripture, can only be a theological discipline, that is, a discipline that starts from faith to be able to reach its object. The essence of Scripture (as an authoritative witness to revelation) will not, in fact, be reached through a historical method in which faith, as human freedom generated and sustained by grace, does not have a role from the beginning (shaping the method itself).

In the development of this chapter, I have paused to consider successively the basic problems that must be dealt with in each of the two dimensions of the interpretation of Scripture: the theological and the historical. In the theological dimension, I have asked how it is possible for faith to be part of the exegetical method if it has been considered, since the time of the Enlightenment, an element that gets in the way of knowledge. As a first approximation, we saw that the exclusion of faith from the critical investigation of the last two centuries has not led to a greater "objectivity". On the contrary, this study has revealed the various philosophical and cultural presuppositions that guided a large part of that investigation, often doing violence to the biblical text.

Moreover, we have been able to see that the exclusion of faith from biblical investigation was related to the claim that exegesis should be governed by the method of the natural sciences. However, the phenomenon to which Scripture attests is human, historical, literary, and religious, and, therefore, the appropriate method to deal with it must be different from the one utilized to study mechanical or natural phenomena. Precisely because he is dealing with a religious phenomenon, the investigator or interpreter cannot remove his freedom from the claim that the object holds: he *must* decide, for truly the religious problem is *his* problem. And this decision, in the case of the Bible, is made, above all, in relation to the historical phenomenon that prolongs the Christian claim in time: the Church. So it is understood that faith can be the most appropriate presupposition to interpret Scripture.

Since faith is the method of knowledge that is appropriate for the object of study that is the Bible, I have taken time to understand better the characteristics of this faith in its practical application to Scripture. In the first place, I have highlighted the uniquely characteristic dynamic of faith in relation to the natural human religiosity that is at the origin of religious creativity. Faith, in its entirety, refers to a spatio-temporally situated event that makes the claim that it is *the* intervention of God in history to reveal himself. The starting point of faith is therefore an event in history. Precisely because of this, it requires people to take a position in relation to it, in its dual status as a historical phenomenon and a religious phenomenon. Secondly, the starting point of faith, a fact that challenges one's freedom (at the same time that it generates and sustains it), implies a challenge to the modern concept of reason as the measure of all things. By its nature, it demands an opening of reason to a fact that it does not possess beforehand, from which something new can come, something *not deducible*. Modern reason, on the other hand, has as one of its basic presuppositions the exclusion of the intervention of God in history. Finally, the affirmation of faith as a method of knowing highlights the role that the moral responsibility of the exegete plays in interpretation, for he is not a mere "scientist" who does not form a part of his investigation (if indeed such is possible in any field).

In the context of the discussion about the moral responsibility of the exegete, I have examined one of the most recent trends in biblical interpretation, especially in the area of the prophets: the one that bases itself on the methods of the social sciences, which I had left unevaluated in chapter 2. Now we have been able to understand that the authors studied, who consider their approach to be neutral precisely because it excludes faith, are guilty of a final act of disloyalty. Above all, they avoid the inevitable decision with relation to Christianity (or Judaism), which, in fact, is in itself a moral position that has its consequences in the results of the exegesis they propose.

In a manner that is more or less obvious, depending on the author, there is an a priori rejection of the uniqueness of ancient Israel and the Christian religion, that is, it is denied that a *discontinuum* has entered into history that breaks the line of the *continuum* on which they want to establish their sociological studies. The Kantian presupposition that only a pure religious faith, a mere rational faith and not a historical faith based only on events, can establish a universal church (have a universal valence) is clearly behind these positions. While in the nineteenth century this presupposition led to defending a natural religiosity (which was projected onto Scripture) in contrast to the positive religions, in the twentieth century it has contributed to the spread of the phenomena of agnosticism and atheism, which additionally share a new form of disloyalty: a lack of commitment to reality and to human experience itself.

The consequences of all these presuppositions are seen in the results of exegesis based on the social sciences, which amount to violence done to the text, since social models are projected onto it (specifically, onto the phenomenon to which it gives testimony) that were created on the basis of ideological categories of the present day. Those social models are not at all "neutral", because they are all indebted to a dialectic and Marxist view of history and its evolution. Moreover, the presupposition of a historical continuum that justifies the application to the past of social models that "work" in the present conceals a fallacy. Man, with his essential factors, remains "immutable" throughout time, but imponderable and unforeseeable factors intervene in history that in fact condition and change the course of that history and of societies, beginning with human freedom itself.

In considering the historical dimension of the interpretation of Scripture, I have insisted on the need for a literary and historical study of it, precisely on the basis of the dynamic of the divine condescension (which reaches its culmination in the redemptive Incarnation) to which Scripture itself attests.[172] This type of study has found its realization in the last two centuries in the historical-critical method, considered by the document *The Interpretation of the Bible in the Church*, by the PBC, to be "indispensable" for the scientific study of the meaning of the ancient texts. Even so, this method is not free of shadows, as we have been able to see in its historical application in the first two chapters of this work. Now that we have come to this point, though, it is not enough to say that if the method is purified of its tendentious hermeneutical choices it can be used objectively, without any a prioris. A method that wants to interpret Scripture, by the very nature of the latter, has no alternative but to start with certain hermeneutical choices. "Objectivity" has been revealed to be an ideal that is naïve and at the same time abstract and unrealistic.

Two clear examples of the presence of hermeneutical choices in the first steps of the historical-critical method are found in the matter of the search for the "original" text, in the textual criticism of the OT, and in the matter of the diachronic or synchronic study of the text, in literary criticism. In both cases we have been able to see hermeneutical choices in action that in fact orient the course of the investigation.

In the textual criticism of the OT, the question of where to put the boundary between literary criticism and textual criticism is decisive. Or, what amounts to the same thing, the question of what text is to be reconstructed. Every form of the text prior to that boundary falls on the side of literary criticism (the study of the sources and the process of formation or redaction of a text). Textual criticism, for its part, is

---

[172] The whole OT can be read in this code of divine condescension: I. Carbajosa, "La progresiva condescendencia de la Palabra de Dios en Israel", in *Palabra encarnada: La Palabra de Dios en la Iglesia*, ed. I. Carbajosa and L. Sánchez Navarro, PD 20 (Madrid, 2008), 15–66.

responsible for reconstructing, on the basis of the textual witnesses, that previously contextualized "original" form. The value given to the Greek version of the LXX, to the Pharisaic community of the first century A.D., or to the Christian community responsible for the NT is decisive in determining "the original" that textual criticism should try to reconstruct. For the Christian exegete, the textual choices that the NT has made in relation to the Scripture of Israel should at least be a factor to take into consideration when deciding what textual form of the OT to read (and this is even more obvious in the field of liturgical usage).

With regard to literary criticism, another decisive hermeneutical choice is the one that must be made about the *level* of the text that we subject to study or interpretation: the text in its final form (synchronic level) or the text in its historical process of formation (diachronic level). It is clear that the two levels do not turn out to be irreconcilable for literary criticism; moreover, they must both be considered by virtue of the nature of Scripture itself. However, *in fact*, interpretation privileges one or the other and orients its study according to this choice (and the conclusions are affected by it). Moreover, the fact that a biblical book is canonical and inspired seems to have much to say about the form of the text that we read or interpret.

In this context, I have brought together the recent discussion, described in the two preceding chapters, concerning the diachronic and synchronic readings, represented by Clines, for the Pentateuch, and by Childs, for the prophets. In order to deal with this matter, I have started with the debate between one of them, Childs, and another prestigious exegete, Barr. The most important conclusion to which I will return here is that the final stage of the text is the only form that can be called canonical and inspired and that, in fact, exercises an essential critical function on the previous stages, which makes the final image of history it produces normative; that is, the complete and true impression of the history of revelation can be perceived in it. Even so, the diachronic study of the text helps us define the outlines of the critical theological judgment of normative value that the final form exercises on the previous material. In this discussion, many factors that have been appearing throughout this chapter come into play, like the normative value of a certain period of history, the canonical interpretation of that period that Scripture gives, the role of tradition and the authority of an ecclesiastical community, the value of the canon and its significance, the notion of inspiration, and so on.

Finally, I have dealt with the relationship between the two Testaments, especially how and in what sense the OT can be read from the NT. I took care of one objection, unfortunately frequent among some Christian exegetes, including Catholics, that claims to see in the Christian reading a kind of violence done to the text, so that an objective or neutral interpretation of the OT must dispense with every historical or literary event subsequent to it.

To illustrate this discussion, I again started with a debate among exegetes, in this case between Childs and Rendtorff, who, when discussing the question of whether the OT gives witness to Christ, touch on the essential factors at stake in this matter. The NT itself, in its relationship with the OT, instructs us about this matter. Indeed, what expands our understanding of the OT is not a careful or more penetrating reading of that same text. Only an "external", surprising, non-deducible, and unforeseeable event, the event of Jesus Christ, opens our understanding to comprehend the Scriptures, so that we can then recognize that they (the OT) give witness of Christ. This last "surprise", the correspondence of Christ with Scripture, which has a normative character, becomes in turn, paradoxically, a truth criterion of the Christian revelation.

What fulfills the OT is not another literary corpus, the NT, but Christ himself, attested in that corpus. Once again, at stake in this matter are the freedom and the moral responsibility of the exegete who has recognized Christ in his own history. The position he takes in relation to the OT will in fact judge the type of faith experience he has. Moreover, faithfulness to the NT requires an understanding of the OT as a witness to Christ, if we pay attention to the very numerous NT passages that illustrate it. The Jewish interpretation of the OT, far from being "neutral", is also based on a series of choices, specifically, that of privileging, among several, the interpretation of the OT that the Pharisaic community of the first century A.D. gave.

As happened to the disciples from Emmaus, it is the encounter with Christ, who is contemporary in his Church through the work of the Holy Spirit, that expands our understanding to comprehend the Scriptures and that teaches us everything in them that refers to him.

General Conclusions

At the beginning of this work I started from the invitation of Pope Benedict XVI to develop an exegesis that was not only historical but also theological. This invitation is based on the two methodological dimensions of the interpretation of Scripture present in DV 12, which, in turn, correspond to the very nature of the Bible as a written and inspired witness of revelation.

The Pope's call is a response to a worrisome situation, character-ized by an ever greater gap between "scientific" exegesis and theology. Speaking in general terms, exegesis produces results that can scarcely be used by theology, and the latter, in turn, constructs its edifice outside of the former, even if it finishes by crowning it with a rosary of biblical citations. In fact, the consequences of this drastic separation constitute one of the most acute problems that has arisen for the understanding of faith in our day, and these consequences make themselves felt in very diverse areas.

In the area of the teaching of Scripture, this radical division con-tributes to sustaining and strengthening the reason-faith dualism with which students of theology, influenced by the cultural context, fre-quently begin their course of study. Exegesis, in the scenario described, is presented as a "scientific", "objective" discipline that operates on a literary work with a method appropriate to it: the historical-critical method. It is, then, a discipline that uses reason methodically and whose results can be verified or confirmed. More or less implicitly, theologi-cal discourse will be presented (or at least perceived by students) as a subsequent step that does not follow if one does not accept a series of premises that go beyond the scientific study of the text: that the text is inspired or that God wants to speak to us by way of a secondary signification, or spiritual meaning, that goes beyond the literal mean-ing, which is the only "objective" meaning that can be scientifically deduced from the text.

Obviously, theological construction that is based on these presuppositions (or that takes them for granted) will not be able to avoid the lingering suspicion that its discourse is not entirely "logical" (in spite of defending the reasonableness of faith) or that it is not based on the facts of Scripture (which, studied "critically", would say things different from what tradition holds). But above all, theological discourse, which is based on faith, would eventually be pushed aside (in the context of the radical division described) into the realm of "believing" (linked to feeling), far from that other territory where the truths of man and history are at stake, which is "knowing". Thus, the drastic separation between "scientific" exegesis and theology would only feed into that other separation—the separation between knowing and believing—with dramatic consequences for the certainty of the faith.

The fields of catechesis and preaching are also affected by this division. Lay Bible instruction reproduces a pattern similar to the one I have described in formal teaching. The results of "scientific" exegesis are popularized in catechesis through Bible studies. However, in the context of the liturgy and preaching, the exegete allows himself a degree of license that would not be allowed in an academic institution because it does not objectively follow from the text. That which is divine or "spiritual" then enters our discourse, but necessarily—once again—it will be perceived as an "addition", something that should be incorporated into the text from the outside. That this is a problem that the Church has been considering for a long time (and the historical journey we have just been through has shown this) is seen by the surprising topicality of the judgment that another pope, Pius X, offered a hundred years ago now, when speaking of the errors of the modernists: "So, when writing history they make no mention of the divinity of Christ, but when preaching in the churches they profess it most strongly. . . . Thus, too, they separate theological and pastoral exegesis from the scientific and the historical" (*Pascendi*; DS 2086).

To mention one final area, the division already discussed is also notable in the relationship between the Old and New Testaments. "Critical" exegesis takes it upon itself to say that the OT is an independent literary corpus that can be understood on its own and that, in fact, belongs to a believing community, the Jewish one, which reads it as a complete whole. Theology may say that the OT is fulfilled in Jesus Christ, and even that the OT gives witness to Christ, but this statement will be perceived, once again, as something that has no basis *in re* (that is, in the books of the OT) but that is based on a confession of faith that is valid only in the context of a believing community (and, furthermore, it would not be suitable to take it out of that context). In this case, there would be serious effects on the certainty of the faith, which since the earliest apostolic times has been surprised at the admirable correspondence between the event of Jesus Christ and the expectation to which the OT attests.

To deal with this serious situation, which Benedict XVI has rightly diagnosed, both in its terms and in its consequences, in this study I have tried to go down two paths that J. Ratzinger (Benedict XVI) himself has indicated at two different times. Both ways aim to attack the root of the problem of the exegesis-theology dualism or, looked at from another perspective, the problem of an exegesis that is only historical and not theological.

The first way was suggested by Ratzinger, then prefect of the Congregation for the Doctrine of the Faith and president of the Pontifical Biblical Commission, in a lecture in New York in 1988. In it, after describing the problem of an exegesis that wants to be called critical and does not accept faith as part of its method, he proposes carrying out a "criticism of criticism" from within critical thought itself. This would be a diachronic reading of the results of the historical-critical method in the different disciplines. A task, Ratzinger then said, that "I do not pretend to be able to achieve . . . alone".[1] By this proposal, he wanted to show that exegesis cannot claim to achieve a level of certainty comparable to that of the natural sciences, with which some like to compare it. In fact, a reading such as the one suggested should clearly show the world of prejudices that have historically conditioned biblical interpretation, making the ideal of objectivity laughable.

This is precisely the task I have tried to carry out in the first part of this work (chapters 1 and 2), in two different areas, both important in the study of the OT. The first area is the investigation of the formation of the Pentateuch, an especially instructive page from the history of exegesis, inasmuch as its central paradigm (the documentary

---

[1] J. Ratzinger, "Biblical Interpretation in Conflict: On the Foundations and the Itinerary of Exegesis Today", in *Opening Up the Scriptures: Joseph Ratzinger and the Foundations of Biblical Interpretation*, ed. José Granados, Carlos Granados, and Luis Sánchez-Navarro (Grand Rapids, 2008), 8.

hypothesis), after a century of practically uncontested domination, is today suffering a very serious legitimacy crisis, to the point that few scholars support it. The second area is that of the study of the figure of the prophet, one of the fields onto which prior religious or cultural understandings have been most powerfully projected.

The possibility of carrying out the diachronic reading of the results of critical exegesis in both areas is today, I must say, easier than it was twenty years ago, when Ratzinger made this suggestion and, of course, much easier than forty, sixty, or eighty years ago. Exegesis has now spent 250 years on the area of the literary criticism of the Pentateuch and almost 150 on the critical study of the prophets. These are more than enough years to look back with understanding and identify a certain journey in step with (and intermingled with) the history of ideas. But there are additional factors that work in our favor.

Indeed, the hermeneutical movement, which bore its best fruit in the second half of the twentieth century, has helped us to understand that no interpretation is neutral and, furthermore, that prior understanding is an essential factor in one's approach to a text. The two world wars did away with the "scientificistic" optimism of the late nineteenth and early twentieth centuries, which exercised such a strong pull on exegesis. The fall of the Berlin Wall in 1989, with the consequent crumbling of ideologies that seemed destined to endure forever, has contributed to a more open cultural context, which has made it possible to criticize paradigms that until then were unassailable. In the area of the Pentateuch, the crisis of the documentary hypothesis (one of the great paradigms of OT interpretation), although it had its origin in the second half of the seventies, did not begin to be an established fact for all exegesis until well into the nineties (still in the twentieth century). It was then that studies began to proliferate that dealt with the question of the methods and their presuppositions, something that was hard to find in previous decades. Finally, the appearance on the scene of the canonical method (which only started to be considered in the eighties), backed by Childs, has made it possible (certainly favored by the cultural context) to call into question one of the basic axioms of the historical-critical method: the diachronic study of the texts. In doing this, the canonical method has shown the relevance of beginning with the final text, which exercises a critical function on the previous stages of redaction.

My diachronic reading of the results of the historical-critical method, in the two areas described, has uncovered very clearly the philosophical and cultural presuppositions that have been decisive in the development of exegesis and its most notable hypothesis. It is truly noteworthy how, on many occasions, those presuppositions led to a kind of myopia in biblical interpretation, so that data that by themselves did not support a certain hypothesis (but rather seemed to contradict it) were brought back into it.

In the case of the formation of the Pentateuch, the presence of different divine names, the existence of duplicates, or contradictions in the same text point toward the composite character of the work, not necessarily toward the existence of four complete and continuous documents. Furthermore, the studies of the history of forms and traditions that Gunkel, von Rad, and Noth carried out after Wellhausen contained elements that, while they supported the composite character of the Pentateuch, directly undermined the hypothesis of four complete documents at its origin. The persuasive force of a model that was comprehensive, together with a certain cultural atmosphere, made it possible for the dominant paradigm simply to strengthen itself by means of the studies mentioned. And this explanatory hypothesis, which bore the valuable seal of being "scientific" (because it started from the objective analysis of literary data), moved through time, firm in its claim to be self-evident, until the cultural conditions and the appearance of a scholar like Rendtorff managed to submit it to examination.

In the area of the prophets, critical investigation sprang from one basic principle: *lex post prophetas*. The passage of time has made it possible to distinguish between the elements of truth that this statement contained and those that did not support it. It is evident that the Law, as we know it today in its different redactions, did not in its totality precede the prophets. However, today it is no longer possible to say that the prophets did not have a tradition before them, and, specifically, a legislative tradition, to which they made reference. This being the case, and the present study has shown it to be so, the religious and philosophical presuppositions of the era were determinative in directing the results of the investigation toward a distorted image of the prophets, who appeared to the eyes of the world to be the creative geniuses of Israel, the initiators of the religion of ethical monotheism. It is clear that in the figure of the prophet the true nature of Christianity was involved. The liberal Protestantism of the late nineteenth century saw in this figure the possibility of vindicating a pure religiosity set free from the chains of the Law and the cult. The prophet would be at the origin of this religion, which was later brought to a climax by Christ and betrayed by the Catholic Church.

In fact, Ratzinger's conclusions when dealing with the diachronic reading of the results of the exegesis of Martin Dibelius and Rudolf Bultmann[2] can serve as a conclusion to my own diachronic reading of the studies of the Pentateuch and the prophets:

> After approximately two hundred years of historical-critical work on the texts, it is no longer possible to spread them out on a single surface and read them side by side. It is necessary to see them perspectivally in the context of their own history. When we do this, we realize that this history is not simply an objectively given story of progress from imprecise findings to precise and objective ones. What emerges into view is that we are dealing also and above all with a history of subjective constellations whose trajectories correspond precisely to the developments of intellectual history and reflect them in the form of interpretations of the text. In the diachronic reading of exegesis, the latter's philosophical presuppositions present themselves readily to view. Looking at things from a distance, the observer finds to his astonishment that what would seem to be rigorously scientific, purely "historical" interpretations turn out in fact to reflect the scholar's own spirit more than they do the spirit of past ages. This need not lead to skepticism, but it should lead to a self-limitation and purification of the method.[3]

Guardini expressed himself very similarly as he carefully analyzed the claim of exegesis to be scientific:

> And similarly here, a later time—often only a decade later, or sometimes even shorter—has seen something change which has been put down with emphasis as scientifically certain. Particularly scientific research—carried out by real men, not their ideology—is indeed prejudiced and apart from that there also exists the strange thing of scientific fashion.[4]

---

[2] Ratzinger bases himself on the doctoral dissertation of Reiner Blank, devoted to the studies of the *history of forms* of both authors: R. Blank, *Analyse und Kritik der formengeschichtlichen Arbeiten von Martin Dibelius und Rudolf Bultmann*, ThDiss 16 (Basel, 1981).

[3] Ratzinger, "Biblical Interpretation in Conflict", 9–10.

[4] R. Guardini, "Holy Scripture and the Science of Faith", trans. Scott G. Hefelfinger, *Letter and Spirit* 6 (2010): 423.

The second way, suggested in this case by Benedict XVI, is that of trying a new synthesis that brings together in a single exegesis—and not in a dualistic form—the two methodological dimensions of the interpretation of Scripture: the historical and the theological. This is the desire the Pope expresses in his Post-Synodal Apostolic Exhortation *Verbum Domini*, conscious of the dramatic consequences of the separation between the two dimensions. The goal is to arrive at an exegesis that is critical and at the same time theological. In fact, a certain type of *exercise* of exegesis is involved, but it is one that will be impossible without serious hermeneutical and theological *reflection*, in view of the conditioning factors, many of which are unconscious, that have so far impeded the desired synthesis.

It is plain that this second task is much more complicated than the first one. And in fact, the times are not as propitious as they are for the diachronic reading of the results of critical exegesis. The negative or self-critical phase, on which Ratzinger's first guideline concentrates, is beginning to show its first results in different areas. The positive labor will undoubtedly be benefited by the results of self-criticism; nevertheless, it will still require much reflection to overcome the dualism between scientific exegesis and theology to which I have so often referred. Ratzinger himself, at the end of the 1988 lecture in which he proposed the first task, gave some notes on "basic elements of a new synthesis",[5] aware that this positive labor "still requires the work of at least another whole generation".[6]

Because of all this, my attempt to contribute to a new synthesis with some reflections can only be a humble one, forming part of the work of the generation to which Ratzinger referred. This attempt is the one I have carried out in the second part of this work (chapter 3), dealing with the characteristic dimensions of the Catholic interpretation of the OT. For this task, it is not enough to affirm the two methodological dimensions of the interpretation of Scripture as DV 12 presents them. Today it is starting to be an established fact for Catholic exegetes that the interpretive task must not stop with the historical-critical dimension but must go as far as theology. However, the larger problem arises when it is time to combine both dimensions into one indivisible

---

[5] Cf. Ratzinger, "Biblical Interpretation in Conflict", 20–29.
[6] Ibid., 8.

synthesis: mere juxtaposition (in which theology always represents the later step) is not enough to free us from the reason-faith and exegesis-theology dualism that threatens us. This dualism cannot be overcome with calls to devotion or with generous attempts to add pious comments to a scripturistic interpretation if faith has not entered into the method from the beginning.

Precisely because of this, my contribution has tried to start with the nature of the object of study, the written and inspired witness of revelation as well as with the very nature of revelation and of faith as the appropriate response of man to God, who is communicating. Understanding the true nature of the object puts us in a position to identify the method that is able to receive this object in all its dimensions.

As a written (human) and inspired (divine) witness, Scripture is characterized by being an accomplishment of the Spirit and at the same time a product of faith (grace-filled and reasonable at the same time). It is not, therefore, a text that can be methodologically accessible (in its historical-critical dimension) without the intervention of a freedom (the faith of the interpreter, a theological dimension) that is able to deal with the symbolic structure with which the truth is given in the witness. Therefore, the historical-critical and theological dimensions depend on one another, not by virtue of a moral appeal or a pious effort, but by virtue of the nature of their object.

Therefore faith must necessarily be involved from the beginning in the shaping of the method, making possible that indivisible unity of the two methodological dimensions that do justice to the nature of Scripture: the historical-critical and the theological. In this synthesis, the freedom of the exegete (that is, his personal involvement, which always entails a moral exercise of responsibility) plays a decisive role. This freedom can no longer be understood as a factor that remains outside of the investigation, in the image of what supposedly occurs in scientific inquiry. On the contrary, it will be decisive because, in fact, only a decision in favor of the event of Christ that remains in time in his Church (by the action of the Holy Spirit), that is, faith (generated and sustained by grace), is able to open the treasures of Scripture.

Thus is uncovered the moral irresponsibility of the exegete who hopes to spare himself the decision concerning his freedom in relation to the Christian event by taking refuge in a "scientific" method. This irresponsibility, beyond being a judgment on the person of the exegete, is an obstacle to knowledge, since it leads to a serious myopia that in fact impedes one's understanding of the text as what it is: a witness of the divine. Decisive questions for exegesis today, like the discussion concerning the diachronic and synchronic methods or the relationship between the OT and the NT, depend in large part on the position the exegete takes in relation to the uniqueness of Christ and his permanence in time.

It is plain that these reflections must take into account, as I have in this study, the cultural atmosphere in which exegesis operates today, which is behind the difficulty in arriving at a new synthesis. The path to overcoming certain modern difficulties in the conception of knowledge, reason, faith, and so forth, must necessarily be involved in the proposal for a new unitary understanding of exegesis. Significantly, Benedict XVI states, "The unity of the two levels at work in the interpretation of sacred Scripture presupposes, in a word, the harmony of faith and reason."[7]

The reflections I have offered, following the guidance of Benedict XVI, make it possible to understand better the general criterion of interpretation that DV 12 gives, which invites people to read and interpret Scripture "in the same spirit in which it was written". It is the grace of faith, in its immanence in the life of the Church, that makes it possible to read Scripture with that same Spirit who was at its origin. The document *The Interpretation of the Bible in the Church*, by the PBC, brings in the same criterion when it states, "Access to a proper understanding of biblical texts is only granted to the person who has an affinity with what the text is saying on the basis of life experience."[8]

The work that is now ending was born of a sincere educational concern, beyond the teaching of the OT in academic centers. To bridge the gap, which has now lasted more than two centuries, between "scientific" exegesis and "believing" theology is an extremely urgent task that will benefit all theology, in a limited sense, and the *intellectus fidei* in general. At stake is no more and no less than the right understanding of faith as well as the avoidance of the reason-faith dualism, in its different variations, which is one of the sicknesses of our time.

---

[7] *Verbum Domini* 36.
[8] PBC, *The Interpretation of the Bible in the Church* II A 2.

Bibliography

Abraham, W. J. *Divine Revelation and the Limits of Historical Criticism*. Oxford, 1982.

Albertz, R. *Religionsgeschichte Israels in alttestamentlicher Zeit*. Göttingen, 1992.

Albright, W. F. "Abram the Hebrew: A New Archeological Interpretation". *BASOR* 163 (1961): 36–54.

———. *Archeology and the Religion of Israel*. 5th ed. New York, 1969.

———. *From the Stone Age to Christianity*. 2nd ed. New York, 1957.

———. *Yahweh and the Gods of Canaan: A Historical Analysis of Two Contrasting Faiths*. London, 1968.

Alonso Schökel, L. "Interpretación de la Sagrada Escritura". In *La Palabra de Dios en la historia de los hombres: Comentario temático a la constitución "Dei Verbum" del Vaticano II sobre la Divina Revelación*, edited by L. Alonso Schökel and A. M. Artola, 385–417. Bilbao, 1991.

———. "Leb". In *Diccionario bíblico hebreo-español*, edited by L. Alonso Schökel, 380–84. Madrid, 1994.

Alt, A. *Der Gott der Väter: Ein Beitrag zur Urgeschichte der israelitischen Religion*. BWANT 3. Stuttgart, 1929.

Alter, R. *The Art of Biblical Narrative*. New York, 1981.

Arendt, H. *The Origins of Totalitarianism*. Cleveland, 1958.

Arkoun, M. "Corano". In *Dizionario del Corano*, edited by V.A., 175–80. Milan, 2007.

Auvray, P. "Comment se pose le problème de l'inspiration des Septante". *RB* 59 (1952): 321–36.

Avalos, H. *The End of Biblical Studies*. New York, 2007.

Barr, J. *The Concept of Biblical Theology: An Old Testament Perspective.* Minneapolis, 1999.

———. *History and Ideology in the Old Testament: Biblical Studies at the End of a Millennium. The Hensley Henson Lectures for 1997 Delivered to the University of Oxford.* Oxford, 2000.

———. *Holy Scripture: Canon, Authority, Criticism.* Oxford, 1983.

———. "Review Article of B. S. Childs, *Introduction to the Old Testament as Scripture". JSOT* 16 (1980): 12–23.

———. "The Synchronic, the Diachronic and the Historical: A Triangular Relationship?" In *Synchronic or Diachronic? A Debate on Method in Old Testament Exegesis,* edited by J. C. De Moor, 1–14. OTS 34. Leiden, New York, and Cologne, 1995.

Barthélemy, D. "L'Ancien Testament a mûri à Alexandrie". *ThZ* 21 (1965): 358–70.

———. "La Place de la Septante dans l'Eglise". In *Aux grands carrefours de la révélation et de l'eségèse de l'Ancien Testament,* 13–28. RechBib 8. Paris, 1967.

Beale, G. K., ed. *John's Use of the Old Testament in Revelation.* JSNT.S 166. Sheffield, 1998.

———. *The Right Doctrine from the Wrong Texts? Essays on the Use of the Old Testament in the New.* Grand Rapids, 1994.

Belli, F. " 'Testimoniada por la Ley y los profetas'. Rom 3,21: Pablo y las Escrituras". *RevAg* 43 (2002): 413–26.

Belli, F., I. Carbajosa, C. Jódar Estrella, and L. Sánchez Navarro. *Vetus in Novo: El recurso a la Escritura en el Nuevo Testamento.* Madrid, 2006.

Benedict XVI. See Ratzinger, J.

Benoit, P. "L'Inspiration des Septante d'après les Pères". In *L'Homme devant Dieu, mélanges offerts au Père Henri De Lubac.* Vol. 1: *Exégèse et Patristique,* 169–87. Théologie 56. Paris, 1963.

———. "La Septante est-elle inspirée?" In *Vom Wort des Lebens: Festschrift für Max Meinertz,* edited by N. Adler, 41–49. Münster, 1951.

Bentzen, A. *Introduction to the Old Testament.* Copenhagen, 1948.

Bertuletti, A. "Esegesi biblica e teologia sistematica". In *La Rivelazione attestata: La Bibbia fra Testo e Teologia: Raccolta di Studi in onore del Cardinale Carlo Maria Martini, Arcivescovo di Milano, per il suo LXX compleanno*, edited by G. Angelini, 133–57. Milan, 1998.

Blank, R. *Analyse und Kritik der formengeschichtlichen Arbeiten von Martin Dibelius und Rudolf Bultmann*. ThDiss 16. Basel, 1981.

Blenkinsopp, J. *The Pentateuch: An Introduction to the First Five Books of the Bible*. New York, 1992.

Blondel, M. *Histoire et dogme: Les Lacunes philosophiques de l'exégèse moderne*. La Chapelle-Montligeon, 1904. Translated into Spanish as *Historia y dogma*. Madrid, 2004, trans. into English in *The Letter on Apologetics and History and Dogma*, Ressourcement: Retrieval and Renewal in Catholic Thought. Grand Rapids, 1995.

Blum, E. *Die Komposition der Vätergeschichte*. WMANT 57. Neukirchen-Vluyn, 1984.

———. *Studien zur Komposition des Pentateuch*. BZAW 189. Berlin and New York, 1990.

Borgonovo, G. "Una proposta di rilettura dell'ispirazione biblica dopo gli apporti della Form- e della Redaktionsgeschichte". In *L'Interpretazione della Bibbia nella Chiesa: Atti del Simposio promosso dalla Congregazione per la Dottrina della Fede. Roma, settembre 1999*, edited by P. Grech, J. N. Aletti, M. Ouellet, and H. Simian-Yofre, 41–63. Atti e Documenti 11. Vatican City, 2001.

Bright, J. *A History of Israel*. 3rd ed. Philadelphia, 1981.

Brueggemann, W. *Theology of the Old Testament: Testimony, Dispute, Advocacy*. Minneapolis, 1997.

Campbell, A. F., and M. A. O'Brien. *Rethinking the Pentateuch: Prolegomena to the Theology of Ancient Israel*. Louisville, 2005.

———. *Sources of the Pentateuch: Texts, Introductions, Annotations*. Minneapolis, 1993.

Carbajosa, I. "El Antiguo Testamento, realidad abierta". In *Entrar en lo Antiguo*, edited by I. Carbajosa and L. Sánchez Navarro, 21–50. PD 16. Madrid, 2007.

———. "La progresiva condescendencia de la Palabra de Dios en Israel". In *Palabra encarnada: La Palabra de Dios en la Iglesia*, edited by I. Carbajosa and L. Sánchez Navarro, 15–66. PD 20. Madrid, 2008.

———. "La recuperación del Antiguo Testamento para la vida de la Iglesia: Estudio de *Dei Verbum* 14". In *Fuente de agua viva: Homenaje al profesor D. Enrique Farfán*, edited by J. Pascual Torró and J. M. Díaz Rodelas, 17–37. SVal 55. Valencia. 2007.

———. "Il Testamento divino offerto alla libertà umana". *Oasis* 7 (2008): 17–21.

Carrasco Rouco, A. "La puesta en cuestión histórico-crítica del testimonio apostólico sobre Jesucristo". *RET* 61 (2001): 207–31.

Carroll, R. P. "Biblical Idolatry: *Ideologiekritik*, Biblical Studies and the Problematics of Ideology". *JNSL* 24 (1998): 101–14.

———. "An Infinity of Traces: On Making an Inventory of our Ideological Holdings: An Introduction to *Ideologiekritik*". *JNSL* 21 (1995): 25–43.

———. *Jeremiah: A Commentary*. London, 1986.

———. "Jeremiah, Intertextuality and *Ideologiekritik*". *JNSL* 22 (1996): 15–34.

———. "On Representation in the Bible: An *Ideologiekritik* Approach". *JNSL* 20 (1994): 1–15.

———. "Whose Prophet? Whose History? Whose Social Reality? Troubling the Interpretative Community Again: Notes Towards a Response to T. W. Overholt's Critique". *JSOT* 48 (1990): 33–49.

———. *Wolf in the Sheepfold: The Bible as Problematic for Theology*. London, 1997.

Carrón Pérez, J. *Acontecimiento y razón: Principio hermenéutico paulino y la interpretación moderna de la Escritura*. Sub 1. Madrid, 2001.

Carter, C. E. "Opening Windows onto Biblical Worlds: Applying the Social Sciences to Hebrew Scripture". In *The Face of Old Testament Studies: A Survey of Contemporary Approaches*, edited by D. W. Baker and B. T. Arnold, 421–51. Grand Rapids, 1999.

Carter, C. E., and C. L. Meyers, eds. *Community, Identity and Ideology: Social Science Approaches to the Hebrew Bible*. Winona Lake, 1996.

Cassuto, U. *The Documentary Hypothesis and the Composition of the Pentateuch*. Jerusalem and New York, 2006.

Castelli, E., et al. *The Postmodern Bible*. New Haven and London, 1995.

Childs, B. S. *Biblical Theology in Crisis*. Philadelphia, 1970.

————. *Biblical Theology of the Old and New Testaments: Theological Reflection on the Christian Bible*. London, 1992.

————. "The Canonical Shape of the Prophetic Literature". *Interp* 32 (1978): 46–55.

————. "Childs Versus Barr: Review of Barr, *Holy Scripture*". *Interp* 38 (1984): 66–70.

————. "Critical Reflections on James Barr's Understanding of the Literal and the Allegorical". *JSOT* 46 (1990): 3–9.

————. "Does the Old Testament Witness to Jesus Christ?" *Evangelium—Schriftauslegung—Kirche: Festschrift für Peter Stuhlmacher zum 65. Geburtstag*, edited by J. Ådna, S. J. Hafemann, and O. Hofius, 57–64. Göttingen, 1997.

————. "Interpretation in Faith: The Theological Responsibility of an Old Testament Commentary". *Interp* 18 (1964): 432–49.

————. *Introduction to the Old Testament as Scripture*. Philadelphia, 1979.

————. *Isaiah*. OTL. Louisville, 2001.

————. *The New Testament as Canon: An Introduction*. Valley Forge, 1984.

————. *Old Testament Theology in a Canonical Context*. Philadelphia, 1985.

————. "A Response". *HBT* 2 (1980): 199–211.

————. "Response to Reviewers". *JSOT* 16 (1980): 52–60.

————. "Retrospective Reading of the Old Testament Prophets". *ZAW* 108 (1996): 362–77.

————. *The Struggle to Understand Isaiah as Christian Scripture*. Grand Rapids, 2004.

Clements, R. E. *Prophecy and Tradition*. Oxford, 1975.

Clines, D. J. A. "Response to Rendtorff". In *Probing the Frontiers of Biblical Studies*, edited by J. H. Ellens and J. T. Greene, 49–55. PTMS 111. Eugene, 2009.

———. *The Theme of the Pentateuch*. JSOT.S. Sheffield, 1978.

Colombo, G. "Grazia e libertà nell'atto di fede". In *Noi crediamo: Per una teologia dell'atto di fede*, edited by R. Fisichella, 39–57. Rome, 1993.

Comisión Teológica Internacional. *El cristianismo y las religiones*. Vatican City, 1996.

Dahmen, U. *Psalmen- und Psalter-Rezeption im Frühjudentum: Reconstruktion, Textbestand, Struktur und Pragmatik der Psalmenrolle 11QPsª aus Qumran*. STDJ 49. Leiden and Boston, 2003.

———. "Psalmentext und Psalmensammlung: Eine Auseinandersetzung mit P. W. Flint". In *Die Handschriftenfunde vom Toten Meer und der Text der Hebräischen Bibel*, edited by U. Dahmen, A. Lange, and H. Lichtenberg. Neukirchen-Vluyn, 2000.

Davies, P. R. *In Search of "Ancient Israel"*. JSOT.S 148. Sheffield, 1992.

De Lubac, H. "Comentario al preámbulo y al capítulo primero". In *La Revelación divina: Comentarios a la constitución dogmática "Dei Verbum"*, edited by H. de Lubac, B. D. Dupuy, et al., 1:183–367. Madrid, 1970.

De Vaux, R. "A propos du second centenaire d'Astruc: Reflexions sur l'état actuel de la critique du Pentateuque." In *Congress Volume: Copenhagen 1953*, 182–98. VT.S. Leiden, 1953.

———. *Histoire ancienne d'Israel*. Paris, 1971.

De Wette, W. M. L. *Dissertatio critica qua Deuteronomium diversium a prioribus Pentateuchi libris, alius cuiusdam recentioris autoris opus esse demonstratur*. Jena, 1805.

Deist, F. E. *The Material Culture of the Bible: An Introduction*. BS 70. Sheffield, 2000.

———. "The Problem of History in Old Testament Theology" *OTWSA* 24 (1981): 23–39.

———. "The Prophets: Are We Heading for a Paradigm Switch?" In *Prophet und Prophetenbuch: Festschrift für Otto Kaiser zum 65. Geburtstag*, edited by V. Fritz, K.-F. Pohlmann, and H.-C. Schmitt, 1–18. BZAW 185. Berlin, 1989.

Dozeman, T. B., and K. Schmid, eds. *A Farewell to the Yahwist? The Composition of the Pentateuch in Recent European Interpretation.* SBLSS 34. Atlanta, 2006.

Duhm, B. *Das Buch Jesaia.* Göttingen, 1892.

———. *Die Theologie der Propheten als Grundlage für die innere Entwicklungsgeschichte der israelitischen Religion.* Bonn, 1875.

Eichhorn, J. G. *Einleitung in das Alte Testament.* Göttingen, 1780–1783.

Ellis, E. E. *The Old Testament in Early Christianity: Canon and Interpretation in the Light of Modern Research.* Tübingen, 1991.

Emerton, J. A. "The Riddle of Genesis XIV". *VT* 21 (1971): 403–39.

Engnell, I. "Prophets and Prophetism in the Old Testament". In *A Rigid Scrutiny: Critical Essays on the Old Testament by Ivan Engnell translated from the Swedish*, edited by J. T. Willis and H. Ringgren, 123–79. Nashville, 1969.

Evans, C. A. "The Function of the Old Testament in the New". In *Introducing New Testament Interpretation*, edited by S. McKnight. Grand Rapids, 2000.

Ewald, H. *Geschichte des Volkes Israels bis Christus.* Göttingen, 1843–1845.

Finkelstein, I., and N. A. Silberman. *The Bible Unearthed: Archeology's New Vision of Ancient Israel and the Origin of Its Sacred Texts.* New York, 2001.

Fisher, B., and R. Weber, eds. *Biblia Sacra iuxta Vulgatam Versionem.* 3rd ed. Stuttgart, 1983.

Frei, H. W. *The Eclipse of Biblical Narrative: A Study in Eighteenth and Nineteenth Century Hermeneutics.* New Haven and London, 1974.

Friedman, R. E. *The Bible with Sources Revealed: A New View into the Five Books of Moses.* San Francisco, 2003.

———. *The Hidden Book in the Bible.* San Francisco, 1998.

Frampton, T. L. *Spinoza and the Rise of Historical Criticism of the Bible*. New York, 2006.

Gadamer, H. G. "Hermeneutik und Historismus". *PhR* 1962 (1962): 241–76.

———. *Truth and Method*. Translated by J. Weinsheimer and D. G. Marshall. 2nd rev. ed. New York, 2004.

García López, F. "De la antigua a la nueva crítica literaria del Pentateuco". *EstBib* 52 (1994): 7–35.

———. *El Pentateuco: Introducción a la lectura de los cinco primeros libros de la Biblia*. IEB 3a. Estella, 2003.

Geddes, A. *Critical Remarks*. London, 1800.

———. *The Holy Bible as the Books Accounted Sacred by Jews and Christians*. London, 1792.

Gerstenberger, E. S. *Theologien im Alten Testament: Pluralität und Synkretismus alttestamentlichen Gottesglaubens*. Stuttgart, 2001.

Gismondi, G. "Epistemologia". In *Dizionario Interdisciplinare di Scienza e Fede: Cultura scientifica, Filosofia e Teologia*, edited by G. Tanzella-Nitti and A. Strumia, 1:486–504. Rome, 2002.

Gnilka J. "Die biblische Exegese im Lichte des Dekretes über die göttliche Offenbarung (Dei Verbum)". *MThZ* 36 (1985): 5–19.

Gordon, R. P. "A Story of Two Paradigm Shifts". In *"The Place Is Too Small for Us": The Israelite Prophets in Recent Scholarship*, edited by R. P. Gordon, 3–26. SBThS 5. Winona Lake, 1995.

Graf, K. H. *Die Geschichtlichen Bücher des Alten Testaments: Zwei historisch-kritischen Untersuchungen*. Leipzig, 1866.

Grelot, P. "La inspiración de la Sagrada Escritura y su interpretación: Comentario al capítulo III". In *La Revelación divina: Comentarios a la constitución dogmática "Dei Verbum"*, edited by H. de Lubac, B. D. Dupuy, et al., 2:15–58. Madrid, 1970.

———. "Sur l'inspiration et la canonicité de la Septante". *ScEc* 16 (1964): 387–418.

————. "Le Texte du Psaume 39,7 dans la Septante". *RB* 108 (2001): 210–13.

Gressmann, H. *Mose und seine Zeit*. Göttingen, 1913.

Gril, D. "Rivelazione e ispirazione". In *Dizionario del Corano*, edited by V.A., 724–30. Milan, 2007.

Guardini, R. "Heilige Schrift und Glaubenswissenschaft". *Die Schild-genossen* 8 (1928): 24–57. Translated into Spanish as "Sagrada Es-critura y ciencia de la fe". In *Biblia y ciencia de la fe*, edited by C. Granados and A. Giménez, 17–66. Madrid, 2007. Translated into English by Scott G. Hefelfinger as "Holy Scripture and the Science of Faith". *Letter and Spirit* 6 (2010): 401–32.

Guitton, J. *Nouvel art de penser*. Paris: Aubier, 1946. Translated into Spanish as *Nuevo arte de pensar*. Madrid, 2001.

Gunkel, H. "Die geheimen Erfahrungen der Propheten". In *Die grossen Propheten*, edited by H. Schmidt, xvii–xxxiv. 2nd ed. Göttingen, 1923.

————. *Genesis*, 3rd ed. GHZAT 1,1. Göttingen, 1910. Translated by Mark E. Biddle as *Genesis*. Macon, Ga., 1997.

————. "Die israelitische Literatur". In *Die Kultur der Gegenwart: Die orientalischen Literaturen*, edited by P. Hinneberg. Berlin and Leipzig, 1906.

————. "The Secret Experiences of the Prophets". *Exp* 9 (1924): 1:356–66; 2:427–35; 3:23–32.

Gunneweg, A. H. J. *Biblische Theologie des Alten Testaments: Eine Religions-geschichte Israels in biblisch-theologischer Sicht*. Stuttgart, 1993.

Hahn, F. "Probleme historischer Kritik". *ZNW* 63 (1972): 1–17.

Haneberg, D. B. *Versuch einer Geschichte der biblischen Offenbarung*. Regens-burg, 1850.

Harrisville, R. A., and W. Sundberg. *The Bible in Modern Culture: Baruch Spinoza to Brevard Childs*. 2nd ed. Grand Rapids, 2002.

Harvey, V. A. *The Historian and the Believer: The Morality of Historical Knowledge and Christian Belief*. New York, 1966.

Hengel, M. "Historische Methoden und theologische Auslegung des Neuen Testaments". *KuD* 19 (1973): 85–90.

Herrmann, W. *Theologie des Alten Testaments: Geschichte und Bedeutung des israelitisch-jüdischen Glaubens*. Stuttgart, 2004.

Hölscher, G. *Hesekiel, der Dichter und das Buch: Eine literarkritische Untersuchung*. BZAW 39. Giessen, 1924.

———. *Die Profeten: Untersuchungen zur Religionsgeschichte Israels*. Leipzig, 1914.

Hoping, H. "Theologischer Kommentar zur Dogmatischen Konstitution über die göttliche Offenbarung *Dei Verbum*". In *Herders Theologischer Kommentar zum Zweiten Vatikanischen Konzil*, edited by P. Hünermann and B.-J. Hilberath, 3:695–831. Freiburg, Basel, and Vienna, 2005.

House, P. R. *Old Testament Theology*. Downers Grove, 1998.

Hupfeld, H. *Die Quellen der Genesis und die Art ihrer Zusammensetzung von neuem untersucht*. Berlin, 1853.

Ilgen, K. D. *Die Urkunden des Jerusalemer Tempelarchivs in ihrer Urgestalt, als Beitrag zur Berichtigung der Geschichte der Religion und Politik aus dem Hebräischen mit kritischen und erklärenden Anmerkungen, auch mancherley dazu gehörenden Abhandlungen*. Halle, 1798.

Jagersma, H. *A History of Israel to Bar Kochba*. London, 1994.

Kähler, M. *Die sogenannte historische Jesus und der geschichtliche biblische Christus*. Leipzig, 1892.

Kaiser, O. *Der Gott des Alten Testaments: Wesen und Wirken: Theologie des Alten Testaments*. Göttingen, 1993.

Kant, I. *Religion within the Boundaries of Mere Reason and Other Writings*. Translated and edited by Allen Wood and George di Giovanni. Cambridge, 1998.

Kaufmann, Y. *The Religion of Israel, from its Beginnings to the Babylonian Exile*. Chicago, 1960.

Kermode, F. "The Argument about Canons". In *An Appetite for Poetry: Essays in Literary Interpretation*, edited by F. Kermode, 189–207. London, 1989.

Kierkegaard, S. *Fear and Trembling and The Sickness unto Death*. Translated by Walter Lowrie. Garden City, N.Y., 1941, 1954.

Klatt, W. *Hermann Gunkel: Zu seiner Theologie der Religionsgeschichte und zur Entstehung der formgeschichtliche Methode*. Göttingen, 1969.

Knohl, I. *The Sanctuary of Silence: The Priestly Torah and the Holiness School*. Minneapolis, 1995.

Köhler, L., W. Baumgartner, and J. J. Stamm. *The Hebrew and Aramaic Lexicon of the Old Testament*. Leiden, 2001.

Kraus, H.-J. *Geschichte der historisch-kritischen Erforschung des Alten Testament*. 3rd ed. Neukirchen-Vluyn, 1982.

Krentz, E. *The Historical-Critical Method*. Philadelphia, 1975.

Kuenen, A. "Critische bijdragen tot de geschiedenis van den Israëlitischen godsdienst: V. De priestelijke bestanddeelen van Pentateuch en Josua". *ThT* 4 (1870): 391–426, 487–526.

———. *The Prophets and Prophecy in Israel: An Historical and Critical Enquiry*. London, 1877.

Kuhn, T. *The Structure of Scientific Revolutions*. Chicago, 1962.

Lemche, N. P. "Rachel and Lea: Or: On the Survival of Outdated Paradigmas in the Study of the Origin of Israel". *SJOT* 2 (1987): 127–53.

Lessing, G. E. "The Education of the Human Race". In *Philosophical and Theological Writings*, translated and edited by H. B. Nisbet, 217–40. Cambridge, 2005.

———. "On the Origin of Revealed Religion." In *Philosophical and Theological Writings*, translated and edited by H. B. Nisbet, 35–36. Cambridge, 2005.

———. "On the Proof of the Spirit and of Power". In *Philosophical and Theological Writings*, translated and edited by H. B. Nisbet, 83–88. Cambridge, 2005.

———. *Philosophical and Theological Writings*. Translated and edited by H. B. Nisbet. Cambridge, 2005.

Liverani, M. *Oltre la Bibbia: Storia antica di Israele*. Rome and Bari, 2003.

Lohfink, N. "Il problema dell'inerranzia". In *La verità della Bibbia nel dibattito attuale*, edited by V.A., 21–63. Brescia, 1968.

———. "Der weibe Fleck in *Dei Verbum*, Artikel 12". *TThZ* 101 (1992): 20–35.

MacIntyre, A. *After Virtue: A Study in Moral Theory*. 3rd ed. Notre Dame, 2007.

Maier, G. *Das Ende der historisch-kritischen Methode*. Wuppertal, 1974.

Martínez Fernández, F. J. *Más allá de la razón secular: Algunos retos contemporáneos para la vida y el pensamiento de la Iglesia, vistos desde Occidente*. Cuadernos 1. Granada, 2008.

McAuliffe, J. D., ed. *Encyclopaedia of the Qur'ān*. Leiden, 2001–2006.

McConville, J. G. *Law and Theology in Deuteronomy*. JSOT.S 33. Sheffield, 1984.

Mendenhall, G. E. "Ancient Oriental and Biblical Law". *BA* 17 (1954): 26–46.

———. *Law and Covenant in the Ancient Near East*. Pittsburgh, 1955.

Menken, M. J. J., and S. Moyise. *The Psalms in the New Testament*. London, 2004.

Moberly, R. W. L. *The Old Testament of the Old Testament*. Minneapolis, 1992.

Molina Palma, M. A. *La interpretación de la Escritura en el Espíritu: Estudio histórico y teológico de un principio hermenéutico de la constitución 'Dei Verbum', 12*. Burgos, 1987.

Mowinckel, S. *Offersang og sangoffer: Salmediktingen i Bibelen*. Oslo, 1951.

———. *Prophecy and Tradition: The Prophetic Books in the Light of the Study of the Growth and History of the Tradition*. Oslo, 1946.

———. *The Psalms in Israel's Worship*. Nashville, 1962.

———. *Religion und Kultus*. Göttingen, 1953.

———. " 'The Spirit' and the 'Word' in the Pre-exilic Reforming Prophets". *JBL* 53 (1934): 199–227.

Moyise, S. *The Old Testament in the Book of Revelation.* JSNT.S 115. Sheffield, 1995.

———. *The Old Testament in the New: An Introduction.* London and New York, 2001.

Nathan, E. "Truth and Prejudice: A Theological Reflection on Biblical Exegesis". *EThL* 83 (2007): 281–318.

Nations, A. L. "Historical Criticism and the Current Methodological Crisis". *SJT* 36 (1986): 59–71.

Niebuhr, H. R. *Radical Monotheism and Western Culture.* New York, 1960.

Nobile, M. *Teologia dell'Antico Testamento.* Turin, 1998.

Noth, M. *Geschichte Israels.* Göttingen, 1950.

———. *The History of Israel.* Translated by Stanley Godman. 2nd ed. London, 1960.

———. *A History of Pentateuchal Traditions.* Translated by Bernhard W. Anderson. Chico, Calif., 1980.

———. *Numbers: A Commentary.* Translated by James D. Martin. Philadelphia, 1968.

———. *Das System der zwölf Stämme Israels.* BWANT 52. Stuttgart, 1930.

———. *Überlieferungsgeschichte des Pentateuch.* Stuttgart, 1948.

———. *Überlieferungsgeschichtliche Studien; die sammelnden und bearbeiten Geschichtswerke im Alten Testament.* 2nd ed. Tübingen, 1957.

———. *Das vierte Buch Mose: Numeri übersetzt und erklärt.* Göttingen, 1966.

Oden, R. A. *The Bible without Theology: The Theological Tradition and Alternatives to It.* San Francisco, 1987.

———. "Intellectual History and the Study of the Bible". In *The Future of Biblical Studies: The Hebrew Scriptures*, edited by R. E. Friedman and H. G. M. Williamson, 1–18. Atlanta, 1987.

Pannenberg, W. *Grundfragen systematischer Theologie: Gesammelte Aufsätze.* Göttingen, 1967.

Penna, R. "Appunti sul come e perchè il Nuovo Testamento si rapporta all'Antico". *Bib* 81 (2000): 95–104.

Perlitt, L. *Vatke und Wellhausen*. BZAW 94. Berlin, 1965.

Peters, T. "The Use of Analogy in Historical Method". *CBQ* 35 (1973): 475–82.

Pontifical Biblical Commission. *The Interpretation of the Bible in the Church*. Vatican City, 1993.

———. *The Jewish People and Their Sacred Scriptures in the Christian Bible*. Vatican City, 2001.

Porteous, N. W. "Record and Revelation". In *Record and Revelation: Essays on the Old Testament by Members of the Society for the Old Testament Study*, edited by H. W. Robinson, 216–49. Oxford, 1938.

Prades, J. "La fe como gracia. Libertad de la fe". In *Diccionario de Teología*, edited by C. Izquierdo, J. Burggraf, and F. M. Arocana, 407–15. Pamplona, 2006.

———. "Un testigo eficaz: Benedicto XVI". In *Dios salve la razón*, edited by Benedicto XVI, G. Bueno, et al., 7–27. Madrid, 2008.

Preuss, H. D. *Theologie des Alten Testaments*. Stuttgart, 1991.

Ratzinger, J. "Biblical Interpretation in Crisis: On the Question of the Foundations and Approaches of Exegesis Today". In *Biblical Interpretation in Crisis*, edited by Richard J. Neuhaus, 1–23. Grand Rapids, 1989. Also translated as "Biblical Interpretation in Conflict: On the Foundations and the Itinerary of Exegesis Today". In *Opening Up the Scriptures: Joseph Ratzinger and the Foundations of Biblical Interpretation*, edited by José Granados, Carlos Granados, and Luis Sánchez-Navarro, 1–29. Grand Rapids, 2008.

———. *Introduction to Christianity*. New York, 1988.

———. *Jesus of Nazareth: From the Baptism in the Jordan to the Transfiguration*. New York, 2007.

Redford, B. D. *A Study of the Biblical Story of Joseph*. VT.S 20. Leiden, 1970.

Renan, E. *The History of the Origins of Christianity. Book I: Life of Jesus*. London, 1890.

Rendtorff, R. "Between Historical Criticism and Holistic Interpretation: New Trends in Old Testament Exegesis". In *Congress Volume: Jerusalem 1986*, edited by J. A. Emerton, 298–303. VT.S 40. Leiden, 1988.

———. *Christen und Juden heute: Neue Einsichten und neue Aufgaben*. Neukirchen-Vluyn, 1998.

———. *Hat denn Gott sein Volk verstossen? Die evangelische Kirche und das Judentum seit 1945: Ein Kommentar*. ACJD 18. Munich, 1989.

———. "Der 'Jahwist' als Theologe? Zum Dilemma der Pentateuchkritik". In *Congress Volume Edinburgh 1974*, edited by L. Alonso Schökel, 158–66. VT.S 28. Leiden, 1975.

———. *Kontinuität im Widerspruch: Autobiographische Reflexionen*. Göttingen, 2007.

———. *The Problem of the Process of Transmission in the Pentateuch*. Translated by John J. Scullion. JSOT.S 89. Sheffield, 1990.

———. "Rezension Brevard S. Childs, *Biblical Theology of the Old and New Testaments: Theological Reflection on the Christian Bible*". In *Sünde und Gericht*, edited by J. Baldermann et al., 359–69. JBTh 9. Neukirchen-Vluyn, 1994.

———. *Theologie des Alten Testaments: Ein kanonischer Entwurf*. Neukirchen-Vluyn, 1999.

———. *Das überlieferungsgeschichtliche Problem des Pentateuch*. BZAW 147. Berlin and New York, 1977.

———. "What Happened to the Yahwist? Reflections after Thirty Years". In *Probing the Frontiers of Biblical Studies*, edited by J. H. Ellens and J. T. Greene, 39–49. PTMS 111. Eugene, 2009.

Reuss, E. *L'Histoire Sainte et la Loi*. Paris, 1879.

Ricoeur, P. "The Canon between the Text and the Community". In *Philosophical Hermeneutics and Biblical Exegesis*, edited by P. Pokorný and J. Roskovec, 7–26. WUNT 153. Tübingen, 2002.

———. *Le Conflit des interpretations: Essais d'herméneutique*. Paris, 1969. Translated as *The Conflict of Interpretations: Essays in Hermeneutics*. Evanston, Ill., 1974.

———. "Contribut d'une réflexion sur le language à une théologie de la parole". In *Exégèse et herméneutique*, edited by V.A., 301–18. Paris, 1971.

———. "Ermeneutica filosofica ed ermeneutica biblica". In *Exegesis: Problèmes de méthode et exercises de lectura*, edited by F. Bovon and G. Rouiller. Neuchâtel, 1975.

———. "Herméneutique de l'idée de révélation". In *La Révélation*, edited by V.A., 15–54. Brussels, 1977.

———. "L'Herméneutique du témoignage". In *Lectures 3: Aux Frontières de la philosophie*, edited by P. Ricoeur, 107–39. Paris, 1994.

———. "Le Sujet convoque à l'École des Récits de Vocation Prophétique". *RICP* 28 (1988): 83–99.

Riehm, E. *Die Gesetzgebung Moses in Lande Moab*. Gotha, 1854.

Roberts, T. A. *History and Christian Apologetic*. London, 1960.

Robinson, H. W. *Inspiration and Revelation in the Old Testament*. Oxford, 1946.

Robinson, J. M., P. Hoffmann, and J. S. Kloppenborg. *The Critical Edition of Q: Synopsis including the Gospels of Matthew and Luke, Mark and Thomas*. Louvain, 2000.

Robinson, T. H. "The Ecstatic Element in O. T. Prophecy". *Exp* 21 (1921): 217–38.

———. *Prophecy and the Prophets in Ancient Israel*. London, 1923.

Rofé, A. *La composizione del Pentateuco: Un'introduzione*. SB 35. Bologna, 1999. Translated as *Introduction to the Composition of the Pentateuch*. Sheffield, 1999.

Römer, T. "The Elusive Yahwist: A Short History of Research". In *A Farewell to the Yahwist? The Composition of the Pentateuch in Recent European Interpretation*, edited by T. B. Dozeman and K. Schmid, 9–27. SBLSS 34. Atlanta, 2006.

Römer, T., and K. Schmid, eds. *Les Dernières Rédactions du Pentateuque, de L'Hexateuque et de L'Ennéateuque*. BEThL 203. Louvain, 2007.

Sanders, J. A. *Canon and Community: A Guide to Canonical Criticism*. Philadelphia, 1984.

———. "Canon as Dialogue". In *The Bible at Qumran: Text, Shape, and Interpretation*, edited by P. W. Flint, 7–26. SDSSRL. Grand Rapids and Cambridge, 2001.

———. *From Sacred Story to Sacred Text: Canon as Paradigm*. Philadelphia, 1987.

———. "The Modern History of the Qumran Psalms Scroll and Its Relation to Canon Criticism". In *Emanuel: Studies in Hebrew Bible, Septuagint and Dead Sea Scrolls in Honor of Emanuel Tov*, edited by S. M. Paul, R. A. Kraft, L. H. Schiffman, and W. W. Fields, 393–411. VT.S 94. Leiden and Boston, 2003.

———. *The Psalms Scroll of Qumrân Cave 11*. DJD IV. Oxford, 1965.

———. "Stability and Fluidity in Text and Canon". In *Tradition of the Text: Studies Offered to Dominique Barthélemy in Celebration of His 70th Birthday*, edited by G. J. Norton and S. Pisano, 203–17. OBO 109. Freiburg and Göttingen, 1991.

———. *Torah and Canon*. Philadelphia, 1972.

Sandmel, S. "The Haggada within Scripture". *JBL* 80 (1961): 105–22.

Schearing, L. S., and S. L. McKenzie. *Those Elusive Deuteronomists: The Phenomenon of Pan-Deuteronomism*. Sheffield, 1999.

Schenker, A. "L'Écriture sainte subsiste en plusieurs formes canoniques simultanées". In *L'Interpretazione della Bibbia nella Chiesa: Atti del Simposio promosso dalla Congregazione per la Dottrina della Fede. Roma, settembre 1999*, edited by P. Grech, J. N. Aletti, M. Ouellet, and H. Simian-Yofre, 178–86. Atti e Documenti 11. Vatican City, 2001.

Schmid, H. H. *Der sogenannte Jahwist*. Zurich, 1976.

Schreiner, J. *Theologie des Alten Testaments*. Würzburg, 1995.

Schweitzer, A. *The Quest of the Historical Jesus*. Translated by W. Montgomery. Revised by J. R. Coates, Susan Cupitt, and John Bowden. Minneapolis, 2001.

Scobie, C. H. H. *The Ways of Our God: An Approach to Biblical Theology*. Grand Rapids, 2003.

Scola, A. *Cuestiones de antropología teológica*. Madrid, 2000.

———. *¿Quién es la Iglesia? Una clave antropológica y sacramental para la eclesiología*. Valencia, 2008.

Segal, M. H. *The Pentateuch: Its Composition and Its Authorship and Other Biblical Studies*. Jerusalem, 1967.

Ska, J.-L. *Introduzione all lettura del Pentateuco: Chiavi per l'interpretazione dei primi cinque libri della Bibbia*. Rome, 1998. Translated by Pascale Dominique as *Introduction to Reading the Pentateuch*. Winona Lake, 2006.

———. "Old and New Perspectives in Old Testament Research". In *The Exegesis of the Pentateuch: Exegetical Studies and Basic Questions*, edited by Jean-Louis Ska, 246–66. FAT 66. Tübingen, 2009.

———. "The Yahwist, a Hero with a Thousand Faces: A Chapter in the History of Modern Exegesis". In *Abschied vom Jahwisten: Die Komposition des Hexateuch in der jüngsten Diskussion*, edited by J. C. Gertz, K. Schmid, and M. Witte, 1–23. BZAW 315. Berlin, 2002.

Spinoza, B. *Theological-Political Treatise*. Cambridge, 2007.

Strauss, D. F. *Das Leben Jesu*. 4th ed. Tübingen, 1840.

———. *The Life of Jesus Critically Examined*. Translated by George Eliot. 4th ed. London, 1902.

Theissen, G. "Historical Scepticism and the Criteria of Jesus Research or My Attempt to Leap Across Lessing's Yawning Gulf". *SJT* 49 (1996): 147–76.

Thompson, T. L. *Early History of the Israelite People*. Leiden, 1994.

Tov, E. *Textual Criticism of the Hebrew Bible*. 2nd ed. Minneapolis and Assen, 2001.

Troeltsch, E. *Gesammelte Schriften*. Vol. 2: *Zur religiösen Lage, Religionsphilosophie und Ethik*. Tübingen, 1922.

Uríbarri, G. "Exégesis científica y teología dogmática: Materiales para un diálogo". *EstBib* 64 (2006): 547–78.

———. "Para una nueva racionalidad de la exégesis: Diagnóstico y propuesta". *EstBib* 65 (2007): 253–306.

Van Seters, J. *Abraham in History and Tradition*. New Haven and London, 1975.

———. *The Life of Moses: The Yahwist as Historian in Exodus-Numbers*. Kampen, 1994.

———. *Prologue to History: The Yahwist as Historian in Genesis*. Louisville, 1992.

———. "The Report of the Yahwist's Demise Has Been Greatly Exaggerated!" In *A Farewell to the Yahwist? The Composition of the Pentateuch in Recent European Interpretation*, edited by T. B. Dozeman and K. Schmid, 143–57. SBLSS 34. Atlanta, 2006.

———. "The Yahwist and the Debate". In *Probing the Frontiers of Biblical Studies*, edited by J. H. Ellens and J. T. Greene, 62–66. PTMS 111. Eugene, 2009.

Vignolo, R. "Metodi, ermeneutica, statuto del testo biblico: Riflessioni a partire da L'interpretazione della Bibbia nella Chiesa (1993)". In *La rivelazione attestata: La Bibbia fra Testo e Teologia: Raccolta di Studi in onore del Cardinale Carlo Maria Martini, Arcivescovo di Milano, per il suo LXX compleanno*, edited by G. Angelini, 29–97. Milan, 1998.

Vischer, W. E. *Die Bedeutung des Alten Testament für das christliche Leben*. Zurich, 1938.

———. *Das Christuszeugnis des Alten Testaments: I. Das Gesetz*. Zurich, 1934. Translated by A. B. Crabtree as *The Witness of the Old Testament to Christ*. Vol. 1: *The Pentateuch*. London: Lutterworth Press, 1949.

Volz, P. *Mose und sein Werk*. 2nd ed. Tübingen, 1932.

Volz, P., and W. Rudolph. *Der Elohist als Erzähler: Ein Irrweg der Pentateuchkritik?* BZAW 63. Giessen, 1933.

Von Balthasar, H. U. *The Glory of the Lord: A Theological Aesthetics*. Vol. 1: *Seeing the Form*. Translated by Erasmo Leiva-Merikakis. San Francisco, 1982.

———. *Theo-Logic*. Vol. 1: *The Truth of the World*. Translated by Adrian J. Walker. San Francisco, 2000.

Von Harnack, A. *Marcion: Das Evangelium vom fremden Gott.* Leipzig, 1920.

———. *What Is Christianity? Lectures Delivered in the University of Berlin during the Winter-Term 1899–1900.* Translated by Thomas Bailey Saunders. 2nd ed. New York, 1903.

Von Rad, G. *Das erste Buch Mose: Genesis: Übersetzt und erklärt.* 10th ed. ATD 2/4. Göttingen, 1976. Translated by John H. Marks as *Genesis: A Commentary.* London, 1963.

———. *Das Formgeschichtliche Problem des Hexateuch.* BWANT 78. Stuttgart, 1938. This essay is included in an English collected volume: *The Problem of the Hexateuch and Other Essays.* Translated by E. W. Trueman Dicken. New York, 1966.

———. *Old Testament Theology.* One-volume edition. Peabody, Mass., 2005.

———. *Theologie des Alten Testaments.* 4th ed. Munich, 1962.

———. *Wisdom in Israel.* London, 1972.

Weber, M. *Das Antike Judentum.* Tübingen, 1921.

Welch, A. T., R. Paret, and J. D. Pearson. "*Ḳurʾān*". In *Encyclopédie de l'Islam,* new ed., edited by P. Bearman et al., 401–35. Leiden, 1960–2005.

Wellhausen, J. *Die Composition des Hexateuchs und der historischen Bücher des Alten Testaments.* 4th ed. Berlin, 1963.

———. *Prolegomena zur Geschichte Israels.* 6th ed. Berlin, 1905. Translated by J. Sutherland Black and Allan Menzies as *Prolegomena to the History of Israel.* Edinburgh, 1885.

Wenham, G. J. "Pondering the Pentateuch: The Search for a New Paradigm". In *The Face of Old Testament Studies: A Survey of Contemporary Approaches,* edited by D. W. Baker and B. T. Arnold, 116–44. Grand Rapids, 1999.

Whybray, R. N. "The Joseph Story and the Pentateuchal Criticism". *VT* 18 (1968): 522–28.

———. *The Making of the Pentateuch: A Methodological Study.* JSOT.S 53. Sheffield, 1987.

Wobbermin, G. *Geschichte und Historie: Über die Notwendigkeit in der Religionswissenschaft zwischen Geschichte und Historie strenger zu unterscheiden, als gewöhnlich geschieht.* Tübingen, 1911.

Zambrano, M. *Hacia un saber sobre el alma.* Madrid, 2000.

Žižek, S., ed. *Mapping Ideology.* London and New York, 1994.

Zubiri, X. *Man and God.* Translated by Joaquín Redondo. Lanham, Md., 2009.

Author Index